Artful

PERSUASION

Artful

PERSUASION

How to command attention,
change minds,
and influence people

HARRY MILLS

AMACOM
American Management Association

New York • Atlanta • Chicago • Kansas City •
San Francisco • Washington, DC • Brussels • Mexico
City • Tokyo • Toronto

Special discounts on bulk quantities of
AMACOM books are available to corporations,
professional associations, and other
organizations. For details, contact Special Sales
Department, AMACOM, an imprint of AMA
Publications, a division of American Management
Association, 1601 Broadway, New York,
NY 10019.

Tel: 212-903-8316.   Fax 212-903-8083.
Web site: www.amanet.org

This publication is designed to provide accurate and authoritive
information in regard to the subject matter covered. It is sold
with the understanding that the publisher is not engaged in
rendering legal, accounting, or other professional service. If legal
advice or other expert assistance is required, the service, of a
competent professional person should be sought.

Library of Congress Cataloging-in-Publication Data

Mills, Harry
    Artful persuasion : how to command attention, change minds,
    and influence people / Harry Mills.
    p. cm.
    Includes index.
    ISBN 0-8144-7063-7
    1. Persuasion (Psychology) 2. Influence (Psychology) I. Title

BF637.P4 M52 2000
153.8'52--dc21

                                                    99-056754

Printing number

10 9 8 7 6 5 4

CONTENTS

PART 3   MINDLESS INFLUENCE

PART 4   PERSUASION AT ITS BEST

Manipulation, Seduction, and Persuasion

Why I Wrote This Book

> "Speech is power:
> speech is to
> persuade, to convert,
> to compel."
> — Ralph Waldo Emerson

I earn my living as a professional persuader. I am what some people call a hired gun. I sell my talents to corporations, governments, and individuals who need help to persuade, sell, or negotiate.

I love it. The bigger the challenge, the more the adrenaline runs. Along the way, I've negotiated on billion-dollar deals, aided the launch of some of the world's best products, and even helped politicians win elections.

It's much easier when your clients include companies such as Toyota, BMW, PricewaterhouseCoopers, and Unilever. These companies appreciate what it takes to win the battle for hearts and minds against formidable competitors.

The Dark Art of Mysterious Influence

Nevertheless, I never cease to be amazed at how few people understand the art of persuasion. A large group of people – 25 percent, pollsters tell us – believe that persuasion is sorcery, a mysterious black art practiced by wizards who masquerade as politicians, advertisers, and spin doctors.

Vance Packard popularised the notion in his 1957 best-selling book *The Hidden Persuaders*. "Many of us are being influenced and manipulated, far more than we realise, in the patterns of our every-day lives," he wrote. He saw motivational research as comparable to "the chilling world of George Orwell and big brother." According to Packard, advertising agencies were tapping into the research of psychoanalysis to create a new type of suggestive and seductive ad.

A Canadian university professor, William Bryan Key, added to the fears when he claimed there was widespread use of what he called subliminal persuasion. He argued that advertisers were using subliminal messages in advertisements. Key claimed hidden messages urging you to buy were being embedded in pictures and print advertisements. At the movies, messages such as "Buy Coke" were being flashed secretly onto the screen at 1/3000 of a second – far too fast for the conscious mind to detect. Customers were being unconsciously manipulated.

Various governments added to the concern when they overreacted by banning subliminal advertising. However, in the over 200 academic papers that have since been published on the power of subliminal messages, *not one* has been able to show that subliminal messages influence what we do at all. Nevertheless, the fears haven't disappeared. In 1990, the rock band Judas Priest found themselves in court for allegedly recording the subliminal message "Do it" on one of their tracks in their 1978 album *Stained Glass.* Two sets of parents had filed suit claiming the message caused their two boys, fanatical Judas Priest fans, to commit suicide.

The band emerged victorious after a Canadian psychologist proved there was no evidence to support Key's ideas, which formed the basis of the accusation. Even so, persuasion for many remains a mysterious, irresistible force that unconsciously shapes their lives. Surveys tell us that 70 percent to 80 percent of people still believe advertisers use subliminal advertising.

Willing Accomplices in Our Own Seduction

The second reason why most people remain ignorant about how persuasion works is that they refuse to admit they are influenced by politicians, salespeople, and advertisers.

It is remarkable how many people believe they are immune to persuasion. They insist that they don't watch ads, that they never listen to politicians, and that they are resistant to all forms of persuasion.

Given that we are bombarded by as many as 1,600 commercial messages a day – that's 100 every waking hour – the claim to immunity is remarkable.

The fact is, none of us is immune to influence (see page xi). Advertisers and other professional persuaders have long known how to get through to those of us who claim to be resistant.

Advertisers, for example, typically flatter those who believe they are too individualistic to fall for a pitch aimed at the mainstream. The simplest trick is to use flattery. The Nike ads or MTV tell the "rebels" they want to win over, "We understand you; you're special. Don't do what everyone else does. Be unique and join us."

There is a moment in Monty Python's *The Life of Brian* that sums up the approach perfectly. The messiah shouts to the crowd, "Don't follow anyone. Think for yourself. You are all individuals." And the crowd shouts back, in unison, "We are all individuals."[1]

Ironically, because of their naïveté, this "rebel" group is often the easiest to persuade – and in the process, they become willing accomplices in their own seduction.

I wrote this book to show that there is nothing inherently mysterious about persuasion. We can all be skilled persuaders if we are prepared to master the techniques and understand what works, what doesn't work, and why.

Moreover, I passionately believe that the best defense against manipulation, propaganda, and ultimately tyranny is a fundamental knowledge of how persuasion works. You only have to visit the Auschwitz and Dachau concentration camps to know the human price we pay for naïveté, gullibility, and ignorance.

HARRY MILLS

How High Is Your Persuasion IQ?

Assess Your Skills as a Persuader

To give you a chance to assess your persuasion abilities prior to reading the book, I've included a *simplified* version of the *Persuasion IQ Test* I use to assess my clients' persuasive abilities. I recommend you complete the test before you read the book. I then suggest you redo the test after reading the book.

Assess your persuasion IQ by answering the following questions. Mark the option that best describes your performance. If your answer is "never," check Option 1. If your answer is "sometimes," check Option 3, and so on.

When you have answered all the questions, total your scores and turn to the "Interpreting Your Results" section to evaluate your performance.

1. I consciously establish my credentials or qualifications before I try to influence somebody. ☐1 ☐2 ☐3 ☐4 ☐5

2. When persuading, I offer proof of how people have been able to trust me or my organization in the past.
☐1 ☐2 ☐3 ☐4 ☐5

3. I consciously make a powerful impression in the first few minutes of any meeting. ☐1 ☐2 ☐3 ☐4 ☐5

4. I consciously use body language to influence others.
☐1 ☐2 ☐3 ☐4 ☐5

5. I constantly interpret other people's body talk.

□1 □2 □3 □4 □5

6. I use mirroring, pacing, and leading techniques to influence others.

□1 □2 □3 □4 □5

7. I monitor what other people say for signs of deception.

□1 □2 □3 □4 □5

8. I use a low pitch when I want my voice to project authority.

□1 □2 □3 □4 □5

9. I vary my vocal tempo and use pauses to create interest and impact.

□1 □2 □3 □4 □5

10. When speaking, I avoid using intensifiers, hedges, and qualifiers.

□1 □2 □3 □4 □5

11. I analyze the words and behavior of the people I want to influence in order to assess the type of information that will persuade them.

□1 □2 □3 □4 □5

12. I analyze the words and behavior of the people I want to influence in order to assess the way they prefer to make decisions.

□1 □2 □3 □4 □5

13. When I sell my ideas, I consciously speak in the language of benefits.

□1 □2 □3 □4 □5

14. When I persuade, I consciously choose powerful attention-grabbing words that have strong, positive, emotional appeals.

□1 □2 □3 □4 □5

15. I use antithesis when I want to create a particularly powerful presentation.

□1 □2 □3 □4 □5

16. As I persuade, I consciously sell what makes my proposition or ideas unique.   [1]   [2]   [3]   [4]   [5]

17. I package my persuasive propositions to appeal to the other person's basic human needs.

[1]   [2]   [3]   [4]   [5]

18. I use repetition in the words and phrases in my speeches to create added impact.   [1]   [2]   [3]   [4]   [5]

19. I use lots of metaphors, analogies, and stories in my presentations to highlight my key points.

[1]   [2]   [3]   [4]   [5]

20. I use humor where appropriate to increase involvement and commitment.   [1]   [2]   [3]   [4]   [5]

21. I consciously limit the number of points I make in any presentation to no more than five.

[1]   [2]   [3]   [4]   [5]

22. Where appropriate, I organize my ideas in a presentation around a thematic structure.

[1]   [2]   [3]   [4]   [5]

23. In a presentation, I grab my audience's attention with a dynamic opening.   [1]   [2]   [3]   [4]   [5]

24. I finish my presentations with a dramatic climax and a call for action.   [1]   [2]   [3]   [4]   [5]

25. I support my arguments with highly credible, well-researched evidence.   [1]   [2]   [3]   [4]   [5]

26. I use novel, vivid case studies to create memorability.

[1]   [2]   [3]   [4]   [5]

27. With important messages, I keep repackaging my ideas and repeating them whenever possible.

1   2   3   4   5

28. I consciously use an argument strategy to refute competing ideas.

1   2   3   4   5

29. I refute competing ideas before they have a chance to gain a foothold.

1   2   3   4   5

30. I inoculate my supporters in advance against competing ideas.

1   2   3   4   5

31. When I cite statistics, I package them for clarity and memorability.

1   2   3   4   5

32. My audiovisual presentations never exceed 20 minutes in length.

1   2   3   4   5

33. My audiovisual presentations are built around one central message.

1   2   3   4   5

34. My visual aids follow the rule: one idea per visual.

1   2   3   4   5

35. My visual aids use more graphics than words.

1   2   3   4   5

36. I tailor the colors I use in my visual aids to my audience's biases.

1   2   3   4   5

37. I vary my choice of media according to the message I want to communicate.

1   2   3   4   5

38. I encourage lots of feedback in discussions to encourage self-persuasion.

1   2   3   4   5

39. I use questions rather than statements to shape discussions.

1　　2　　3　　4　　5

40. I deliberately use disturbing questions when I want to make the other person uncomfortable with the status quo.

1　　2　　3　　4　　5

41. Where appropriate, I use leading and rhetorical questions to influence a presentation or meeting.

1　　2　　3　　4　　5

42. I actively listen to people to reflect the content and feelings of what they've said.

1　　2　　3　　4　　5

43. I analyze my audience in advance to determine my persuasion strategy.

1　　2　　3　　4　　5

44. I alter my persuasion strategy and change my material and approach when persuading different audiences.

1　　2　　3　　4　　5

45. When there is a strong opposition to my proposals, I plan for gradual, step-by-step persuasion.

1　　2　　3　　4　　5

46. I consciously use a persuasion strategy that systematically promotes my strong points and downplays my weaknesses.

1　　2　　3　　4　　5

47. When I am negotiating or selling, I always ask for more than I expect to get.

1　　2　　3　　4　　5

48. When I am negotiating to buy, I offer less than I expect to pay.

1　　2　　3　　4　　5

49. I consciously grant people favours knowing they will feel obliged to reciprocate in kind later.

1 2 3 4 5

50. When I want someone to make a large order or commitment that I know will meet resistance, I start by asking for a much smaller order or commitment. I then build on this, asking for a much bigger order or commitment later.

1 2 3 4 5

51. When I want people to stand by their commitments, I try to get them to make their commitments publicly or on paper.

1 2 3 4 5

52. I consciously tap the power that comes from titles or positions of authority I hold.

1 2 3 4 5

53. I consciously dress to communicate authority, competence, and professionalism.

1 2 3 4 5

54. When I possess exclusive information, I sell its scarcity value to those I'm trying to influence.

1 2 3 4 5

55. When I promote something, I stress that what I'm selling is popular, standard practice, or part of a trend.

1 2 3 4 5

56. I consciously associate myself with products, people, or companies that the people I'm trying to influence admire or emulate.

1 2 3 4 5

57. I emphasise the similarities I share with the people I want to influence.

1 2 3 4 5

58. I consciously use my friends as a referral network to build business or influence. ☐1 ☐2 ☐3 ☐4 ☐5

59. I consciously praise and flatter others to increase my influence with them. ☐1 ☐2 ☐3 ☐4 ☐5

60. I take advantage of situations where the person I want to influence is under pressure to "unthinkingly" agree with my proposals. ☐1 ☐2 ☐3 ☐4 ☐5

Interpreting Your Results

The prime purpose of this assessment is to allow you to identify the areas you need to improve so you can refer to the relevant sections in this book to further refine your skills.

SCORE	PERSUASION IQ
280–300	**Exceptional:** You are a persuasion marvel. If this was an intelligence test, you'd be a genius. If you're not in a successful career in sales, politics, diplomacy, law, or business, you should consider a career move. Watch out for complacency.
240–279	**Superior:** You are a talented persuader in many areas but lack the refinements displayed by exceptional persuaders.
180–239	**Adequate:** You know and practice many of the basics of persuasion. However, you can significantly decrease your number of missed opportunities by extending your skills and awareness.
UNDER 179	**Deficient:** Your persuasion skills are weak. You struggle getting what you want. You are also likely to be vulnerable to exploitation by unethical persuaders. Life is full of missed opportunities.

Acknowledgments

I owe a tremendous debt to my many clients and seminar participants who have helped to test and refine the materials.

I want to especially thank all those who agreed to review the manuscript in its various drafts. I thank people here in alphabetical order:

Rod Alford, Scott Archibald, John Baird, Kim Barkel, Paul Bell, Chris Beuth, Margo Black, Pat Blades, David Butler, Bryce Campbell, Alastair Carruthers, Robert Cattel, Mike Chan, Ed Cooley, Ron Cooper, Alistair Davis, Jillian de Beer, Anne de Salis, Wayne Deeth, David Evans, Grahame Evans, Brad Goddings, Michael Guggenheimer, James Hall, Keith Harris, Warwick Harvie, Philip Hines, Garry Hora, Geer Iseke, Vic Johnston, Tim Jones, Mandy Kells, Roger Kerr, Alan Kirby, Horst Kolo, Gerri Learmonth, Colin Lee, John Link, Errol Lizzamore, Phil Lloyd, Chris Marshall, Phil McCarroll, Ian Macdonald, Gary McIver, Viv McGowan, Patrick Middleton, Craig Mills, Rada Millwood, Stephanie Moore, Spencer Morris, Ross Morten, Julian Nalepa, Phil Neilson, Mick O'Driscoll, Mike O'Neil, Grant O'Riley, Jim Palmer, Debbie Pattulo, Peter Russell, Pam Sharp, Trudy Shay Petty, Jim Sherwin, Alan Simpson, Daljit Singh, Mike Skilling, Russell Smith, Paul Steele, Vicki Steele, Peter Stone, Mike Suggate, Gaynor Thomas, Ken Thomas, Shane Tiernan, Roy Trimbel, Christine Tubbs, Michael Ulmer, Elizabeth Valentine, Cathy Wagner, Jane Walker, John Walker, Lesley Walker, Mark Wallwork, Brian Walshe, Peter Watson, Murray Wham, Bryce Wilkinson, Lee Wilkinson.

This book would not exist if it hadn't been for Jan Harrison, my office manager. Thank you for everything.

Finally there is my wife, Mary Anne, and my two loving daughters, Alicia and Amy. Their love and support give meaning to everything I do.

Part 1

HOW PERSUASION WORKS

"When dealing with people, remember you are not dealing with creatures of logic, but with creatures of emotion, creatures bristling with prejudice and motivated by pride and vanity."

DALE CARNEGIE

Thoughtful Persuasion, Mindless Influence

1

The Two Routes to Successful Persuasion

THE PATH TO PERSUASION

What Is Persuasion?

Persuasion is the process of changing or reinforcing attitudes, beliefs, or behavior.

> *"The object of oratory is not truth but persuasion."*
> — *Thomas Babington Macaulay*

We respond to persuasive messages in two ways: thoughtfully and mindlessly. When we are thoughtful, we listen hard to what the persuader is saying; we weigh the pros and cons of each argument. We critique the message for logic and consistency, and if we don't like what we hear, we ask questions and call for more information. When we are in the thoughtful mode, the persuasiveness of the message is determined by the merits of the case.

When we respond to messages mindlessly, our brains are locked on automatic. We don't have the time, motivation, or ability to listen intently. So instead of relying on facts, logic, and evidence to make a judgment, we take a mental shortcut and rely on our instincts to provide us with cues as to how to respond.

Take a television debate between two politicians as an example. If you were in the thoughtful mode, you would listen hard to both sides and make your mind up based on the discussion of issues and the quality of evidence.

If you were in the mindless mode – say, half watching while entertaining friends – you would rely on simple cues. Typically, the cues that influence us most in situations like this are the attractiveness of the speakers, the reactions of our friends, and the pleasure or pain associated with agreeing with their arguments.

The Two Routes to Persuasion

Psychologists Richard Petty and John Cacioppo have labeled the thoughtful and mindless routes to persuasion as central and peripheral. In the central route, the message receiver actively thinks about the message and rationally analyzes all the logic and evidence presented.

In the peripheral route, the message receiver spends little time processing the content. The mind activates a decision trigger, which tells the receiver to say yes or no. The triggers are largely emotionally driven, and the receiver relies on simple cues or heuristics.

The organization of this book is built around these two routes to successful persuasion.

Listener's Two Routes to Persuasion

Thoughtful Persuasion	Mindless Persuasion
Is motivated to listen and is able to evaluate	Lacks motivation or ability to listen
Has high involvement	Has low involvement
Actively processes information	Uses passive processing and automatic decision triggers
Weighs pros and cons of evidence	Doesn't use counterarguing and doesn't search for persuasion cues
Uses reason and logic	Uses little intellectual analysis and is instinct- and emotion-driven
Has lasting attitude change and is resistant to other changes	Has temporary attitude change and easily changes mind

The Persuasion Effect

The Four Patterns of Influence

THE PERSUASION EFFECT

Management Professor Charles Margerison has identified four conversation patterns that occur when two people try to influence each other.[1]

1. Persuasion effect

The first pattern he calls the persuasion effect. Here, one side successfully persuades the other persons to adopt or agree to their position (see Figure 2.1).

Figure 2.1 The influencer successfully persuades the receiver to move to his or her position.
Source: Adapted from Charles J. Margerison, *If Only I Had Said...,* Mercury, 1987, p. 77.

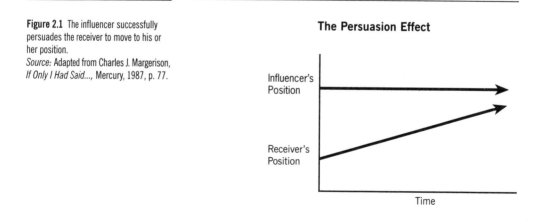

The Persuasion Effect

Influencer's Position

Receiver's Position

Time

The central focus of *Artful Persuasion* is on the persuasion effect. It shows you how to get the other person to agree with and support what you want to do.

"Agreement is brought about by changing people's minds – other people's."

— *S. I. Hayakawa*

2. Negotiation effect

If you can't persuade the other party to accept your position totally, you start to negotiate. In a typical negotiation, you give a little, and they give a little. The result is a negotiated compromise (see Figure 2.2).

Figure 2.2 Through negotiation, both parties take steps to close the gap between them.
Source: Adapted from Charles J. Margerison, *If Only I Had Said...*, Mercury, 1987, p. 78.

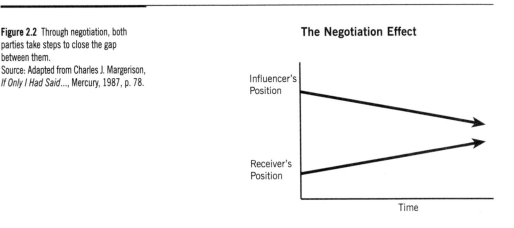

The Negotiation Effect

Influencer's Position

Receiver's Position

Time

Skilled persuaders are usually prepared to negotiate where straight persuasion isn't possible. Continued cooperation and win-win relationships usually involve give and take.

In *Artful Persuasion*, there are lots of tips on how to get the other side to negotiate and how to negotiate from a position of strength.

3. Fixation effect

Fixation occurs when both sides take up fixed positions and refuse to move, regardless of what the other side says (see Figure 2.3).

The fixation effect is remarkably common. Watch two supporters of different political parties argue their respective positions. Both sides hammer away, trying to convince the other side to move, but neither party moves. Instead, they normally harden their positions.

Artful Persuasion shows you how to avoid the fixation trap.

Figure 2.3 Both parties take fixed positions and conduct a meeting that reinforces their original differences.
Source: Adapted from Charles J. Margerison, *If Only I Had Said ...*, Mercury, 1987, p. 75.

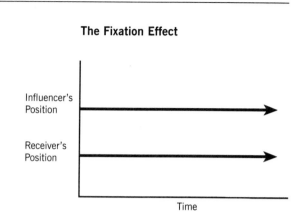

The Fixation Effect

Influencer's Position

Receiver's Position

Time

4. Polarization effect

Polarization occurs when the gap increases the more you talk (see Figure 2.4). Polarization typically takes place when both sides unfairly attack the other side's position, refusing to listen to the other side's arguments. As both sides try to establish their superiority, polarization occurs.

Artful Persuasion shows you how to prevent polarization from occurring and how to win over someone who is openly hostile.

Figure 2.4 The more the two parties talk, the further apart they move.
Source: Adapted from Charles J. Margerison, *If Only I Had Said ...*, Mercury, 1987, p. 74.

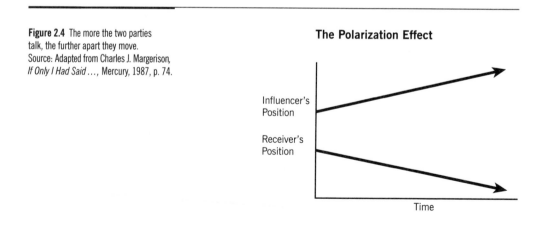

The Polarization Effect

Influencer's Position

Receiver's Position

Time

For a summary and comparison of the four conversation patterns of influence, see Figure 2.5.

Figure 2.5
Source: Adapted from Charles J. Margerison, *If Only I Had Said ...,* Mercury, 1987, p. 74-76, 77-78.

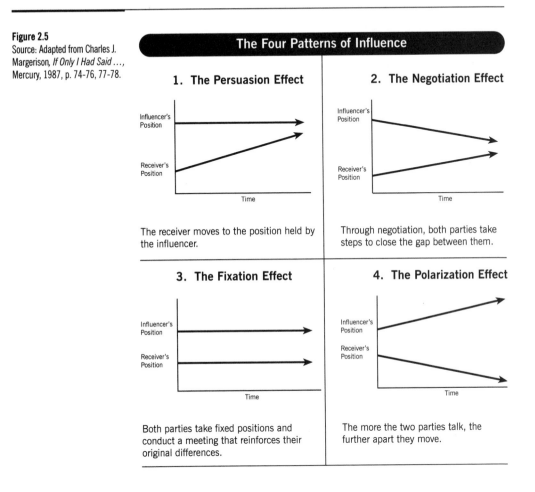

Part 2

THOUGHTFUL PERSUASION

"Get your facts first, then you can distort

them as you please."

MARK TWAIN

Foxes, Bloodhounds, and Donkeys

The Three Types of Influencers

THE THREE TYPES OF INFLUENCERS

Influencers can be divided into three groups: foxes, bloodhounds, and donkeys.

Foxes

Foxes are at heart devious. Ruthlessly competitive, they exploit influence opportunities to deceive and manipulate others. Life for true foxes is a contest: They win; you lose.

> *"The trouble with the rat race is that even if you win, you're still a rat."*
> — *Lily Tomlin*

When foxes manipulate, they focus on the short term. If they are selling, they focus on the current sale. They don't care how their behavior might damage their long-term reputation as long as they close the deal in front of them. Like their close cousins the wolves, they can dress up in sheep's clothing.

Bloodhounds

Bloodhounds are detectives of influence. They recognize the influence opportunities inherent in any situation and legitimately take advantage of them. Influence opportunities are not good or bad in themselves; they are opportunities to build mutual gain.

Bloodhounds are win-win-motivated. They use influence opportunities to create synergy, where one and one equal three. They also think about the long-term implications of anything they do. They appreciate that a reputation built over years can evaporate in minutes with the wrong tactics.

Beware: Some bloodhounds are closet foxes.

Donkeys

Because they are stubborn, unwilling to learn, and inflexible, donkeys botch most of their influence opportunities. Typically they fumble their way through meetings, presentations, and negotiations.

Meetings derail in confusion and argument; presentations fail to convince. Negotiations that have the potential to be win-win turn into lose-win or lose-lose.

Donkeys usually lack the skill to recognise the influence opportunities inherent in any situation. They also lack the techniques to skilfully manage an influence opportunity through to its best conclusion.

Turning Donkeys into Bloodhounds

Can you turn a donkey into a bloodhound? Yes, you can. Most donkeys simply don't know how to analyze or manage an influence opportunity. Donkeys who belong to this group lack knowledge and need training.

A second group of donkeys has a natural distaste for using influence. They see influencing and persuading as unethical manipulation. Donkeys of this type can usually be won over with education and training. Most become enthusiastic bloodhounds when they learn that if you truly believe in the merits of your proposal, you are letting your customers or coworkers down when you fail to persuade.

The last group of donkeys is much harder to change. If someone is truly inflexible and cannot see the world through any other person's eyes, he or she is doomed to remain a donkey.

Turning Foxes into Bloodhounds

Foxes fall into two groups. The first type of fox has become a fox because of an overriding ambition to succeed. Such people would like to be able to look themselves in the mirror in the morning and play win-win, but in a dog-eat-dog world, they believe good guys finish last – so they follow the way of the fox.

Most people in this group have a limited repertoire of skills. In negotiations, they lack the skills to turn a win-lose haggle into a win-win agreement. This group can be converted, but its members often need intensive training.

The second group of foxes may be irredeemable. These foxes are genuine Machiavellians: They lack trust, they don't care about other people's needs, and they delight in contests where they win and you lose. Training will do little for this group. What they need is a character transplant.

The Transformation of Abraham Lincoln

My favorite example of a fox who was transformed into a bloodhound is Abraham Lincoln. The Lincoln of history is a different one from the Lincoln of legend. According to legend, Lincoln's emergence as a statesman was one long triumphal march. This is not so. In *Honor's Voice, the Transformation of Abraham Lincoln,* Douglas Wilson, the director of the International Center for Jefferson Studies at Monticello, traces Lincoln's life in the 1830s and 1840s from bumpkin to knowledgeable politician.

Although "honest Abe" was honest by frontier standards, Lincoln was at times a sharp, slippery, and unsavory politician. Lincoln discredited opponents by writing anonymous newspaper columns in which he viciously accused opponents – often unjustly – of hypocrisy, duplicity, and dishonesty.

According to Wilson, Lincoln's anonymous newspaper articles show a Lincoln who "could be abusive" and "reckless with the truth." Wilson said, "The Lincoln of the newspaper columns had a far less savoury and respectable character than his public persona."[1] Even so, Wilson shows that Lincoln constantly battled his inadequacies to transform himself from an at-times devious country politician into a statesman of extraordinary political ability and moral greatness.

Persuasion Starts with Credibility

How to Build Trust and Sell Your Expertise

THE CREDIBILITY FORMULA

"One can stand as the greatest orator the world has known, possess the quickest mind, employ the cleverest psychology, and have mastered all the technical devices of argument, but if one is not credible one might just as well preach to the pelicans."[1]

> *"To be persuasive, we must be believable. To be believable, we must be credible. To be credible, we must be truthful."*
> — Edward R. Murrow

These words come from Gerry Spence, arguably one of America's greatest trial lawyers. In a criminal career spanning forty years, Gerry Spence has not lost a single case before a jury.

Spence believes that, to persuade, we must be believable, and to be believable, we must be credible. Spence's views are supported by a wealth of research. Credibility rests on two pillars: trust and expertise.

This enables us to picture credibility as a formula:

Trust + Expertise = Credibility

The Pillar of Trust

When persuaders lack integrity, we discount everything they say. Whenever we listen to a professional persuader – a lawyer, a salesperson, or a diplomat – among the first questions we ask are: Can I trust this person? Do I believe him or her? Is he or she sincere?

The Munich Deceit

When British Prime Minister Neville Chamberlain first met Adolf Hitler in September 1938, trust was a central issue.

Hitler wanted to take over Czechoslovakia. He had already secretly mobilized the German army to attack Czechoslovakia, but his army needed until the end of September to prepare. If he could hoodwink the Czechs into delaying their mobilization, the German army could take the country by surprise.

Hitler persuaded Chamberlain that if the Czechs gave up the Sudetenland (a German-speaking region of Czechoslovakia), he would live in peace and never make another territorial demand.

Chamberlain, desperate to avoid war, foolishly believed him. He wrote to his sister: "[Hitler] was a man who could be relied upon when he had given his word."[2]

The Munich Agreement that followed allowed Germany to occupy the Sudetenland. A few months later, Hitler broke his word and invaded the rest of Czechoslovakia. When Hitler attacked Poland in September 1939, there were no talks. What little trust there had been had evaporated. Britain and France declared war on Germany, and World War II began.

The Secret of Eloquence

Chamberlain didn't survive the humiliation that followed Munich. He was forced to resign in May 1940 and was replaced by one of the twentieth-century's greatest orators and persuaders – Winston Churchill.

Rarely, if ever, had a national leader taken over at such a desperate hour. An inspired Churchill declared in his inaugural address as prime minister to the British House of Commons: "I have nothing to offer but blood, toil, tears and sweat."

Churchill's mentor for speaking was an Irish-born U.S. politician named Bourke Cockran, one of America's greatest orators who also coached President Franklin Roosevelt. (He was also Churchill's mother's lover.)

Churchill once asked Cockran: "Bourke, what is the secret of eloquence?" Bourke replied: "Believing in what you are talking about." Cockran summed it up: "Sincerity – never speak what you don't believe."[3]

The word sincerity comes from the Latin *sincerus,* which literally means *without wax.* In ancient times, unethical pillar carvers used wax to mask their mistakes or to hide flaws in the marble. Only after many years of weathering did the wax fall out to reveal the deception practiced by the long-gone carver. Thus, a sincere person was *without wax,* or uncamouflaged.

It makes sense for us to respond to a persuasive message by questioning the speaker's integrity. Usually we test the speaker's bias by asking what the speaker personally stands to gain – in other words, what is in his or her self-interest.

If we think the message is biased, we can carefully analyze the message or dismiss it, depending on the circumstances. Professional persuaders, therefore, work hard to appear unbiased and trustworthy.

Acting Against Your Self-Interest

One way persuaders appear trustworthy is by apparently acting against their own self-interest. If we are convinced that communicators have nothing to gain and perhaps something to lose by persuading us, we will trust them and they will be more credible.

Suppose, for example, a convicted heroin smuggler delivers a talk on how unfair the justice system is; he argues that criminals are the victims of an unjust social system. Would he influence you? Probably not. Most people would view him as biased and untrustworthy.

But imagine that he argued that the criminal system was too soft, that sentences were too short, and that prisoners should do hard labor while inside because only then would prison act as a deterrent. Would he influence you now?

Experiments run by Elliot Aronson, Elaine Walster, and Darcy Abrahams suggest he would. In one experiment in which a criminal (an actor called Joe "The Shoulder") called for more lenient courts, he was totally ineffective. Indeed, he caused opinions to harden in the opposite direction. But when he was calling for tougher, more powerful courts, he was very persuasive – as persuasive as a respected justice official arguing the same case.[4]

One of the most persuasive spokespeople for the antismoking lobby in the United States is Patrick Reynolds. Patrick Reynolds, who inherited $2.5 million from the R.J. Reynolds Tobacco Company founded by his grandfather, has urged victims of smoking-related illnesses to sue the tobacco companies for damages.[5]

Similarly, J. Robert Oppenheimer, who helped lead the Los Alamos project that developed the first atomic bomb, became a very convincing spokesperson for the antinuclear movement when he warned against the further spread of nuclear technology.

Conversely, self-interest often affects judgment. The great Russian composer Tchaikovsky called the great German composer Brahms a "giftless bastard." In his diary, Tchaikovsky admitted, "It annoys me that this self-inflated mediocrity is hailed as a genius."

As consumers of persuasion, it pays us to audit every message for bias. Always question a communicator's motives.

Using a Front Group to Create Trust

Corporations face the same credibility problems as individuals. "Any institution with a vested commercial interest in the outcome of an issue has a natural credibility barrier to overcome with the public and media," says Merill Rose, executive vice president of the public relations firm Porter/Novelli.[6]

Because of the trust issue, it has become increasingly common in the United States for corporations and industry groups to work through front groups. A front group, usually made up of a coalition of interested groups and hired experts, can publicly promote what a corporation wants while claiming to speak for the public interest.

The Killing of Clinton's Health Care Reforms

The best example of the corporate world using front groups to gain trust or credibility and move public opinion has to be the public relations blitz staged to kill Clinton's health care reforms.

During the 1992 presidential campaign, opinion polls showed widespread support for Clinton's plan to introduce universal health insurance. Opposed to the reforms were the pharmaceutical industry, the insurance industry, and the American Medical Association.

To succeed, the campaign opposing reform had to appear as though it had massive grassroots support. So, a number of citizens' organizations were created and funded to attack Clinton's plan on a number of fronts.

One of the most prominent groups was the Coalition for Health Insurance Choices (CHIC). The coalition proclaimed it was "a coalition of thousands of Americans, drawn from every walk of life and every corner of the country, who are concerned about health care reform." In reality, it was a front group for the Health Insurance Association of America. In a series of television advertisements produced by this group, two ordinary Americans, "Harry and Louise," shared their personal fears about the prospect of guaranteed health care.

Another grassroots front group, RxPartners, publicly campaigned against the possibility of government-imposed price controls on pharmaceutical drugs. RxPartners was a front group for a number of companies, which included Bristol-Myers Squibb, Eli Lilly, Hoffman-LaRoche, Searle, Upjohn, and Warner Lambert.

With a massive multimillion-dollar budget, the various front groups were able to fund huge direct-mail and telephone campaigns to spread fears that government health care would bankrupt the country, reduce the quality of care, and take away choice.[7]

By 1994, the various campaigns had achieved their aims. In a last-ditch effort to save face, Clinton's supporters drastically scaled back their health care plans, but even these couldn't win enough political support. "Never before had private interests spent such vast sums to defeat an initiative launched by a president," wrote Thomas Scarlett in *Campaigns and Elections* magazine.[8]

Increasing Trust While Decreasing Bias

Researchers into persuasion have also discovered ways you can increase a person's apparent trustworthiness while decreasing the apparent bias of a message. One technique is to make sure the target person or audience is absolutely convinced that the person doing the speaking is not trying to persuade them.

Suppose a property investment broker calls you with a hot tip on a newly listed property. Will you purchase the property? It depends. You might see the broker as an expert and this might induce you to buy, or you could see the broker as biased, given that he or she stands to make a sizeable commission.

But suppose you accidentally overhear your broker telling a colleague about a property just listed. Because the broker was not trying to influence you, you are very likely to be convinced.[9]

In the same way, "hidden camera" advertisements on television are designed to make us believe that the testimony of the person being filmed is unbiased and trustworthy.[10]

The Law of Candor

Marketing gurus Al Ries and Jack Trout believe truth is such a powerful, persuasive weapon in advertising that they call it the "law of candor."

Ries and Trout argue, "One of the most effective ways to get into a prospect's mind is to first admit a negative and then twist it into a positive."[11]

Take Avis Rental Cars. For years, Avis promoted its high quality. Claims in "Finest in rent-a-cars" advertisements simply didn't ring true. How could Avis have the finest rent-a-car service when Hertz was clearly the market leader?

> *"I've a great gimmick. Let's tell the truth."*
> — *Bill Bernbach*

Then Avis admitted it was No. 2. The advertisements declared, "Avis is No. 2. We try harder."

The advertising claims were now credible. Avis, which had lost money for thirteen straight years, suddenly began to make money.

"Candor is very disarming," say Ries and Trout. "Every negative statement you make about yourself is instantly accepted as a truth. Positive statements, on the other hand, are looked at as dubious at best. Especially in an advertisement."[12]

Advertising agency Doyle Dane Bernbach (DDB) used the "law of candor" to create a remarkable campaign for Volkswagen, starting in 1960.

Many of the advertisements took the novel approach of knocking the product (see Figure 4.1). Here are some of the headlines used:

- Ugly is only skin-deep.
- Think small.
- Lemon.
- The 1970 VW will stay ugly longer.

The campaign was built around what the Beetle actually was: small, simple, economical, reliable, and (except to VW addicts) ugly. In 1968, the VW Beetle sold 423,000 units in the United States – more than any other single automobile had ever sold. The campaign's success is even more remarkable when you consider that the U.S. market at the time was dominated by big gas-guzzling cars.

Figure 4.1 This "Lemon" advertisement for Volkswagen in the United States formed part of one of the most brilliant, successful ad campaigns ever created. The campaign was revolutionary because of the way the VW Beetle was advertised for what it was rather than hyped beyond credibility.
Source: Doyle Dane Bembach, New York.
Courtesy: Volkswagen.

The Volkswagon campaign was created by the New York agency Doyle Dane Bernbach, founded by Bill Bernbach. Bernbach had a simple attitude to truth in advertising:

"The truth isn't the truth until people believe you, and they can't believe you if they don't know what you're saying, and they can't know what you're saying if they don't listen to you, and they won't listen to you if you're not interesting, and you won't be interesting unless you say things imaginatively, originally, freshly."[13]

Some years ago, Scope took on Listerine in the mouthwash market, with a pleasant-tasting mouthwash attacking Listerine's horrible taste. Listerine's answer: "The taste that you hate twice a day." This allowed the company to sell the idea that because Listerine tastes like a disinfectant, it must kill lots of germs.

Ries and Trout end with a cautionary note: "The law of candor must be used with great skill. First your negative must be widely perceived as a negative. It has to trigger instant agreement with your prospect's mind. Next you have to shift quickly to the positive. The purpose of candor is not to apologize. The purpose of candor is to set up a benefit that will convince your prospect."[14]

Ed Koch Wins with Candor

Public relations expert Roger Ailes (who served as an adviser to both Ronald Reagan and George Bush), in his book *You Are the Message,* shows how New York City's Mayor Ed Koch used candor to increase his credibility:

In 1980, Ed Koch appeared on one of those Sunday "newsmaker" programs in the aftermath of the city's financial crisis. Koch had spent $300,000 to put up bike lanes in Manhattan. As it turned out, cars were driving in the bike lanes, endangering the bikers.

Meanwhile, some bikers were running over pedestrians because the pedestrians didn't know the bike lanes were there or didn't understand how they worked. It was a mess. The Mayor was coming up for re-election, and four or five journalists now had Koch cornered on this talk show. The whole purpose was to rip the Mayor's skin off for the bike lanes and for spending money foolishly when the city was nearly broke.

The trap was set. One reporter led off with, "Mayor Koch, in light of the financial difficulties in New York City, how could you possibly justify wasting $300,000 on bike lanes?"

Cut to Koch. Tight close-up. Everybody was expecting a half-hour disaster. Koch smiled and he said, "You're right. It was a terrible idea." He went on, "I thought it would work. It didn't. It was one of the worst mistakes I ever made." And he stopped.

Now nobody knew what to do. They had another twenty-six minutes of the program left. They all had prepared questions about the bike lanes, and so the next person feebly asked, "But, Mayor Koch, how could you do this?" And Mayor Koch said, "I already told you, it was stupid. I did a dumb thing. It didn't work." And he stopped again. Now, there were twenty-five minutes left and nothing to ask him. It was brilliant.[15]

The Power of Confession

Public relations professionals know a confession coming from your mouth is not nearly as damaging to trust as an exposure coming from an opponent.

Ronald Reagan. When President Reagan campaigned for reelection against Walter Mondale in 1984, the first of the television debates started badly. The seventy-three-year-old President appeared tired and confused. Everyone expected Mondale to make Reagan's advanced age a central issue.

During the second debate, Reagan went on the offensive, raising the age issue: "and I want you to know that I will not make age an issue of this campaign. I am not going to exploit my opponent's youth and inexperience."

It was a brilliant line. Everyone laughed – Reagan had taken charge of the issue and used humor to admit weakness. And the media used it as a lead quote the next day.[16]

Richard Nixon. Perhaps Richard Nixon could have avoided becoming the only U.S. President ever to resign from office. Noted U.S. trial lawyer and author of *How to Argue and Win Every Time* Gerry Spence thinks so. Spence believes President Nixon could have avoided Watergate by simply admitting, "I know about this whole messy thing. It got out of hand when zealous people, who believed in me, did the wrong thing. I wish to God it never happened. I hope the American people will forgive me."[17]

The irony is that the evidence shows Nixon knew full well the importance of being honest. The White House tapes record that on April 16, 1973, Nixon instructed John Dean, the White House counsel, on how to give evidence during the Watergate investigation.

Said Nixon, "Tell the truth. This is the thing I have told everyone around here – tell the truth …! If you are going to lie, you go to jail for the lie rather than for the crime. So believe me, don't ever lie."

History records Nixon didn't follow his own advice.

Union Carbide

The trouble is, in times of crisis the temptation is to keep quiet. When the poisonous gas methyl isocyanate leaked from Union

Carbide's plant in Bhopal, India, in late 1984, the chairman of Union Carbide, Warren Anderson, flew to Bhopal to demonstrate his concern. Some 7,000 people died from the accidental poison leak; 200,000 people were reported injured.

However, back in the United States, Anderson's public relations handler soon blew Union Carbide's credibility. Here is part of the press conference led by the company's director of health, safety, and environmental affairs:

Reporter: I think you've said the company was not liable to the Bhopal victims?

Director: I didn't say that.

Reporter: Does that mean you are liable?

Director: I didn't say that either.

Reporter: Then what did you say?

Director: Ask me another question.[18]

Isuzu

The easiest way to destroy your credibility is to oversell or exaggerate. The daily bombardment of advertising, sales pitches, and political hype has made us highly sceptical.

Salespeople need to address this problem. When some 3,000 U.S. business decision makers were asked, "What is the *highest* degree to which you trust any of the salespeople you *bought from* the previous 24 months?" only 4 percent answered "completely" while over 60 percent answered "barely" or "not at all."[19]

When it comes to surveys on professional credibility, few occupations rank consistently lower than car salespeople. When it comes to trust, car salespeople compete for bottom rank with politicians.

As a result, research shows 85 percent of Americans hate going to a dealership to buy a car. The image is so bad that advertising agency Dell, Femina, Travisano & Partners was able to take the sleazeball image of the car salesperson and turn it into a tongue-in-cheek, attention-grabbing campaign for Isuzu automobiles.

The campaign, first launched in 1986, starred Joe Isuzu as a grinning, oily salesperson. Joe made outrageous claims for his Isuzu: "It costs $9 a car. It can climb Mount Everest." At the same time, the words "He's lying" were superimposed on the screen. The print advertising declared, "Big Joe is a liar." Of course, the commercial pushed Isuzu's key features, which, compared to Joe Isuzu's lies, came across as understated truths.

Adweek called the award-winning campaign revolutionary for its willingness to lie outrageously about a product and then correct the lie with a message superimposed simultaneously on the television screen.

Perhaps it also shows that lying is so much a part of our culture that open references to lying are, surprisingly enough, refreshingly honest.[20]

Under the Radar Screen

Exaggerated claims by advertisers and other promoters have created a huge credibility problem for professional persuaders. According to the Pretesting Company, from 1986 to 1996 advertising believability in the United States plummeted from 61 percent to 38 percent. Disillusioned consumers no longer trust claims that proclaim "We're the best" and "We're no. 1."

Advertising gurus and authors of *Under the Radar*, Jonathan Bond and Richard Kirshenbaum believe every consumer has a built-in advertising radar shield. "Marketing radar is a defensive mechanism that helps us screen out the 1,500 commercial messages we are exposed to every day."[21] And the key to getting under that radar screen is credibility.

In 1994, Mercedes dropped a plan to use the slogan "Simply the best car in the world" after extensive testing. Even though many people passionately believe that the Mercedes is the best car in the world, the slogan was a turnoff for potential buyers. The only way a car company today can claim to be the best with any credibility is to cite the ratings given by an independent third-party rating firm such as J.D. Power & Associates.[22]

Truth: The "New" Marketing Weapon

Fortune magazine reports advertisers are rediscovering the power of truth as a marketing weapon. The magazine reports that Clean Shower has dramatically increased its sales with a campaign based on truth and honesty. The Clean Shower ad campaign urges consumers not to use too much. A radio spot says, "Don't overdo it. With Clean Shower, less is more; don't use too much – a little is all it takes." It then adds, "When was the last time you heard a company tell you to use just a little bit of their product? I mean, we're geniuses over here."[23]

Paul Lukas, *Fortune* columnist and author of *Inconspicuous Consumption*, notes, "There is no denying the cleverness of the ad. By capitalizing on consumer cynicism generated by decades of marketing manipulations, this commercial essentially turns the notion of planned obsolescence on its head simply by acknowledging its existence."

Anita Roddick and the Body Shop

When words and deeds don't match, a credibility issue can quickly turn into a major scandal. When Anita Roddick, who built the Body Shop on values of honesty and integrity, was accused of selling products that had been tested on animals in 1994, it was the worst possible publicity the company could receive.

Dubbed the "Mother Theresa of capitalism," Roddick had publicly proclaimed the Body Shop's opposition to animal testing. In her biography *Body and Soul,* she had attacked the beauty industry as liars and cheats.

When Roddick's integrity was attacked, the Body Shop responded badly to the media by reacting indignantly. The company could have admitted it had a problem with third-party suppliers. The Body Shop then could have set up an advisory board to monitor the suppliers or introduce third-party certification. If it had taken actions such as these, it might have limited the damage to its reputation and set about rebuilding the icon status the Body Shop had as a brand.[24]

The message for professional persuaders is: Don't exaggerate or oversell. Even if you really have a miraculous product or service, temper your claims.

Point Out the Disadvantages

One of the best ways to increase your trustworthiness is to openly admit the weaknesses or disadvantages associated with your proposals. It is a deceptively disarming technique. The best salespeople increase their credibility by pointing out the disadvantages or the risks associated with their product.

"It is hard to believe that a man is telling the truth when you know that you would lie, if you were in his place."

— H. L. Mencken

Here is a salesperson selling a mutual fund in emerging markets:

I appreciate the fact that you're attracted by the fantastic returns this fund has enjoyed in the last year, but I want to tell you I wouldn't feel comfortable if I didn't warn you about the downside risks.

First, this fund could easily drop 25 to 30 percent in a bad year. Could you sleep at night if you experienced that sort of risk? Second, this is not a fund for short-term investors. If you're not prepared to stay the course for at least five years, don't invest. Finally, if you need this fund to produce a regular annual income, this is not the fund for you.

Salespeople who sell this way sell more, get many client referrals, and experience much less buyer remorse when the product doesn't perform as expected.

Selling on Commission

One of the reasons buyers distrust salespeople's motives is that buyers know many are paid on commission. As buyers, people therefore suspect the motives that lie behind any recommendation to buy.

If you are not on commission, make sure you let the customer know. Don't turn it into a major issue; simply mention it during the conversation at an opportune moment.

If you are on commission, you have to *prove* to your client you are prepared to put his or her interests ahead of yours – even when it means losing a commission.

As a professional persuader, it is not enough simply to be trustworthy. In the highly skeptical world we live in, you have to provide demonstrable proof of your credibility.

THE PILLAR OF EXPERTISE

Once trust has been established, it is much easier to build the second pillar of credibility – expertise.

In one experiment carried out at an Australian university, a man was introduced as a guest speaker from Cambridge University in England. However, his expertise was represented differently to each class. To the first class, he was introduced as a student, to the second class as a demonstrator, to the third class as a lecturer, and to the fourth class as a senior lecturer; to the fifth class, he was introduced as a professor.

After each class, the students were asked to estimate his height. Remarkably, with each increase in expertise, the same man grew in stature by an average of half an inch. As a "professor," he was perceived as two and a half inches taller than as a student.[25]

Academic titles, of course, confer expertise and status. An opinion voiced by an expert in a particular field carries more weight than that given by an amateur.

Experts typically establish their authority by displaying their credentials. Doctors, dentists, lawyers, and other professionals hang their qualifications on their office walls to impress us.

The Language of Expertise

Experts demonstrate their expertise with mastery of their subject's jargon. One estimate claims a typical professional learns at least

3,000 new technical words related to his or her career. Within a group, jargon operates as a verbal shorthand that allows members of the group to communicate quickly and precisely.

Experts enhance their expertise by writing articles and books. Being referred to, endorsed, or quoted on paper suggests expert status.

John F. Kennedy. John F. Kennedy wrote two books: *Why England Slept* and *Profiles in Courage*. Both played key parts in establishing Kennedy's credentials, first as a junior politician and later as a national statesman.

The first, *Why England Slept* (published in 1940), helped establish John Kennedy as a potential politician. Father Joseph Kennedy persuaded family friend and journalist Arthur Krock to turn John's very ordinary undergraduate thesis on English foreign policy in the 1930s into a book.

After much rewriting, the book appeared in July 1940 just one month after young John's graduation from college. Just before it was published, his father wrote to him, "You would be surprised how a book that really makes the grade with high class people stands you in good stead for years to come."[26]

Joseph got his friend Henry Luce, the *Time-Life* publisher, to endorse the book by writing the introduction. "I cannot recall a single man in my college generation," Luce wrote, "who could have written such an adult book on such a vitally important subject."[27]

Father Joseph's influence with the media ensured that the book received good reviews. Luce put John's picture in *Time* magazine; to make the book a best-seller, Joseph Kennedy quietly purchased 30,000 copies and stored them at his home.

By 1955, John Kennedy was established as a first-term New England senator looking to achieve national prominence and win the Democratic Party's nomination for the vice presidency. While recovering from a back operation, John enlisted the help of a team of historians and aide Ted Sorenson to write *Profiles in Courage*. The book, published in 1956, profiled members of the Senate who had made principled, often unpopular, courageous decisions.

Again, father Joseph helped out with the publicity. Reviewers lavishly praised the book, and more than one linked the young senator to the idealism extolled therein. One reviewer exclaimed, "It is refreshing to have a first-rate politician write a thoughtful and persuasive book about political integrity."

Profiles quickly became a best-seller and won the Pulitzer Prize. Historian Thomas Reeves says, "The young senator was now more widely recognized and highly regarded than ever. He was thought to be a deep thinker, an important writer, a conqueror of adversity and a politician of the highest promise."[28] About four years later, John Kennedy was elected President of the United States.

Selling Expertise

No one appreciates the power of print to build a reputation better than McKinsey's, the world's most profitable management consultancy group. In 1995, McKinsey's earned $1.5 billion in fees. Since 1980, McKinsey staff have churned out over fifty books. They also publish the *McKinsey Quarterly*, which rivals the *Harvard Business Review* in quality.

In 1981, Tom Peters and Robert Waterman, McKinsey consultants, produced a book from a McKinsey internal research project describing the practices of America's best companies. Full of racy anecdotes and written in simple, easy-to-read, jargon-free language, *In Search of Excellence* leaped onto the best-seller list. Within three years, it had sold 5 million copies.

The longer *In Search of Excellence* stayed on the best-seller list, the more widely Peters and Waterman were quoted and interviewed. Within a month, business magazines and newspapers were labeling Peters and Waterman gurus. At the same time, their incomes from individual daily fees spiraled to $50,000.

Within a short time of the publication of *In Search of Excellence,* critics pointed out that Peters' and Waterman's star companies were badly underperforming: Two-thirds of the companies they had cited as excellent in 1982 were now underachieving. Perhaps Peters' and Waterman's advice was suspect.

However, in his book *Thriving on Chaos,* Peters, who had by now left McKinsey's and set up his own consulting group, performed a clever about-face. He declared, "There are no excellent companies," that the world was embroiled in revolution and that businesses needed to remake themselves if they were to survive. The market responded to Peters' openness: *Thriving on Chaos* spent sixty weeks on the *New York Times* best-seller list.

Testimonials Substantiate Expertise

If you pick up a popular management or investment book, you'll find the covers and first few pages often laced with endorsements or testimonials from experts or influential authorities.

One of the most powerful weapons salespeople can use on a prospect is a collection of testimonial letters from satisfied customers. Letters such as these are doubly powerful because the public commitment involved in giving a written testimonial makes the endorser even more likely to stay loyal to the salesperson.

Printed endorsements or testimonials from experts are especially powerful. I remember scanning the dozens of investment titles in one of New York's Barnes and Noble bookstores. I picked up *Bogle on Mutual Funds* and flipped through the pages. It was full of graphs and statistics; it looked to be heavy-going – just the sort of book to cure a case of insomnia. But there on the front cover was an endorsement by Warren E. Buffett, arguably the world's most successful investor. In large, bold print, his endorsement read: "This is the definitive book on mutual funds – comprehensive, insightful and – most important – honest."

The foreword was written by economics guru and Nobel Laureate Paul Samuelson. I reasoned that neither of these two men would endorse a suspect product; this had to be a good read – so I purchased four, one for me and three for friends.

THE THREE LEVELS OF CREDIBILITY

Credibility must be built on three levels (see the credibility analysis tool kit). At the first level, you have to build your personal credibility. This involves selling yourself, demonstrating your mastery of issues, and speaking with flair and style.

At the second level, you have to sell the credibility of your ideas. If your propositions are controversial, you'll need valid evidence supported by independent research.

At the third level, you have to sell the credibility of the organization you represent. To be successful in persuasion, you normally have to be effective on all three levels.

The Credibility Tool Kit

The Credibility Analysis Tool Kit is designed to help you establish credibility with the people you're looking to influence. To assess your credibility with the people you want to persuade, follow the six steps set out below:

1. List all the people you need to influence on the Credibility Ratings List.
2. Plot the people you've just listed on to the Credibility Matrix.
3. Measure how each person perceives your expertise and trust on a scale of 1 to 10.
4. Now, transfer the measurements from the Credibility Matrix back to the Credibility Ratings List.
5. Finally, add the trust and expertise scores together for each person to compile a single credibility score from 1 to 10. If you are registering 5 or below in the trust or expertise category, you'll need to take some credibility-building initiatives.
6. Use the list of Credibility-Building tactics to complete the Credibility Strategy Planner.

Credibility Ratings List

Target (name and role)	Expertise (1 to 10)	Trust (1 to 10)	Credibility Score (1 to 20)

© Harry Mills

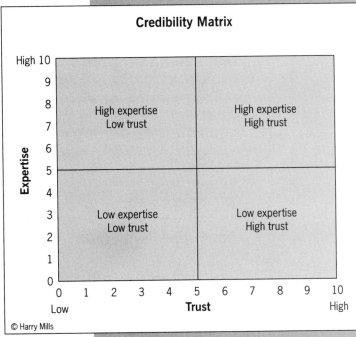

Credibility Matrix

High expertise
Low trust

High expertise
High trust

Low expertise
Low trust

Low expertise
High trust

Expertise

Trust

Low — High

© Harry Mills

Credibility-Building Tactics

Problem: Low Expertise

- Publish and distribute third-party testimonials that endorse your position.

- Persuade an outside recognized expert or guide to publicly endorse and validate your ideas.

- Write and publish relevant articles or a book.

- Hire a publicity agent or PR consultant and regularly comment on industry issues.

- Win invitations to speak at key industry or professional forums.

- Publicly celebrate early successes – even if they are small – as proof your ideas are right.

- Learn to speak with flair, with humor, and in quotable sound bites on mundane issues. The press always look for experts who speak in sound bites with flair and humor.

- Hire a coach or attend an intensive course to update you on the cutting-edge thinking in your field.

Problem: Low Trust

- Be reliable. Do what you promise and publicize your achievements. We distrust unreliable people and discount everything they say.

- Be rational. It's much easier to trust someone who makes decisions based on reason rather than emotion.

- Be receptive. It's much easier to trust someone who is receptive to our needs and concerns.

- Don't oversell or exaggerate. Underpromise and overdeliver. Manage expectations by always delivering more than you promise.

- Use a disciple who is trusted and respected, to actively promote your reliability.

- Use candor. Openly admit the downside of your proposals. Admit your failures and weaknesses.

- Use a credible front group to endorse your position when you or your organization is perceived to be biased on major issues.

Credibility Strategy Planner

Expertise Issues	Action Required

Expertise Issues	Action Required

PERSUASION
POINTERS

1 Don't be afraid to display or promote your qualifications. Qualifications confer status and expertise.

2 Build your reputation on openness and honesty. People with dishonest reputations are not believed even when they tell the truth.

3 Don't oversell your position with exaggerated claims. Exaggerations weaken the rest of your case.

4 Never claim more than you think your audience will believe. Your product or service may be the best, but if you can't convince the audience, you're better off to moderate your claims.

5 Where appropriate, point out the disadvantages in your product or service. It gives credibility to everything else you say.

6 Never assume that people trust you. Take every opportunity to prove that your word is your bond.

7 Use the power of print to increase your credibility by being quoted. A well-written book in your area of expertise, endorsed by fellow experts, can boost your reputation enormously.

8 Build a portfolio of reputable third-party endorsements and testimonials.

9 Look to build your credibility on three levels:
   A. Your personal credibility
   B. The credibility of your ideas
   C. The credibility of your organization

First Impression, Best Impression

The Art of Image Management

IMAGE MANAGEMENT

Image Management and Politicians

Most people associate image management and the visual packaging of politicians with the rise of television.

The Visual Packaging of Abraham Lincoln

The visual packaging of politicians, however, dates back to the midnineteenth century and the invention of the photograph. Abraham Lincoln's election chances were visibly enhanced in 1860 by an impressive-looking campaign photograph doctored by the prominent New York photographer Matthew Brady.

Lincoln, a gangly man with a protruding Adam's apple and deeply furrowed face, was less than photogenic. So, Brady modified Lincoln's appearance with a couple of photographic tricks and retouched the print to remove his harsh facial lines. The embellished photograph made Lincoln look much more physically attractive; according to photographic historian Susan Kismeric, "Lincoln credited Brady's portrait in large part – for his election to the presidency."[1]

FDR's Great Deception

Lincoln's efforts at image management were minor compared to those of Franklin D. Roosevelt. From 1910 when he entered politics until his death in 1945 while serving a record fourth term as President, Roosevelt worked continuously on perfecting the art of image management.

Roosevelt's supreme challenge as an image maker came in 1921 when he was struck down by polio and was turned into a wheelchair-bound paraplegic. His political career seemed over. His mother advised him to give up politics. How could Roosevelt, wheelchair-bound, communicate the strength and vitality that voters would expect in a political leader?

Roosevelt rejected the advice to give up politics and set about projecting an image of health and vitality. While campaigning for the governorship of New York in 1928, he perfected a technique that conveyed the impression he could walk by shifting his weight back and forth between a cane on one side and his son Elliott on the other.

To hide his disability, Roosevelt campaigned from cars and trains. He only once referred to his polio in public, and the press went along with his request for voluntary censorship. He never allowed himself to be photographed in his wheelchair. Out of a total of 35,000 photographs in the presidential library, only 2 show Roosevelt in a wheelchair. Author Hugh Gregory Gallagher states, "No newsreels show him being lifted, carried or being pushed in his chair. Among the thousands of political cartoons and caricatures, not one shows the man as physically impaired."[2]

Gallagher both titled his book and calls Roosevelt's successful twenty-five-year campaign to convey vigor *Franklin D. Roosevelt's Splendid Deception.*[3] The deception turned his disability into a nonissue and allowed Roosevelt to lead the United States through the Depression and World War II.

Roosevelt must surely go down in history as one of the twentieth century's greatest communicators. Ronald Reagan, who as President earned the title of the Great Communicator for his nonverbal skills, was mesmerized by Roosevelt's personal magnetism and nonverbal skills. "Reagan," says public relations historian Stuart Ewen, "found Franklin D. Roosevelt's empathic and strikingly accessible presence electrifying. Years later communications lessons learned from Franklin D. Roosevelt were never forsaken."[4]

Roosevelt was also the absolute master of using the radio to influence voters. During his first ten months in office, he spoke directly to the nation on twenty occasions. Roosevelt's labor secretary Frances Perkins said, "His voice and his facial expressions were those of an intimate friend."[5] Perkins watched families listening to Roosevelt's fireside chats laugh and cry as Roosevelt related a funny story or tragic tale.

The 1950s marked the end of the golden age of radio and ushered in the new television age – with a new set of challenges for image makers.

The Kennedy–Nixon Debates

A milestone in television broadcasting came on September 26, 1960, with the first-ever U.S. presidential television debate between Richard Nixon and John F. Kennedy in Chicago.

The polls had Nixon and Kennedy running neck and neck: Nixon 47 percent, Kennedy 47 percent. Nine out of ten American families now owned a television set, and the viewing audience would be the largest ever assembled. The television confrontation was expected to be decisive.

Nixon knew he had problems with television. His notorious five o'clock shadow made him look grim and pallid, even after shaving. Nevertheless, Nixon believed he could rely on his verbal skills. In face-to-face debates, he rarely ever lost.

Kennedy prepared diligently, spending hours answering possible questions prepared by his staff. Nixon refused to practice; no one could tell him what he needed to know.

The signs were ominous for Nixon from the moment he arrived at the television studio. The gathered photographers flocked to take pictures of the young, good-looking Kennedy. When the moderator, Howard K. Smith, introduced the two candidates, Richard Nixon looked, according to author of *Kennedy and Nixon* Christopher Matthews, like an "ill-at-ease, unshaven, middle-aged fellow recovering from a serious illness. Jack Kennedy, by contrast, was elegant in a dark, well-tailored suit that set off his healthy tan."[6]

Verbally Nixon handled himself well. Americans who tuned in to their radios rather than their television sets later rated Nixon a clear winner. But this was the age of television, and the images – the nonverbal body language – that were projected across millions of television screens had an impact. According to Matthews, "Each time Kennedy spoke, Nixon's eyes darted toward him in an uncomfortable mix of fear and curiosity."[7] In stark contrast, Kennedy's body language projected strength and confidence.

Nixon's close adviser Henry Cabot Lodge, watching the last few minutes of the debate, remarked despondently, "That son of a bitch just lost the election."[8]

Kennedy won the great debate decisively: A total of 43 percent of the viewers gave it to Kennedy, 29 percent called it even, and only 23 percent favored Nixon. In the all-important opinion polls, Kennedy pulled ahead. On election day, Nixon lost by just 103,000 votes out of more than 68 million votes cast. "For the rest of his life, Nixon would refuse even to look at the tapes."

The Kennedy–Nixon debates highlighted the importance of nonverbal communication like nothing else that had gone before.

Image Management and Body Language

The importance of nonverbal communication was further highlighted by the publication of the research of a UCLA professor, Albert Mehrabian. On the basis of two studies carried out in 1967, Mehrabian claimed that the impact of nonverbal body language could be measured precisely.

Mehrabian said we are perceived three ways:

1. 55 percent   visually   (body language)
2. 38 percent   vocally   (tone of voice)
3. 7 percent   verbally   (spoken words)

When you add the visual and vocal components together, you are left with the conclusion that nonverbal communication accounts for 93 percent of the impact of a message. By contrast, the verbal component accounts for just 7 percent of the impact (see Figure 5.1).

The 93 percent nonverbal – 7 percent verbal split amazed everyone. But few questioned the research, and the finding soon found its way into virtually every popular book on communication, resulting in an enormous impact on the advice and training given to all persuaders. Many spin doctors, image consultants, and speech trainers still claim it doesn't matter whether you are making a presidential address or proposing marriage, it is your body language that has the most impact.

If you accept the 93 percent figure at face value, then words are essentially unimportant: It's not what you say; it's how you say it.

However, Mehrabian's figures have been discredited as "exaggerated and suspect" by top nonverbal scholars such as Judee Burgoon, David Buller, and Gill Woodall.[9] The saying, "It's not what you say; it's how you say it" is at best a half-truth.

A review of over 100 studies shows the following:[10]

- Words are much more important than Mehrabian's research claims.
- Statistics that suggest the impact of a message can be split into fixed percentages are fundamentally misleading. The relative impact of nonverbal and verbal communication is very dependent upon the persuasive context and therefore varies dramatically from presentation to presentation.

Here is a three-point summary of the latest research on the impact of body language on persuasion:

1. If you are making a presentation in which establishing credibility, making an initial impression, or building a relationship is the prime purpose, then your body language will have the greatest impact (see Figure 5.1).

2. If you are making a presentation, such as a face-to-face sale or negotiation, which is information-heavy, then words become much more important; indeed, they may be the most important components (see Figure 5.2).[11]

3. In most persuasive situations in which your body language and words clash, your audience will rely on your body language for their interpretation. In his television debate with Kennedy, Nixon delivered a mixed message; his body language clashed with his words. The audience turned to the negative body language for their interpretation.

Figure 5.1 The impact of body language varies with the setting. At a social function, the impact of body language will be all-important. The actual message will be of minimal importance.

The Impact of Body Language

Building a Relationship
Content of message unimportant

Figure 5.2 During an important presentation, the message will often be of critical importance. In information-heavy presentations, the content is often more important than the body language.

The Impact of Body Language

Important Presentation
Message critically important

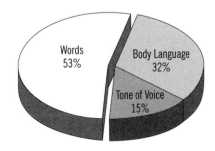

The First Impression

When we meet someone for the first time, we do the following:

1. Scan their face and eyes.
2. Look at their body.
3. Examine what they are wearing.
4. Listen to their tone of voice.
5. Shake their hands, if appropriate.
6. Listen to their words.

If you don't connect with your first impression, you may never connect. The saying, "You don't get a second chance to make a first impression" has some scientific basis. Research shows it takes just two minutes to make your first impression; within four minutes people have made up their minds and the initial impressions are locked in. It can take six to eight meetings to overcome a bad initial impression.

First impressions can undoubtedly mislead us. Both Winston Churchill and Neville Chamberlain didn't take Adolf Hitler seriously at first. Why? Hitler's posturing, absurd little mustache, and slicked-down hair made him look stupid. In the same way, Bill Gates was probably underrated by some of his early competitors because of his "nerd" or "geek" appearance.

The Art of Image Management

In today's world of visual media, few professional persuaders leave image management to chance. Margaret Thatcher employed the services of ex-Mars marketing man Gordon Reece. "[Compare] photographs of her taken in 1975 when she became Conservative Party leader with those taken during and after the 1979 General Election.... She had her teeth capped. She changed her hairstyle to give it a gentler line."[12]

Virtually all of today's political leaders have been made over at some point. Australia's prime minister John Howard is typical. His eyes have been tweaked, his teeth whitened and capped.[13]

The Amazing Hillary Clinton

When it comes to successful image management, few can match Hillary Clinton. When she first moved to Little Rock, Arkansas, in 1976 with new husband Bill, Hillary wore granny-style clothes and coke-bottle glasses, and she opted to retain her maiden name, Rodham. Locals called her Bill's hippie wife.

When Bill Clinton lost his bid for reelection as governor in 1980, Hillary underwent the first of a series of makeovers. She straightened her hair, began wearing contact lenses, and dressed in power suits. On the campaign trail, she dutifully played the role of political wife, rapturously listening to Bill's every word. She even changed her name, calling herself Mrs. Bill Clinton.

With Hillary's support, Bill won reelection in 1982 and subsequently served four more terms.

When the Clintons campaigned for the presidency in 1992, Hillary initially campaigned as an equal partner with strong views of her own. The press called her the co-candidate. But when the polls turned sour at the prospect of a feminist First Lady, Hillary took the advice of her image consultants and did an abrupt turnaround. She ditched the power suits, lightened her hair, and dressed in more feminine outfits. She began campaigning as a mother and even boasted publicly about her low-fat cookie recipe. In the meantime, Hillary successfully confronted allegations about Bill's infidelity.

As First Lady, she failed in her attempts to reform the U.S. health care system and faced ridicule for communicating with the dead Eleanor Roosevelt through a spirit medium.

The glaring publicity of husband Bill's affair with Monica Lewinsky in 1998 must have left her humiliated and bitter, but Hillary continued to stick with Bill. In public, she acted as if nothing had happened. When walking with Bill, "she squeezed his hand, joking and laughing at every photo opportunity."[15] In the 1998 midterm elections, she won plaudits for her marathon cross-country campaigning efforts. Crowds crammed into her evangelical rallies; her public approval ratings soared to 70 percent.

Then she amazed everyone by becoming the first First Lady to pose for *Vogue* – fashion's most influential magazine. The results were stunning: Dressed in a velvet evening gown, the Cinderella of 1974 had turned into a radiant, relaxed, and self-composed cover model. No wonder *Economist* magazine calls her "the amazing Mrs. Clinton."

Health and Vitality

Elected politicians worldwide are "absolutely manic" about looking healthy, says political scientist Michael Jackson. Watch the politicians during winter, he advises. "It is not that they don't get sick, they don't appear when they're ill."[16] They can't afford to appear frail.

Part of the reason for Nixon's television defeat in 1960 was his frail appearance on television while recovering from an illness. Kennedy, who actually had a history of ill health, looked as fit and healthy as an Olympic athlete.

CEO Image Management

Unlike politicians, chief executives don't have to monitor opinion polls, but they do have to watch their share price. "The chief executive is the major determinant of the stock price," says leadership guru Warren Bennis.

Hugh Zurkuhlen, analyst with Salomon Bros., Inc., says, "The short-term impact of a chief executive's personality on the stock price is incredible.... A CEO's presentation and personality have a lot to do with how analysts and portfolio managers view a company." "Many analysts," reports *USA Today*, "say the faces behind the figures can tell them how a company is run and headed. They look for intelligence, substance and candor. But if they also get a touch of pizzazz, warmth and humor, they just might fall in love with the company."[17]

An Intercultural Caution

While all cultures share the same basic emotions, our body language varies enormously. Take eye contact as just one example. Americans, British, Canadians, Australians, and New Zealanders favor direct eye contact. In Japan, Korea, and Thailand, prolonged eye contact is considered rude.

Even within similar cultures, there are important differences. When President George Bush toured Australia, he flashed the "V" for victory sign from the back of his limousine to the watching crowds. It was meant to be a friendly gesture, but the next day Bush's picture made front-page news in Australia. The headlines read, "President Insults Australians."

Bush didn't know that the "V" sign he gave – a backward one, with the back of his hand facing the crowd – means "up yours, mate!" in Australia. The correct form, popularized by Winston Churchill, is with the palm facing outward.[18]

HOW TO USE BODY LANGUAGE

Here are six guidelines to help you manage your body language when influencing:

1. Face the other person squarely.
2. Assume an open posture.
3. Lean forward.
4. Maintain eye contact.
5. Touch.
6. Relax.

1. Face the other person squarely.

Most people focus on your face as their first cue to gauge your attitude, feelings, and emotional state. Show interest by looking directly at the other person. Tilt your head slightly to one side, arch your eyebrows, and nod intermittently to show you understand or agree. The key is to stay relaxed; a tense face is a rigid face. We listen and trust people who express their emotions through an animated face.

Of all the facial expressions, the smile is the most powerful. According to Julius Fast, the author of *Body Language in the Workplace*, the "smile is the most direct way of saying I like you,...

I'm happy in your presence.... It conveys a subtext of trust and caring."[19] It also projects warmth and confidence and is a key to establishing rapport. Make sure your facial expressions match your message. Sending mixed messages weakens your influence.

2. Assume an open posture.

When you adopt an open posture, you convey warmth and receptivity, and you increase your chances of winning the other person over.

Leading negotiating authorities Gerard Nierenberg and Henry Calero found in their research that whenever negotiations went well, seated participants unbuttoned their coats, uncrossed their legs, sat forward in their chairs, and moved closer to the other side. This "getting together cluster" was usually accompanied by words that stressed common needs and the positive advantages of agreement.

On the other hand, if they crossed their arms and legs, they were adopting a negative or defensive posture. Locked ankles and clenched fists also communicated defensiveness.[20]

The way that you stand and walk is also important. An upright stance conveys competence, pride, and confidence; slumped shoulders communicate vulnerability, uncertainty, and uneasiness. The way you walk can convey a variety of messages. Broadly speaking, people who walk rapidly and swing their arms appear goal-oriented.

In 1986, a reporter wrote that President Reagan would emerge from behind a closed door at the White House, then "stride purposely down a long, red-carpeted corridor, then finally bound onto a platform." The subtext was communicated before he spoke: vigour, authority and ease.[21]

Churchill was famous for striding quickly, with his hands on his hips. The nonverbal message: Make way; here I come.

3. Lean forward.

When you lean forward in a chair, with your hands on your

knees or lightly clasped, you are indicating interest to the other party. You are also showing that you are listening and are ready to proceed.

If, however, you sit back in your chair with your hands sharply "steepled" (joining fingers like a church steeple), you are indicating indifference. A barrier, such as a desk, between you and the other party can also add to the negative feelings.

4. Maintain eye contact.

If you want to communicate interest and empathy, look the other person in the eye. When we like someone or find them interesting or appealing, we look at them a lot – research shows about 60 percent to 70 percent of the time. Our pupils dilate at the same time. Hostility is also associated with sustained eye contact, but the pupils constrict so the look feels like a stare.

Exactly where people look when they talk to each other signals the type of relationship they have.

When we are nervous, we avoid eye contact – our eyes typically meet the other person's less than 40 percent of the time. As a result, other people feel uneasy or distrust us.

Watch a TV news anchor in action. TelePrompTers allow TV anchors to read newscopy that rolls over the lens of the camera. As a result, they seem to make eye contact with you in your living room, thus relating to you the listener.

Texaco's $2.5 Billion Eye-Contact Disaster. The commercial costs of failing to establish eye contact were dramatically illustrated in a huge claim Pennzoil brought against Texaco. Pennzoil charged Texaco with illegally interfering in a contract it had with Getty Oil. During the trial, the Texaco lawyers thought Pennzoil's counsel were trying to win over the jury by telling their witnesses to "always make eye contact and joke with them."

To establish the point that the issues were too serious to be joked about, Texaco counsel instructed their witnesses to be serious and to *avoid* all eye contact with the jurors.

It was an unintelligent and very costly mistake. The jury granted Pennzoil over $2.5 billion in damages plus interest – the largest damage award ever in U.S. history. In interviews after the verdict, the jurors said, "Those Texaco witnesses never looked at us once. They were arrogant and indifferent. How could we believe them?"[22]

When staring an opponent down, eyes can be used as a weapon. Margaret Thatcher was well known for using her eyes to stare an opponent down. According to her biographer Andrew Thompson, when Thatcher was upset by an interviewer, "The eyes narrowed, the coldness of the eyes became quite terrifying and the very temperature in the room seemed to chill."[23]

The infamous priest Rasputin's mesmerizing hold over Czarina Alexandra in prerevolutionary Russia was attributed to his penetrating, hypnotic stare. The mass murderer Charles Manson was notorious for his threatening stare.

5. Touch.

In our culture, the most acceptable form of contact between two people is a handshake. In virtually every business and social setting, a handshake is the safest and most positive way to convey friendliness and warmth.

Keep your handshake firm and brief. Apply moderate pressure, hold for three to five seconds, then release.

A limp handshake always suggests disinterest. Females in particular loathe limp handshakes. Everyone dislikes the limp "dead fish" grip, so always make sure your hand is dry and your handshake firm.

The "vise grip" handshake rarely goes down well in business; neither does the "power play" handshake in which one person tries to dominate with his or her hand on top. If someone does this to you, don't restore the balance by using similar tactics. It's much better to register mentally the other person's attempt to dominate and store it away for future reference.

Keating Hugs the Queen. Touch is also used as a mark of status. Generally speaking, higher-status people are more likely to touch; lower-status people are more likely to be touched. The British tabloids screamed outrage when Australian Prime Minister Paul Keating placed his arm around Queen Elizabeth II. Social commentators noted it was simply another symbolic act marking the declining status of the British monarchy in Australia.[24]

The Queen of Hearts. Before Princess Diana, the British royal family had a reputation for physically keeping their distance. Then came Diana – wife of the heir to the British throne and one of the most glamorous and beautiful women in the world – cuddling, hugging, holding, and comforting AIDS, leprosy, cancer, and land-mine victims. As the patron/head of over 300 charities, Diana was able to use her influence to raise hundreds of millions of dollars for charity and cause the world to sit up and take action to ban land-mines.

Her enormous influence was demonstrated when 2 million mourners packed London for her funeral while an extraordinary 2.5 billion worldwide watched the funeral on television.

The Prince of Hearts. The public reaction to her death even influenced her former husband, Prince Charles, to change his "buttoned-up" public image. Within six months of her death, the British tabloids were praising Charles's "new gentle touch" when he followed Diana's lead and reached out to young AIDS victims on a tour of Asia.[25]

6. Relax.

A comfortable, relaxed, yet attentive pose lets the other person know that you are ready to listen. A relaxed posture signals openness while a tense, rigid posture indicates defensiveness.

Don't slouch or appear bored; do try to avoid fidgeting and other random movements, which communicate impatience, boredom, and nervousness.

Page 59 covers the Quickscan process on how to speed-read people.

Checklist of Body Language/Gestures

One of the biggest mistakes you can make when observing body language is to make judgments on that basis, or ignoring the context. Gestures come in clusters and should always be interpreted this way. Use these checklists to identify the common patterns of behavior:

Openness

- Warm smile
- Unfolded arms
- Uncrossed legs
- Leaning forward
- Relaxed body
- Direct eye contact with dilated pupils
- Open palms
- Unbuttoned/removed coat (for men)
- Hands to chest (for men)

Aggressiveness

- Furrowed brow
- Sustained eye contact with contracted pupils (stare)
- Pointing your glasses at someone
- Clenched fists
- Arms spread out while hands grip edge of table
- Leg over arm of chair
- Squinting eyes
- Downward-turned eyebrows
- Pointed index finger
- Strong palm-down thrusting or knuckle-crunching handshake
- Hands on hips when standing
- Moving in on the other person's personal space

Dominance

- Palms down
- Straddling chair – sitting with chair back serving as shield
- Feet on desk
- Physical elevation above the other person
- Strident, loud voice
- Leaning back in chair with both hands supporting head
- Strong palm-down thrusting or knuckle-crunching handshake
- Leg over arm of chair
- Using desk as physical barrier

Defensiveness

- Little eye contact
- Corners of lips turned down
- Rigid body
- Clenched hands
- Palm to back of neck
- Tightly crossed arms
- Wrinkled brow
- Tightly pursed lips
- Head down
- Tightly crossed legs/ankles
- Scratching below earlobes or side of neck

Boredom or Indifference

- Blank stare
- Lack of eye blinking
- Head in palm of hand
- Repetitive finger or foot tapping
- Little eye contact
- Drooping eyes
- Crossed legs
- Doodling

Readiness

- Good eye contact
- Seated, leaning forward with hands on mid-thighs or knees
- Lively facial expression
- Standing with coat open and pushed back with hands on hips (for men)
- Alert facial expression
- Close proximity
- Sitting on edge of chair
- Nodding in agreement

Frustration

- Staring into space
- Running fingers through hair
- Kicking at ground or imaginary object
- Short in-and-out breaths
- Wringing of hands
- Tightly closed lips
- Rubbing back of neck
- Deep breaths
- Tightly clutched hands
- Pacing

Confidence

- Steepling (joining fingers like a church steeple)
- Feet on desk
- Leaning back with hands joined behind back of head
- Proud, erect stance with hands joined behind back
- Head up
- Stretched legs
- Physically elevating oneself
- Leaning back in chair
- Continuous eye contact
- Chin forward

Nervousness, Uncertainty

- Weak, clammy handshake
- Constant throat clearing
- Hands covering mouth while speaking
- Poor eye contact
- Nervous laughter
- Tapping fingers on table
- Sighing
- Crossed arms and legs
- Fidgeting in chair
- Fiddling with objects or clothing
- Pacing
- Smoking
- Biting or picking fingernails or cuticles

DRESSING FOR SUCCESS

People judge us by the clothes we wear. Studies show that the ways we dress are read by others "as statements of deep and personal values – whether those who observe us consciously know it or not."[27]

Dress and Political Image

If you dress in clothes that others regard as conservative, they are highly likely to label you a political conservative. If you dress neatly, people trust you more.

In class-conscious Great Britain, former Labour Party leader Michael Foot was always identified by the scruffy duffel coat he wore everywhere – even to a formal Remembrance Day event – in marked contrast to the immaculate, double-breasted suits most Labor Party politicians wear today.

Power Dress

Impressions of authority are central to persuasion. The right clothes can allow you to communicate authority, competence, and professionalism. Uniforms, judges' wigs, and doctors' white coats all communicate authority. The business suit does the same thing. In the business world, suits remain overwhelmingly the dress of influence. The common "power colors" of blue, black, and charcoal gray communicate strength and competence. The dark-blue pinstripe suit communicates the greatest sense of authority of all.

Although casual dress is weaving its way into the corporate world, such dress must be used with great caution. Many customers still associate casual dress with a casual attitude.

When large numbers of women first joined the workplace, the standard advice was to dress as much like their male colleagues as possible. The advice now is to dress for credibility. For career seekers, this translates into dressing for the position you aspire to. Look at what the people you want to influence are wearing and be guided by their tastes.

Women are more likely to be criticized for inappropriate dress. "When a man gets up to speak, people listen, then look," says U.S. news correspondent Pauline Frederick. "When a woman gets up, people look, then, if they like what they see, they listen."

Frederick exaggerates. President Clinton's Secretary of State, Madeleine Albright, arguably one of the most powerful women in the world, has rarely, if ever, been praised for her looks or her dress style. Her influence comes from her charm, intelligence, relationship building, and persuasive skills.

MIRRORING, PACING, AND LEADING

When people have deep rapport, the body language on both sides is synchronized in the same way a baby's heartbeat becomes synchronized with that of his or her mother.

Mirroring

Often when two people are talking, they will move into virtually identical postures. Without really being aware of it, they will cross their arms or sprawl back in a chair, each forming a virtual mirror image of the other.

In most influence settings, when people share the same view, they often share the same body posture. When the dominant influencer in a group changes his or her body position, the other group members will usually alter their positions to match. If someone in the group opposes the others, his or her body language will clash as well.

If you are speaking to a small group, the degree to which the other people mirror your posture tends to match the intensity of rapport they feel toward you. Mirroring occurs naturally and unconsciously, but skillful persuaders can make conscious use of it.

Mirroring Margaret Thatcher

When Margaret Thatcher first came to power, few bureaucrats could tune in to her needs, but top British civil servant Sir Bernard Ingham was a master of the mirroring process. Ingham – who runs a master class in influence – exerted an enormous hold over Thatcher by aligning his projected self-image to her perceived self-image.

Mary Bragg, author of *Reinventing Influence,* says Thatcher "saw herself as a 'can do' politician, and so she wanted to be surrounded by men and women who would give her the 'can do' image. Rather than offer her the traditional civil service message of 'it can't be done,' Ingham turned himself into a 'can do' civil servant and played Thatcher's perceived self-image straight back to her."[28]

Mirroring Breathing Patterns and Speech

Once you've established a deep level of rapport, you'll find the other person will mirror your breathing patterns and rate of speech. If the person you are trying to influence is breathing slowly, slow down your own breathing until it matches the pace of the other person.

Most people find it takes a lot of practice to learn to mirror breathing patterns. However, it's much easier to mirror the other person's speech in speed, volume, or intonation. A caution! Be subtle; otherwise, people will think you're mimicking them. And don't do it if it means you have to change your own speech pattern dramatically.[29]

Mirroring Language

One of the best ways to build rapport through mirroring is to use the specialist vocabulary or jargon of the person whom you are trying to influence. Most great sellers consciously use their client's vocabulary or jargon when presenting.

Here are examples of a stockbroker selling to an accountant and to an architect; notice how the stockbroker weaves the vocabulary of her client into the conversation:

Example one: Selling stocks to an accountant. "I've *analyzed* your portfolio and think you should consider selling some stocks. The *figures* show that some of your holdings are weak. When you *add up* my ideas I'm sure you'll agree."

Example two: Selling stocks to an architect. "I've *analyzed* your holdings and see some need to change the *structure* of your portfolio of stocks. I've a few ideas that will give you a better *foundation* and better support. As you review the *blueprint,* I'm sure you'll agree."[30]

Words in these examples have been italicized to make a point, but anyone who wants to establish deep rapport must be able to speak his or her audience's language.

Mirroring Posture

In an important meeting, you can mirror the other person's posture. The key is to position your body in a way that is similar to that of the person you're trying to influence. It doesn't mean you should literally mirror the other person, matching move for move and position for position, which irritates and offends. It means approximating his or her position. For example, if the other person is sitting with legs crossed, you can cross your arms while keeping your feet flat on the floor. In other words, be subtle.

Pacing

Can you establish rapport with someone whose body language is aggressive? Yes, you can. But first, you have to get on the same wave length by mirroring that person for a few minutes. Chat about something you have in common. Then continue to mirror the other person for a few minutes until you feel you have established rapport. This ongoing mirroring, in which you subtly change your position and gestures to stay in tune with the other person, is called pacing.

Leading

Once your rapport is strong, you are ready to try to lead, to change that person's body language by changing your own. Change your posture for, say, up to thirty seconds; watch to see if the other person adjusts his or her posture. If the person doesn't change, you are moving too fast. Return to a softer version of the other person's negative style, and wait for a few more minutes before you try to lead him or her again.

Quickscan: How to Speed-Read Another Person

It is highly dangerous to make snap decisions based on body language, but often we have no choice. We simply don't have the time or opportunity to put in the desired preparation. If you have to speed-read a person or group, use the Four-step Quickscan process:

Step One: Scan for context.
First, it pays to scan the surrounding environment. Look at the setting; look for general patterns in the appearance and behavior of people.

Step Two: Concentrate on the key traits.
Once you have an idea of the background, you should focus on the person or people you want to study. Mentally draw up a list of four to six key traits you want to observe, and focus on these.

Step Three: Magnify the critical features.
Having focused on the key traits, you need to bring them into sharper focus, zoom in on these critical features, and examine them in minute detail.

Step Four: Interpret for meaning.
Finally, look for patterns in the clues. What do they suggest? Suspend judgment as long as possible. Look for ways you might be able to test your assumptions.[26]

VOCAL DELIVERY

Few of the great silent film stars survived the arrival of the talking movies in 1927. They simply lacked verbal impact. Even the great Ruldolph Valentino couldn't overcome his small, squeaky voice.

The Power of Vocal Control

In 1985, Peter Blanck and his associate researchers proved that California juries were twice as likely to convict defendants in criminal trials when judges knew of defendants' prior felony convictions, even though the law forbids judges to share that information with juries. How could that be? The researchers found that when the judges gave their final instructions to the jury in cases involving previously convicted defendants, the judges' words lacked warmth, tolerance, and patience; the judges, communicated their negative attitudes via their tone of voice.[31]

Voice – Your Calling Card

If you sound energetic and confident, you will very likely be viewed as energetic and confident. If you sound weak and timid, you will probably be seen as weak and timid. If you sound shrill and strident, people will probably treat you that way. Your voice can reveal how relaxed or tense you are or how tired you are; it can even indicate your emotional state.

Here are five tips on how to produce a confident, commanding voice:

1. Vary your pace to generate interest.

Smart persuaders vary their vocal tempo. Watch a persuasive speaker: He or she can speak fast enough to excite and energize the audience and can slow his or her pace down to create a mood of anticipation.

If you speak too slowly, you'll be seen as boring, tired, or incompetent. A top expert witness, who knows his or her subject backward and forward, will speak more quickly whereas an expert who is unsure on an issue will automatically slow down.

Studies show listeners prefer a faster-than-average speaking rate to a slower-than-average rate. The right pace is slow enough to follow, but quick enough to be interesting.

Most speakers average 120 to 180 words a minute. There is no ideal speed; great speakers' rates of delivery vary greatly. Franklin Roosevelt spoke at 110 words a minute, President Kennedy raced along at 180 words a minute; in one speech, he was clocked at a record-breaking pace of 327 words a minute. Martin Luther King,

Jr. began his "I Have a Dream" speech at 92 words a minute and finished at 145 words a minute. The best rate depends upon the speaker's style and message.[32]

2. Use a low pitch to project authority.

A lower pitch is interpreted as authoritative and influential. It is hard to think of any successful professional persuaders with high-pitched "Minnie Mouse" voices. George Bush nearly destroyed his 1988 presidential campaign by speaking at a high, strained pitch. Until he sought vocal training, he was labeled a "wimp." Similarly, Margaret Thatcher took voice lessons to lower her pitch in an effort to sound more authoritative.

President Reagan was the master. According to professor of linguistics Suzette Haden Elgin, "Reagan's wonderful . . . deep baritone has always been sufficient for people to like him and vote for him even when they disagree with the words the voice is saying."[33] Former White House speechwriter and political columnist William Safire says, "Ronald Reagan's delivery could lift a bad speech by the scruff of the neck, shake it and make it sing."[34]

Inflection is when you raise or lower the pitch as you speak. A persuader's vocal inflections influence our choice of whether to accept or reject what we hear. Think of the sentence "I did not say I stole the money." Read it aloud, each time stressing a different word:

"I did not *say* I stole the money" leaves open the possibility you did the stealing.

"I did not say *I* stole the money" implies you know who did.

"I did not say I stole the *money*" makes it sound as if you did steal something, but not necessarily the money.

Broadcasters are trained to complete sentences with a slight downward inflection. In general, downward inflections communicate confidence, authority, and certainty. Upward inflections, on the other hand, suggest doubt and uncertainty.[35]

3. Control the loudness.

To have an impact, you first have to be heard easily and comfortably. A "megaphone" voice, however, annoys, irritates, and offends. An overly soft voice not only can't be heard, but also conveys meekness and timidity.

The key is to vary your volume by stressing the most important words and phrases. If you want to dramatize a moment, first try lowering the volume. It usually has much more impact than a raised voice.

4. Sharpen your articulation.

Clearly articulate each sentence, phrase, and word; clear, crisp words convey confidence and competence. Sloppy speech, on the other hand, is associated with poor education, laziness, and nervousness. Clear, crisp language is, of course, easy to follow and listen to. Inarticulate speech, by contrast, generates misunderstanding and confusion.

5. Master pauses for impact.

"Bond . . . James Bond." The anticipation here is created by the pause. As Mark Twain said, "There is nothing so powerful as the rightly timed pause."

Persuasive speakers use pauses for emphasis, effect, and mood. President Kennedy's famous line, "Ask not what your country can do for you . . . ask what you can do for your country," is much more powerful when it is delivered with a pause in the middle. Try reading it without the pause and see how it loses its impact.

Pauses can alert your audience to pay attention to a special point, as if you had said, "Listen to this." Much of the power of the pause comes from its subtlety. Here is a lawyer delivering a simple statement to a jury: "The truck was traveling . . . 70 miles per hour when it hit the girl."

The longer pause focuses the attention on the car's speed, without the lawyer having to be overly dramatic. If the lawyer wants to emphasize the girl, all he or she has to do is shift the pause: "The truck was traveling 70 miles an hour when it hit . . . the girl." [36]

The key is to pause: in front of the point you want to emphasize. The greatest mistake speakers make is not pausing long enough for maximum effect. Count one – two – three – four when pausing, and be sure to maintain eye contact during the pause.

John Howard

Poor vocal skills are a serious liability. Australian prime minister John Howard stands out as a professional persuader whose poor vocal skills cost him votes and influence. When Howard reads a speech, he sounds wooden and labored. He has never learned to read a script or master the television autocue. As a result, he prefers to speak off-the-cuff. Even so, he still stumbles and uses weak phrasing.

LIES AND DECEPTION

Sex, Lies, and the President

Newsweek called it the "scandal of the decade." [37] President Bill Clinton stood accused of having an affair with twenty-four-year-old former White House intern, Monica Lewinsky.

On January 26, 1998, Clinton delivered a forceful public denial. Emphasizing every word, he said, "I did not have sexual relations with that woman."

Was Clinton lying? Yes, he was. But at the time, public opinion was split. Clinton's terse comments were even run by a BBC television production team, through a computer software program that analyzes speech patterns. The results shown on a BBC television science program showed Clinton was *technically* telling the truth. But telltale patterns in his voice also indicated "some guilty knowledge," said the Israeli inventor of the Truster lie detector, Amir Lieberman. President Clinton's speech pattern indicated he could have used a deliberately narrow definition of "sexual relations," meaning sexual intercourse but not oral sex. [38]

Politicians have always been masters of deception. The master of the "dark arts" of influence, Machiavelli, advised his master to be "a great feigner and dissembler."

Natural Liars

We are no longer surprised if politicians lie. In his book *Telling Lies*, University of California psychologist Dr. Paul Ekman says any politician "who is agile in handling questions at news conferences, with a glistening TV or radio image, has the conversational talents to be a natural liar."[39]

Ekman says, "Natural liars, should be able to capitalize upon their talents in certain professions — as actors, salesmen, trial lawyers, negotiators, spies or diplomats."[40]

Born Liars

Are we born dishonest? Amazingly, researchers have discovered that "people have genes for lying."[41] A study of 1,819 Hawaiians found that, of fifty-four different personality traits, family members most imitated each other in the way they lied. "Family members deceive in similar ways," concludes science writer Daniel McNeill, "because of their genes."[42]

The evidence suggests that lying in the workplace is endemic. A 1997 survey of 200 sales managers, carried out by *Sales and Marketing Management* magazine, revealed widespread deception:[43]

- 49 percent of surveyed managers said their reps have lied to customers.
- 34 percent say they've heard reps make unrealistic promises to customers.
- 22 percent say their reps have sold products their customers didn't need.
- 30 percent say customers have demanded a kickback for buying their product or service.

The survey, states *Sales and Marketing Management*, shows "a market place sullied by unethical behavior."[44]

In his book *Telling Lies*, Dr. Paul Ekman says, "There are two primary ways to lie; to *conceal* and *falsify*. In concealing, the liar withholds information without actually saying anything true. In falsifying, the liar takes an additional step. Not only does the liar withhold true information, but presents false information as if were true."[45]

Lies Are Difficult to Detect

If lying is so common, every influencer needs to be able to ferret out the untruths and find the truth using all the skills of an investigative reporter.

The problem is that when it comes to detecting lies, we are not very good. In a study carried out at the University of California, Ekman found most of the people we expect to be skilled lie detectors – police detectives, judges, and lawyers – are 45 percent to 60 percent accurate in spotting lies. This is no better than the rate of the average citizen when it comes to detecting lies. The only group in Ekman's study who did better than chance were Secret Service agents – and even they were only 64 percent accurate.

A recent Dutch study asked prisoners, police, prison guards, customs officers, and students to list signs of lying. The prisoners easily outscored the other groups, perhaps, researchers said, because they were more practiced in bluffing and conning.[46]

Training in lie detection, however, can make a huge difference. Lie-catching scores usually improve from 50 percent to over 80 percent.

Closely observing nonverbal signals is the key to lie detection. "Everyone knows that when we use words, we can say whatever we want and easily conceal the truth," says Ekman, "but it takes extraordinary skills to deceive the trained eye with our face, voice and body."[47]

We can spot a liar by watching for clues to deceit (see page 70). Pay attention to the nonverbal "leakages" that come out in body language through the face, body, voice, and words:

Face

When our emotions are aroused, our facial muscles begin to twitch automatically. Liars, therefore, focus a lot of their efforts on managing their facial expressions since they know that is what others look at.

Liars' eyes provide a number of useful clues for the suspicious listener. Liars avert their gaze to reduce anxiety levels. Liars' eye pupils also dilate, and blinking reduces. "The eye is traitor of the heart," said poet Thomas Wyatt. When clues from the mouth and the eyes clash, the eyes prevail.

Liars often display a marked reluctance to sit or stand face-to-face. Some will turn away from you or even try and hide behind a desk or physical object.

Liars smile less; when liars do smile, they resort to forced smiles. When we spontaneously smile, the muscles beneath our eyes create skin wrinkles. Forced smiles do not alter these muscles. Forced smiles also distort one side of the face more than the other. The forced smile appears more quickly, is held longer, and then fades away irregularly.

Body

Liars often try to keep their hands still or out of sight by significantly decreasing their hand-movements. Deceivers often engage in more frequent self-touching by continually touching their nose, chin, or mouth.

Confident, honest people stand erect or sit up straight. Liars, because of their insecurity, slouch more and often put their hands in their pockets.

Voice

Liars raise the pitch of their voices, especially at the end of a sentence. When liars talk, they hesitate more by leaving gaps in their speech. Liars are also sometimes inclined to mumble and speak inexpressively.

Words

Not surprisingly, liars avoid making factual statements; they use generalizations instead of specific statements. Liars depersonalize their answers and avoid using the pronouns *I* and *we*. When President Nixon was accused of wrongdoing in the Watergate affair, he did not say, "I did not do that." He replied, "The President would not do such a thing."

Liars also depersonalize their answers by giving you their attitude on a subject rather than giving a direct answer.

Liars avoid giving direct answers to questions. Their answers circumvent the question. Look at how Ronald Ziegler, President Nixon's press secretary during the Watergate crisis, avoided answering reporter Helen Thomas's questions:

> *Thomas:* Has the President asked for any resignations so far and have any been submitted or are on his desk?
>
> *Ziegler:* I have repeatedly stated, Helen, that there is no change in the status of the White House staff.
>
> *Thomas:* But that was not the question. Has he asked for any resignations?
>
> *Ziegler:* I understood the question and I heard it the first time. Let me go through my answer. As I have said, there is no change in the status of the White House staff. There have been no resignations submitted.

Ziegler did not want to be caught lying in public so he avoided answering the question directly.

To cover guilt, shrewd liars display indignant outbursts. In 1960 Israeli prosecutors discovered whenever the Nazi mass murderer Adolf Eichmann screamed, "Never! Never! Never! Herr Hauptmann" or "At no time! At no time!" he was lying.

Liars are also inclined to add in phrases such as "to be perfectly honest" and "to tell you the truth." These phrases are called "metatalk. "

Liars often exaggerate. When they use numbers, liars often fall into "the number trap." They use rounded numbers rather than specific figures, and all the numbers they use appear to be multiples of each other.

Liars make unconscious slips. They say one thing when they mean to say another. The great psychologist Sigmund Freud called these, slips of the tongue. Slips, he said, are not accidents; they are a "mode of self betrayal." For example, someone who intends to say, "This was a tough assignment; it took me all weekend to write it" might slip up and say, "This was a tough assignment. It took me all weekend to *copy* it."

Liars' answers can sound too good to be true. In the O.J. Simpson trial, prosecution witness detective Mark Fuhrman claimed under oath that he had never used a specific racial epithet. Virtually no one, including the jury, believed him. He would have been far more credible if he had confessed to occasionally using racial epithets. Later on, the defence was able to use a taped conversation to prove that he was a liar and discredit him.

Liars also give more information than necessary. Liars, to cover up their deceit, oversell. They go on and on when a short answer would be sufficient.

Perhaps the most damning proof of deceit is the verbal contradictions that even the most skilled liars make. In another part of the conversation or at a later meeting, they contradict an earlier statement.

THE THREE-STEP
LIE DETECTION PROCESS

Gerhard Gschwandtner, the editor of *Personal Selling Power* magazine, has developed a useful set of three guidelines to help persuaders detect lies:[48]

1. Watch for contradictions and verbal mistakes. People often forget what they have said in a previous meeting. Memory lapses and slips of the tongue often result in contradictions. Write these contradictions down. However, never assume a verbal slip is a lie; it may simply be an act of carelessness.

2. Compare two different conversations. Examine the discrepancies between what the person says at two different meetings. For example, a prospective partner displays a little nervousness when you ask questions about the financial success of one of his previous ventures. He pauses for a moment, then delivers a confident answer, supported by a broad smile. During a second meeting, you return to the same subject. However, this time the pause is more prolonged, the answer more convoluted, and the pitch of his voice higher.

Although you have no proof that your prospective partner is lying, the wide discrepancy between the two meetings indicates you need to delve deeper.

3. Watch for clashes between verbal and nonverbal messages. When you listen to the other person, watch his or her voice, eyes, and hands. Listen for a rising voice pitch; watch for reduced hand movements and increased self-touching gestures. If there is a gap between what people say and what their bodies express, carefully monitor the verbal information.

Common Clues to Deceit

Here is a checklist of the common signs of deception. Remember, there is no single gesture, posture, or facial expression that is in itself proof of deceit. There are only clues to leakage and deception. A facial clue, therefore, needs to be supported by confirming clues from the face, body, voice, and words.

1. Face

- Avoids eye contact.
- Pupils dilate and blinking reduces.
- Does little smiling.
- False smiles linger longer and end abruptly.
- Smile appears forced.
- Eyes seem vacant.

2. Body

- Gestures and words don't match.
- Uses fewer arm and hand movements to illustrate points.
- Uses increased self-touching of nose, chin, and mouth.

3. Voice

- Raises voice pitch.
- Increase pauses and hesitations.
- Has slower speech.

4. Words

- Avoids making factual statements.
- Uses generalizations instead of specifics.
- Words seem forced.
- Takes longer to answer questions.
- Uses briefer answers than normal.
- Has more um's and uh's.
- Is inclined to mumble and speak inexpressively.
- Statements sound like questions.
- Avoids using pronouns *I* and *we*.
- Implies rather than gives an answer.
- Avoids direct answers.
- Uses phrases such as "to be perfectly honest," and "to tell you the truth."
- Claims sound too good to be true.
- Reasoning sounds implausible.
- Numbers mentioned are rounded and sound the same or are multiples of each other.
- Is prone to verbal outbursts which leak information.
- Has verbal slips of the tongue.

CHAPTER 5

PERSUASION
POINTERS

① Always make sure your body language matches your verbal communication. When your body language and words clash, your body language will have the greater impact.

② You rarely get a second chance to make a favorable impression. It only takes four minutes to lock in a negative impression.

③ To create rapport using body language, face the other person, assume an open posture, lean forward, maintain eye contact, and shake hands.

④ Always present yourself in the most advantageous way possible. Dress to communicate authority, competence, and professionalism.

⑤ To deepen rapport, mirror the other person's posture, language, and rate of speech.

⑥ Control your tone of voice, speed of delivery, pitch, and volume to project confidence and authority. Use pauses for impact.

⑦ To detect deceit, look for contradictions and verbal mistakes. Watch for clashes between the verbal and nonverbal messages.

Reading the Other Person

6

How to Use Personality Type to Persuade

▌ PERSONALITY TYPE AND BEHAVIOR

While we come in all shapes and sizes, we are not as different as most of us like to think. Scholars of Personality Type have found that our behavior is surprisingly predictable and have identified a number of personality types into which we all fit.

The idea of personality type goes back over seventy years to the work of Swiss psychologist Carl Jung. Jung said there were three personality preference scales and eight Personality Types. Two American women, Katharine Briggs and her daughter Isabel Myers, expanded on Jung and developed the Myers Briggs Type Indicator (MBTI). Their research revealed there were four personality preference scales and sixteen distinct personality types.

Personality Type and Persuasion

Over the past decade, millions of people have taken the MBTI. In the process, professional persuaders have discovered the value of Personality Type. Professional persuaders, especially salespeople, have found that Personality Type is one of the best predictors of human behavior. Research on personality type reveals that different personality types prefer to be persuaded in different ways. A knowledge of Personality Type helps you:

- Identify how the people you want to persuade like to be persuaded
- Identify what kind of information the people you want to convince take notice of and remember
- Identify how the people you want to influence make decisions
- Talk your clients' or audience's language
- Quickly build the rapport required for successful persuasion.

With this information, it's so much easier for a professional persuader to tailor his or her presentation to meet the other person's precise needs.

THE FOUR SCALES OF PERSONALITY TYPE

Personality Type can be measured on four scales; each of these scales is a continuum between two extremes:

1. How and where we get our energy from (the Extrovert-Introvert Scale)

    (E) Extrovert   Introvert (I)

2. What type of information we pay attention to (the Sensor-Intuitive Scale)

    (S) Sensor   Intuitive (N)

3. How we make decisions (the Thinker-Feeler Scale)

    (T) Thinker   Feeler (F)

4. How we resolve issues (the Judger-Perceiver Scale)

    (J) Judger   Perceiver (P)

The opposite ends of each scale are called preferences. Most of us have a built-in bias toward one preference. People at the opposite ends of a scale are usually very different from each other. A strong extrovert, for example, is usually much more talkative and outgoing than an extreme introvert, who is usually both much less talkative and more reflective. However, the strongest introvert is usually quite capable of very strong extroverted behavior. A strong introvert, for example, can still be a superb trainer and presenter, activities normally associated with extroverts.

However, we are most comfortable when working or communicating in the way that comes naturally to our personality type. Indeed, research shows that, under stress, we tend to revert to personality type.

The four scales yield eight preferences; these preferences combine to create sixteen possible combinations of personality types.

It is easiest to view these in a chart (see below). Personality Type uses a preference's first letter as a form of shorthand. For example, an extrovert is called an E; an introvert is called an I. (Note: An intuitive is called an N because an I is the shorthand label for an introvert.)

The 16 Personality Types			
ISTJ	ISFJ	INFJ	INTJ
ISTP	ISFP	INFP	INTP
ESTP	ESFP	ENFP	ENTP
ESTJ	ESFJ	ENFJ	ENTJ

Scale 1: How and Where We Get Our Energy From (Extrovert-Introvert Scale)

The first scale measures how we are energized. Extroverts are energized by the company of others. When their batteries need charging, they mix with friends and colleagues. By contrast, introverts energize themselves by seeking solitude and reflecting alone.

When it comes to working on a project, extroverts like involving others in the planning and implementation; introverts prefer to work alone and think through the challenges in isolation.

Extroverts communicate by thinking and working through a problem out loud; they like to talk matters over with others. Introverts don't usually speak as much as extroverts. Introverts prefer privacy; they tend to reflect and pause before giving an opinion.

Because extroverts like the company of others, they are normally much more comfortable in a public role, exposed to the glare of continual public scrutiny. Introverts appear more secretive. Because they value their privacy, introverts let only their closest friends share their secrets.

About 75 percent of Americans are extroverts; the remaining 25 percent are introverts.

Read through the checklist below; choose the preference that best describes your behavior.

Extovert-Introvert Checklist

Extroverts	Introverts
▪ Think aloud	▪ Reflect, then talk
▪ Communicate enthusiastically	▪ Keep feelings to themselves
▪ Are talkative	▪ Listen more than talk
▪ Dominate conversation	▪ Need to be drawn out
▪ Share personal facts more readily	▪ Keep personal information private
▪ Prefer face-to-face meetings	▪ Like written memos and reports
▪ Speak rapidly when giving information	▪ Pause when answering questions
▪ Are at ease communicating with groups	▪ Like to communicate one-on-one

Which preference seems to describe you best?

_____ Extrovert (E)   _____ Introvert (I)

Scale 2: What Type of Information We Pay Attention To (Sensor-Intuitive Scale)

The second scale describes the way we prefer to receive information. Sensors pay attention to facts and details. By contrast, when listening to a presentation intuitives like to get the big picture first; the details can come later.

Sensors rely on information that is practical and useful, but intuitives like to learn new things through general concepts.

Sensors are oriented to the present; they like to live life focused on today. Intuitives consider the implications and possibilities of a situation rather than the facts and details. They are future- rather than present-oriented.

Sensors process their information through their five senses – what they see, hear, touch, taste, and smell – hence the label sensors. Intuitives absorb their information through their sixth sense – their intuition – hence the label, intuitives. The latter often rely on their gut feeling or hunch.

Personality Type experts Paul Tieger and Barbara Barron-Tieger say that, "Sensors see the trees while Intuitives see the forest." The Tiegers also use a photographic metaphor to demonstrate the differences in focus between sensors and intuitives. Imagine, they say, a photographer taking a picture with a zoom lens. "The photographer is shooting a person in front of a huge panoramic view of a mountain range. With Sensors, it's as if they turn the lens until the person in the foreground (the detail) is in sharp focus, while the view behind (the big picture) is blurry. With Intuitives, it's just the opposite: they turn the lens so that the view (the big picture) behind the person is in focus, but the person in the foreground (the detail) is blurry and out of focus." [1]

Some 65 percent of the U.S. population are sensors; intuitives represent 35 percent.

Read through the following checklist; choose the preference that best describes your behavior.

Sensor-Intuitive Checklist

Sensors	Intuitives
■ Present facts, evidence, examples first	■ Present the "big picture" ideas first
■ Ask lots of "what" and "how" questions	■ Ask lots of "why" questions
■ Use lots of specific examples	■ Talk about general concepts
■ Are interested in short-term, practical applications	■ Are interested in the long-term picture and future possibilities
■ Like step-by-step information and detailed descriptions	■ Like using metaphors and analogies
■ Value real-life experiences	■ Are interested in hunches and imaginative insights

Which preference seems to describe you best?

_____ Sensor (S)   _____ Intuitive (N)

Scale 3: How We Make Decisions (Thinker-Feeler Scale)

The third scale measures the different ways we make decisions or reach conclusions.

When it comes to making a decision, thinkers are driven by facts, logic, and reason. They like to weigh the pros and cons of an issue. If the facts point to the need for a tough decision, so be it – even if it means upsetting or hurting the feelings of others. For thinkers, the truth (as they see it), is of central importance.

When feelers make a decision, the emotions or feelings of others who will be affected are of central importance. For feelers, all feelings are important, and decisions should be made based on both facts and sympathy. Feelers are persuaded more by a strong emotional call than cold, hard logic. For feelers, tact is as important as truth.

If the thinker can be described as head over heart, the feeler can be described as heart over head. Whereas most thinkers would be proud to be called tough-minded, feelers would take pride in being called tender-hearted.

The U.S. population is split 50/50 between thinkers and feelers.

Read through the following checklist; choose the preference that best describes your behavior.

Thinker-Feeler Checklist

Thinkers	Feelers
■ Use cold, hard facts and logic to persuade others	■ Persuade others with personal, emotionally presented examples
■ Present meeting goals and objectives first	■ Start with pleasantries, then summarize areas of agreement
■ Weigh the pros and cons of each example	■ Talk about the value of each alternative
■ Demonstrate objectivity and are often critical	■ Empathize and appreciate other viewpoints
■ Believe feelings are only valid if they are logical	■ Believe all feelings are valid
■ Are task-focused	■ Are relationship-focused

Which preference seems to describe you best?

——————————— Thinker (T)   ——————————— Feeler (F)

Scale 4: How We Resolve Issues (Judger-Perceiver Scale)

The last scale describes the way we like to plan and organize our lives.

Judgers prefer to make decisions quickly. They like to be decisive; uncertainty and indecision create anxiety. On the other hand, when it comes to making decisions, perceivers prefer to keep their options open. They prefer to hold off decisions until they absolutely have to make them.

Judgers like to be in control; they like stepping in and taking charge. Perceivers are much more happy than judgers to let others take charge and run the show.

Judgers are time-conscious and like to be punctual and to work under deadlines. Time for the perceiver is a renewable resource; deadlines are meant to be flexible.

Perceivers do not like to be overly organized and often have trouble locating things or staying organized. Judgers are likely to believe a "cluttered desk indicates a cluttered mind"; a perceiver believes an "empty desk is the symbol of an empty mind." Judgers value organization; they like a "place for everything and everything in its place."

Judgers make up about 60 percent and perceivers about 40 percent of Americans.

Read through the following checklist; choose the preference that best describes your behavior.

Judger-Perceiver Checklist

Judgers	Perceivers
Prefer to make decisions quickly and like to be seen as decisive	Like to keep options open – may procrastinate
Like to set schedules and deadlines	Feel restricted by schedules and deadlines
Like to complete projects	Prefer to start projects
Negotiate from fixed positions and are sometimes dogmatic	Are flexible about positions and are sometimes seen as wishy-washy
Focus discussions on content	Focus discussions on process
Like meetings to reach a conclusion	Are happy for meetings to remain inconclusive
Believe time is a fixed resource and deadlines are important	Believe time is renewable and deadlines are elastic

Which preference seems to describe you best?

————————— Judger (J)　　————————— Perceiver (P)

The following diagram sums up what we've discussed so far.

Summary of the Four Personality Types

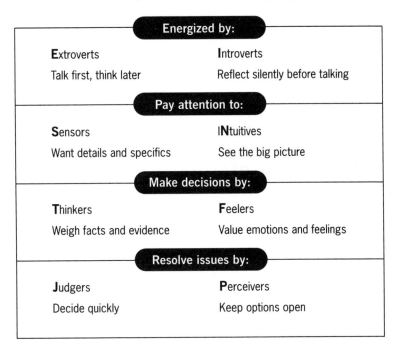

Energized by:

Extroverts

Talk first, think later

Introverts

Reflect silently before talking

Pay attention to:

Sensors

Want details and specifics

INtuitives

See the big picture

Make decisions by:

Thinkers

Weigh facts and evidence

Feelers

Value emotions and feelings

Resolve issues by:

Judgers

Decide quickly

Perceivers

Keep options open

HOW TO USE PERSONALITY TYPE WHEN PERSUADING

To determine a Personality Type quickly, ask yourself four questions:

1. Does the person I want to persuade usually prefer to talk about an issue out loud before acting (extrovert) or prefer to reflect on a problem before talking and acting (introvert)?

2. When listening to a presentation, does the person I want to persuade pay attention to specific and detailed information (sensor) or respond to the global or big picture (intuitive)?

3. When making a decision, does the person I want to persuade base a decision on the quality of facts and evidence (thinkers) or consider first the impact on people's values and feelings (feelers)?

4. Does the person I want to persuade prefer to proceed quickly once a decision has been made (judger) or prefer to keep options open (perceiver)?

The key when persuading is to remember different Personality Types prefer to be persuaded in different ways.

As a persuader, you are not going to know the Personality Type of everyone you want to convince. However, most people reveal enough clues through their behavior to allow you to approximately match your style to their preferences.

THE FOUR KEY INFLUENCING STRATEGIES

It also pays to remember that, for most persuaders, the critical information you need for successful persuasion relates to the middle two personality scales: the sensor-intuitive scale and the thinker-feeler scale.

When you narrow your focus to the SN and TF scales, you discover there are only four combinations or functional pairs: ST, SF, NT, and NF.

By focusing on just these four combinations, you come up with four key influencing strategies (see below).

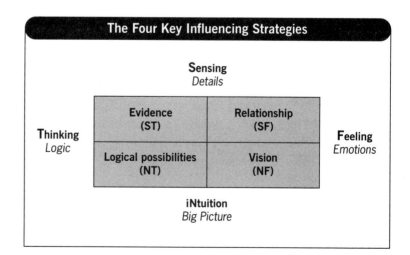

The Four Key Influencing Strategies		
	Sensing *Details*	
Thinking *Logic*	Evidence (ST)	Relationship (SF)	**Feeling** *Emotions*
	Logical possibilities (NT)	Vision (NF)	
	iNtuition *Big Picture*	

To be effective, choose one of these options:

To influence an ST: Concentrate on the evidence and present a step-by-step, logical analysis. In essence, focus on the evidence.

To influence an SF: Concentrate on the details and show how these details will affect the people involved. In essence, focus on the relationship.

To influence an NT: Present an overview first, and offer a series of well-analyzed, practical options. In essence, focus on the logical possibilities.

To influence an NF: Present the big picture and demonstrate how your proposal will impact people's lives, values, and feelings. In essence, help the other person realize his or her vision.

A Final Caution

If this has been your first look at Personality Type, you should now attend a workshop on MBTI run by an accredited MBTI trainer and take the full test.

To evaluate someone's Personality Type, see page 83. For the personality types of some famous people, see page 84.

When assessing personality type, always remember that people of the same or similar personality type usually have little trouble communicating with each other. "The converse is also true," write personality type experts and authors Paul D. Tieger and Barbara Barron-Tieger. "In general, the more different your type ... the greater the likelihood of miscommunication."[2]

The golden rule in personality type communication is: "Do unto others as they would like done unto them."[3] In other words, always speak the other person's language.

Speed-Type Analysis

Energized by:

Extroverts
Talk first ☐

Introverts
Reflect silently ☐

Pay attention to:

Sensors
Want details ☐

i**N**tuitives
See big picture ☐

Make decisions by:

Thinkers
Weigh facts ☐

Feelers
Value emotions ☐

Resolve issues by:

Judgers
Decide quickly ☐

Perceivers
Keep options open ☐

Type:

☐ ☐ ☐ ☐

The Four Key Influencing Strategies

Evidence (ST)	Relationship (SF)
Logical possibilities (NT)	Vision (NF)

Persuasion Strategy

Personality Types of Famous People

ISTJ	ISFJ	INFJ	INTJ
■ George Washington ■ George Bush ■ Herbert Hoover ■ Harry Truman	■ Michael Jordan ■ Robert D. Lee ■ Queen Elizabeth II ■ William Howard Taft	■ Oprah Winfrey ■ Mother Teresa ■ Martin Luther King, Jr. ■ Jimmy Carter ■ Princess Diana	■ Hannibal ■ Susan B. Anthony ■ Thomas Jefferson ■ John F. Kennedy ■ Woodrow Wilson
ISTP	**ISFP**	**INFP**	**INTP**
■ Keith Richards ■ Ernest Hemingway ■ Millard Fillmore ■ Zachary Taylor	■ Michael Jackson ■ Paul McCartney ■ Ulysses S. Grant ■ Wolfgang Mozart ■ John Travolta	■ Anne Frank ■ William Shakespeare ■ Jacqueline Kennedy ■ John F. Kennedy, Jr.	■ Socrates ■ Albert Einstein ■ Dwight Eisenhower ■ Gerald Ford ■ Adolf Hitler
ESTP	**ESFP**	**ENFP**	**ENTP**
■ Madonna ■ Jack Nicholson ■ James Buchanan ■ Franklin Pierce	■ Bob Hope ■ Goldie Hawn ■ Arsenio Hall ■ Pablo Picasso	■ Mark Twain ■ Meg Ryan ■ Ronald Reagan ■ Leon Trotsky	■ Tom Hanks ■ Theodore Roosevelt ■ Winston Churchill
ESTJ	**ESFJ**	**ENFJ**	**ENTJ**
■ Elliot Ness ■ Lyndon Johnson ■ Joseph Stalin ■ John D. Rockefeller	■ Don Knotts ■ Sally Field ■ Bill Clinton ■ William McKinley ■ Rev. Billy Graham	■ François Mitterand ■ Abraham Lincoln ■ Mao Tse-tung ■ Ross Perot ■ Nelson Mandela	■ Franklin D. Roosevelt ■ Richard Nixon ■ Gen. Norman Schwarzkopf ■ Margaret Thatcher

Source: Joe Butts. www.typelogic.com.

Power Talk!

How to Give Words Added Impact

WORDS DO MATTER

The Jesuit and the Benedictine

A Jesuit priest and a Benedictine monk shared a problem. Both were addicted chain-smokers, and they had to spend large portions of their day praying, all the while craving a smoke.

After talking about their problem, they agreed to discuss it with their respective superiors and report back the following week.

When they met again, the Jesuit asked the Benedictine how the meeting had gone. "Disastrously," he replied. "I asked the Abbot, 'Will you give me permission to smoke while I'm praying?' and he was furious. He gave me fifteen extra penances as a punishment for my irreverence. But you look happy, my brother, what happened to you?"

The Jesuit smiled. "I went to my rector, and asked, 'May I have permission to pray while I am smoking?' Not only did he give me permission, but he congratulated me on my piety."[1]

Like the Jesuit, successful persuaders know how to extract value out of every word. Numerous studies show that speakers with good verbal skills come across as more credible, competent, and convincing.

On the other hand, speakers who hesitate, lack fluency, and use powerless language lack credibility and come across as weak and ineffective.

English – The Super-Language for Persuaders

"English is the great vacuum cleaner of language: it sucks in anything it can get."
— *David Crystal*

If there is a super-language for persuaders, it surely has to be English. With over 615,000 words, English gives the skilled persuader virtually an infinite choice of word combinations – and each year another 5,000 new words are added to the pool.

Shakespeare alone created hundreds of new words. "If you 'have seen better days' and are 'poor but honest'; or 'haven't slept a wink' because someone has 'made you mad' – you are not only speaking English, you are speaking Shakespeare."[2]

One popular myth says the size of a person's vocabulary is about two-thirds the size of Shakespeare's vocabulary, whose plays contain about 30,000 words. But many more words exist than appear in Shakespeare, and many speakers probably know twice as many words as Shakespeare did. According to Oxford University linguist Jean Aitchison, an educated, mature speaker of English can call on at least 50,000 words.[3]

POWER TALK

Powerful persuaders are highly articulate, skilled wordsmiths. They speak what communications authority George Walther calls power talk.[4] Power talkers have the following characteristics:

Power talkers use affirmative language. They talk positively. When they want something, they use words that communicate precisely what they expect to happen. Suppose if, for example, they want an unenthusiastic worker to complete his or her report. Instead of saying:

> "*If* you finish the report tonight, we'll all celebrate by going out for a drink."

They say:

"*When* you finish your report tonight, we'll all celebrate by going out for a drink."

Power talkers speak assertively. When talking, they describe themselves, their beliefs, and their achievements positively and confidently.

Instead of saying:

"Well, it's only my opinion, of course, and I could be wrong, but I would say …"

They say:

"I believe …"

Power talkers accept responsibility. Power talkers avoid the language of victimization. Rather than blame others when they speak, they take control and accept responsibility for their circumstances. They use their words to shape the circumstances in which they find themselves.

Instead of saying:

"That's not my department. You'll have to talk to someone else to help you."

They say:

"I'll help you myself. I'll get the person responsible to ring you."

Power talkers talk win-win. Power talkers use win-win phrasing to create cooperation and synergy. When negotiating, they try to turn win-lose into win-win.

Instead of saying:

"That's not practical; it'll never work."

They say:

"That's a new approach; let's talk it through and see where we end up."

Power talkers speak decisively. Smart persuaders are straight talkers. They don't waffle; they get straight to the point and say exactly what they mean. Decisive speakers project credibility and confidence.

Instead of saying:

> "I think this will probably solve your needs. Hopefully, this will give you what you are looking for."

They say:

> "This is going to fit your needs exactly. I know this will give you exactly what you want."

Power talkers speak the language of integrity. Power talkers convey integrity by avoiding phrases that make people question their sincerity and honesty.

Instead of saying:

> "To be perfectly honest, we had to reprimand Kevin for poor performance."

They say:

> "We had to reprimand Kevin for poor performance."

Power talkers avoid intensifiers. Intensifiers such as *very, definitely,* and *surely* do the opposite of what they are supposed to do.

Australian Prime Minister John Howard is notorious for weakening his language with *very.* Look at how all the *verys* Howard uses make him sound weak and ineffective:

June 1995: "I am going to have to work *very, very* hard to win."
February 1996: "I am really getting *very, very* happy about this campaign."
March 1996: "I feel *very, very* deeply and *very* personally the responsibility that has been given to me."

Power talkers avoid hesitations and fillers. Powerless speakers hesitate a lot and rely on fillers such as *uh, umm,* and *well.* Fillers communicate uncertainty and a lack of confidence.

Power talkers avoid tag questions. When you add a question to the end of the statement, it is called a tag question. "This plan will cost too much, don't you think?" is a tag question. Tag questions communicate uncertainty and damage credibility.

Power talkers avoid disclaimers. Disclaimers are introductory expressions that ask the listener to show understanding or to be tolerant. "I'm not an expert in this field, but …" is a classic disclaimer. Disclaimers challenge the listener to disagree with you and question your expertise.

Power talkers avoid hedges and qualifiers. When we are unsure of something or are afraid to assert ourselves, we use hedges and qualifiers. Instead of saying "I liked that proposal," we become uncertain and say "I *sort* of liked that proposal."

Power talkers avoid irritators. Irritators are phrases that annoy the listener while conveying vagueness, uncertainty, and incompetence. If you say, "I know I'm not communicating this clearly, but you know what I mean," you are effectively saying, "I can't be bothered clarifying my thoughts."

Power talkers try not to be overly polite. Powerless speakers use *please* and *thank-you* too often. Overpoliteness conveys timidity and uncertainty.

If you have made a mistake or inconvenienced someone, an apology is appropriate. However, if you say, "I apologize – we had a power failure," you are apologizing for a situation over which you had no control. It is better to simply state the problem and detail your solution.

WHAT'S IN IT FOR ME?

Whether you are selling a product, service, or an idea, it always pays to remember that the person you are trying to convince always wants to know, What's in it for me? You'll never convince anyone verbally until you answer that question. Compare the appeal of the promotion "Apples contain vitamins and natural sugar" with "An apple a day keeps the doctor away."[5] The first speaks the words of the apple grower; the second appeals to the needs of the buyer.

Sell the Sizzle, Not the Steak

From early in their careers, salespeople are taught that to make a sale they must first show how their product or service can meet a prospect's needs. This requires a knowledge of the features and benefits of what they are selling and an understanding of the difference between the two.

Features are the facts that describe both what the product is and how it is made or works. Benefits, on the other hand, are statements of ways in which the product's features will help the prospect. Here is a list of some computer features with their associated benefits:

Computer Features and Their Benefits

Features	Benefits
Pentium III microprocessor	Lets you both work faster and use the latest video and graphics applications
10-gigabyte hard drive	Holds more program and data files, giving you more power and flexibility
EV900 19" monitor	Gives you increased viewing area without taking any more desk space than a 17" monitor

Features are cold, remote, and impersonal; benefits are warm and tempting. While prospects can be interested in features, it is benefits that cement the sale.

For this reason, you hear sales trainers urging their classes to "sell the sizzle, not the steak," "sell the tan, not the sun," and "sell the envy, not the car."[6]

Appeals and Basic Human Wants

Once you have a list of benefits, you have to decide which appeal will do the best selling job. Marketers talk about positioning the product in the prospect's mind. Bob Stone, professor of direct marketing at Northwestern University, believes, "People respond to any given proposition for one of two reasons: to gain something they do not have or to avoid losing something they now possess."[7]

Bob Stone's list of basic human wants is found below. He created this list for professional copywriters working in the direct-marketing industry, but it is a useful checklist for any persuader to use when determining the appeal of a persuasive proposition.

What Motivates Us to Act	
The Desire to Gain	**The Desire to Avoid Loss**
To make money	To avoid criticism
To save time	To avoid loss of possessions
To avoid effort	To avoid physical pain
To achieve comfort	To avoid loss of reputation
To have health	To avoid loss of money
To be popular	To avoid trouble
To experience pleasure	
To be clean	
To be praised	
To be in style	
To gratify curiosity	
To satisfy an appetite	
To have beautiful possessions	
To attract the opposite sex	
To be an individual	
To emulate others	
To take advantage of opportunities	

Source: Bob Stone, *Successful Direct Marketing Methods*, NTC Business Books, 1994, p.379.

Henry Kissinger the Salesman

All persuaders should think in terms of features and benefits. Few people think of Henry Kissinger, Secretary of State for Richard Nixon, as a salesman, but much of his "shuttle diplomacy" time was spent getting two sides in a dispute to see the benefits of coming to an agreement. For his exceptional skills as a negotiator, he was awarded the Nobel Peace Prize in 1973.

The Unique Selling Proposition (USP)

Advertisers spend much of their time looking for something in a product or service that makes it unique. They call it the USP – the unique selling proposition. The idea of the unique selling proposition came from Roger Reeves, the adman who produced the television commercials for Eisenhower's presidential campaign.

One of the longest-running and most famous subscription letters ever run by the *Wall Street Journal* is successful because it sells its uniqueness. The letter reads:

"It's a publication *unlike* any other ... It is a *unique* publication. It is the country's *only* national business daily. Each business day it is put together by the *world's largest* staff of business-news experts."[9]

American Express has also built its success on selling its uniqueness. Its most famous and successful sales letter reads:

"As you know, card membership is accorded only to those who have achieved a certain measure of financial success. That's because ... unlike credit cards ... *we do not set a spending limit in advance.*"[10]

Like the *Wall Street Journal* and American Express, all successful persuaders package their words to focus on the differences that set them apart from the competition. Politicians, in particular, look for policies and issues that can differentiate them from their opponents.

How to Create a USP

A USP will enhance the audience appeal of most presentations. Garrett Soden, veteran communication specialist and author of *Hook, Spin, Buzz,* argues, "It's best to build a USP backwards: start with a proposition (or promise of a benefit), then think of its selling benefits, and finally say why it's unique."[11] This stops you from developing unique selling points and benefits that are of no interest to your audience.

To draw up a USP, ask these three questions:

1. What benefits will my audience get from my proposition?

2. What proof or evidence can I offer to show it will work?

3. What is unique or different about my proposal?

> *"There is only one way under high heaven to get anybody to do anything. And that is by making the other person want to do it."*
>
> *- Dale Carnegie*

Volvo and Safety

A unique selling proposition can easily be turned into the focal point of a brand. When car buyers think Volvo, they think safety: safety is Volvo's USP. No other carmaker has been able to differentiate itself on safety like Volvo (see Figure 7.1).

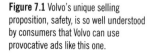

Figure 7.1 Volvo's unique selling proposition, safety, is so well understood by consumers that Volvo can use provocative ads like this one.

Psycholinguistics

Words are rarely neutral in their impact. The great Swiss psychologist Carl Jung discovered that words are full of symbols. By a symbol, he meant something that sparks an emotional reaction deep inside our subconscious. Scholars who study how words affect our minds and emotions are called psycholinguists.[12]

Words often carry emotional meanings that extend beyond their dictionary definitions. Compare the words *denomination, sect,* and *cult.* All have much the same literal meanings and all are groups of people who share common religious beliefs, but the emotional baggage each word carries is very different.

When most people hear the word *denomination,* they usually think of a mainstream, respectable group such as the Roman Catholics or Presbyterians. When they hear the word *sect,* they think of a less acceptable group with radical leanings. When they hear the word *cult,* they think of fanaticism: the Jonestown tragedy, the killings at Waco, or the Heaven's Gate mass suicide.[13]

Words can alter our moods, attitudes, and feelings. The childhood playground cry "Sticks and stones may break my bones, but words will never hurt me" couldn't be more wrong.

In one experiment, the word "hopeless," printed in large letters, was projected onto a movie screen. Different people were then asked to look at it for a few minutes. The negative associations of the word soon had an impact. People's faces changed; in some cases, their pulse rate dropped. In contrast, printed words like "patience" and "courage" had the opposite effect.[15]

Baby Versus Fetus

"The basic tool for the manipulation of reality is the manipulation of words. If you can control the meaning of words, you can control the people who must use the words."
— *Philip K. Dick*

Most trial lawyers appreciate the critical importance of words. In one notable case, an abortionist and the woman who had had the abortion were charged with manslaughter because the abortion occurred late in the pregnancy.

The prosecution set the tone by talking about the death of the "baby boy" and the loss of a "human being." In retaliation, the defence called on the judge to order the prosecution to stop using the words "baby boy" and substitute the word "fetus." They argued the words "baby boy" implied a living human being. By getting the word "fetus" substituted for "baby boy," they were able to distance the defendants from the wrongdoing.[14]

Positive and Negative Words

There are positive and negative words. Positive words make us feel confident, secure, and comfortable; negative words make us feel uneasy or depressed.

Before he was elected to the powerful position of Speaker of the House of Representatives, Newt Gingrich published a pamphlet titled "Language, a Key Mechanism of Control." In it, he advised fellow Republicans to use "positive governing words" for themselves and negative words to describe their opponents. His list of positive words includes challenge, choice, dream, family, freedom, pride, reform, unique, passionate, and strength. The negative list includes betray, decay, failure, lie, shallow, threaten, crisis, greed, sick, and destroy.[16]

Ac-cent-tchu-ate the positive

You got to ac-cent-tchu-ate the positive
Elim-my-nate the negative
Latch on to the affirmative
Don't mess with Mister In-between.

Johnny Mercer's words echo the advice of most public relations experts and advertisers. Put a positive spin on your message.

Psychologist Daryl Benn studied how advertisers use positive words and slogans to sell different brands of aspirin.

Brand A proclaims it is 100 percent pure. It further claims that government tests have shown that no other pain remedy is stronger or more effective than Brand A. Benn notes what the advertisement omits is that the government tests also showed that no brand was weaker or less effective than any of the others.

Brand B advertises it is "unsurpassed in speed – no other brand works faster." The same government tests showed Brand B works no faster than regular aspirin.

Brand C declares it uses the ingredient "that doctors recommend." The government tests reveal the special ingredient is nothing more than regular aspirin.[17]

The advertisements work psychologically because the positive spin leads us to infer almost mindlessly that the advertised brand is the best. When we examine the words in detail, the bias is obvious, but advertisers know much of the time we absorb messages unconsciously.

Attention-Grabbing Words

Studies show that out of the half-million or more words you can choose from, there are sixteen that really grab your attention (see page 97).

The sixteen words that really sell

benefit	guarantee	money	results
easy	health	new	safe
free	how to	now	save
fun	love	proven	you/your

With the number of catalogs, brochures, and advertisements we get bombarded with, you would expect these words to become stale and dated. But the continual testing carried out by the $95 billion direct-mail industry shows the same words continue to work – despite being used time and time again. Without going overboard, you should work these words into your presentations and proposals.

Out of the top sixteen attention-grabbing words, two stand out beyond the others – *new* and *free*:

1. It's New.

There is something irresistible about the word *new*. Step into any room and ask, "Did you hear the news?" I guarantee virtually everyone will sit up and listen. Advertisements containing news are recalled by 22 percent more people than ones without news. John Caple's bible of advertising techniques, *Tested Advertising Methods*, urges, "If you have news, such as a new product, or a new use for an old product, be sure to get that news into your headline in a big way."[18]

It's not uncommon to see the word *new* used in a headline and then repeated up to half a dozen times in the body of one-page advertisement. You'll also find advertisements, brochures, and sales letters littered with words and phrases that suggest news, such as "introducing," "announcing," "now," "the first," "at last" and "finally."

Politicians have long appreciated the power and the potency of the word *new*: Franklin Roosevelt called his program the "New

Deal," Kennedy described his vision as the "New Frontier," Reagan promised a "New Beginning," and Clinton tried to differentiate himself with a "New Covenant."

The message for persuaders is: Highlight what's newsworthy in your proposal. The changes you highlight don't have to be revolutionary; even something old can be made newsworthy. If you're stuck with your traditional way of doing things while everyone else is changing, you can say, "We've made a new commitment to stick with our traditional method, which we believe is superior."[19]

2. It's free.

Have you ever wondered why advertisements, catalogs, and direct mail keep using the phrase "free gift"? The word *free* is redundant; a gift, by definition, is free. The reason we don't mind the addition of "free" is that we love the notion of getting something for nothing, with the result that advertisers use the word *free* whenever they can. Research in direct mail shows three times as many people respond to "free gift" compared to just "gift."

For the moment, imagine you own a direct-mail business selling golf balls. The success of your mailing campaign will depend on the way you phrase your offer. You have come up with three ways to present the same offer:

1. Half price!
2. Buy one – get one *free!*
3. 50 percent off!

Each statement makes the same offer, but testing shows number 2 ("Buy one – get one *free!*") outpulls numbers 1 and 3 by 40 percent.[20] Such is the pulling power of the word *free*. Indeed, professor of direct marketing at Northwestern University Bob Stone says, "Free gift offers ... outpull discount offers consistently."[21]

Labeling

Since few words are neutral, the words we use to label others can have a great impact. In the 1930s, Hitler and the Nazis started calling the Jews "vermin," "sludge," "garbage," "lice," "sewage," "insects," and "bloodsuckers."

Name-calling is dangerous because it gets people to reject ideas and groups before they ever listen to the facts behind an issue: Environmentalists are labeled "ecoterrorists"; business development proposals are rejected simply because they come from "big business"; spokespeople for business are called "corporate hucksters"; convenience food is attacked as "junk food"; and advertising is dismissed as "propaganda."

> *Sticks and stones can break your bones, but words can make your blood boil."*
> *– Cullen Hightower*

Saddam Hussein: The New Hitler.

Before the Persian Gulf War in 1991, the U.S. Congress debated America's involvement. Those who supported sending U.S. troops to the Gulf labeled Saddam Hussein the new Hitler. They likened Saddam's gassing of the Kurds to Hitler's gassing of the Jews and Iraq's invasion of Kuwait to Germany's invasion of Czechoslovakia and Poland. The lesson was clear: Hitler had to be stopped; so too should Saddam.

President Bush latched onto the Hitler label, even hinting that Saddam might face a Nuremberg-style trial following the war. A Gannett Foundation study found over 1,000 mentions of Saddam Hussein as Hitler from August 1, 1990, to February 28, 1991, in the print media. The Hitler image certainly helped mobilize U.S. public opinion; during and immediately after the Gulf War, President Bush's approval rating soared to 90 percent.[22]

The success of the Hitler label allowed Bush to turn what was a complex crisis into a simple fight between good and evil. President Bush told Congress, "I have resolved all moral questions in my mind: this is black versus white, good versus evil."

The Hitler analogy also served to emphasize the military solution over the diplomatic one; after all, Hitler had to be crushed by force and so did Saddam.

The Hitler label backfired when critics of Bush said if Saddam really was a Hitler, why did Bush allow him to continue to remain in power? Even so, the Hitler label stuck. When President Clinton ordered U.S. troops to prepare for another attack on Iraq in early 1998 (this time because Saddam was refusing to allow UN arms inspectors to search key sites for hidden biological, chemical, and nuclear weapons), Saddam was again portrayed as a Hitler who couldn't be trusted.

Glittering Generalities

"Words, like eye glasses, blur everything that they do not make more clear."
— Joseph Joubert

Sometimes persuaders deliberately avoid using specific language. Politicians often face mixed audiences who hold strong conflicting views. To win over the audience, they use glittering generalities. *Glittering generalities* are "purr words" that have positive associations but are essentially ambiguous. The full meaning is left to the imagination of the individual listener.

Propaganda analyst Aaron Delwiche calls glittering generalities "name-calling in reverse. While name-calling makes us form a judgment to reject and condemn, the glittering generality device seeks to make us approve and accept without examining the evidence."[23] Examples include "freedom of choice," "fiscal responsibility," "responsibility in taxation," and "peace with honor."

Take the phrase "fiscal responsibility." Politicians of all persuasions preach fiscal responsibility, but what precisely does it mean? To some, fiscal responsibility means that the government should run in the black, that is, spend no more than it earns in taxes. Others believe it means controlling the growth of the money supply.[24]

Euphemisms

When persuaders name-call and use glittering generalities, they are trying to win over their audience with emotionally suggestive words. However, in some situations when the truth is unpalatable, the persuaders attempt to pacify an audience by taking the sting out of the words and making them bland and euphemistic.

Since war always has an ugly side, military-speak is full of euphemisms. In the 1940s, America changed the name of the War

Department to Department of Defense. Under President Reagan, the MX missile was renamed the *Peacekeeper*. During wartime, civilian casualties are called "collateral damage."

The comedian George Carlon notes that "in the wake of the First World War, traumatized veterans were said to be suffering from *shell shock*. The short, vivid phrase conveys the horrors of battle – one can practically hear the shells exploding overhead. After the Second World War people began to use the term *combat fatigue* to characterize the same condition. The phrase is a bit more pleasant, but it still acknowledges combat as the source of discomfort. In the wake of the Vietnam War, people referred to *post-traumatic stress disorder*: a phrase that is disconnected from the reality of war altogether."[25]

THE MAGIC OF ANTITHESIS

Read these five famous, popular quotations. What makes them so memorable and quotable?

1. One small step for man, one giant leap for mankind.
   – Neil Armstrong, on first stepping on the moon, July 1969

2. Ask not what your country can do for you – ask what you can do for your country.
   – John F. Kennedy, Inaugural Address, January 1961

3. Let us never negotiate out of fear, but let us never fear to negotiate.
   – John F. Kennedy, Inaugural Address, January 1961

4. When the going gets tough, the tough get going.
   – Popular saying

5. Do not let us speak of darker days; let us speak of sterner days. These are not dark days: they are great days – the greatest days our country has ever lived.
   – Winston Churchill, address, Harrow School, October 1941

All five quotations exploit a clever rhetorical device used by memorable communicators called *antithesis*.

In an antithetical statement, opposing meanings are juxtaposed in the same sentence. Picture a sentence as a seesaw with the two parts balancing each other on opposite sides.[26] We'll use one of literature's most famous lines, taken from Charles Dickens's classic *A Tale of Two Cities*, as an example (see below).

An Antithetical Statement "Seesaw"

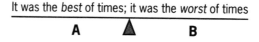

It was the *best* of times; it was the *worst* of times

      A   B

Here Dickens uses two opposites – "best" and "worst" – to create one of English literature's most powerful lines. The Dickens best-worst antithesis works because it uses simple, easy-to-understand words and it is short and balanced. The complete statement is only twelve words long; the two sides of the antithesis are perfectly balanced with six words each.

The AB-BA formula

Highly skilled speechwriters can create a more complex form of antithesis that the classical Greeks called *Chiamus*. Professor of communications and expert on presidential rhetoric Ronald Carpenter calls this the "AB-BA reversal."[27]

Let's use it to analyze Kennedy's most quoted line and antithesis (see below).

Kennedy's Antithetical "Seesaw"

Ask not what your *country* can do for *you* – ask what *you* can do for your *country*.

    A   B   B   A

Notice how the two most important words in the first half, "country" and "you," are twisted 180 degrees in the second half to create a totally different – and opposite – meaning.

Another popular Kennedy quote taken from the same speech – "Let us never *negotiate* (A) out of *fear* (B), but let us never *fear* (B) to *negotiate*" (A) – also exploits the AB-BA formula.

The AB-BA antithesis is difficult to master. The key rule to remember, says Carpenter, is that "the second half of an AB-BA reversal must evoke a meaning opposite or different from that in the first half."[28]

Kennedy Versus Reagan

Have you ever pondered why Ronald Reagan, often called the Great Communicator, left so few memorable quotes? Why don't we quote Reagan the way we quote Kennedy?

Kennedy and Reagan make for an interesting comparison. Both were extraordinarily popular in office and both were gifted speakers, yet while most of us can readily quote a number of Kennedy sayings, we struggle to quote Reagan. If we do, it's normally one of his humorous one-liners.

Presidential rhetoric expert Ronald Carpenter blames Reagan's speechwriters – in particular, their use of antithesis.

Many of Kennedy's most memorable and quotable lines are antitheses. The most powerful and inspiring antitheses typically end on the upbeat; they accentuate the positive. Kennedy's most-quoted line is memorable because it ends with the positive declaration of "ask what you can do for your country."

In contrast, Reagan's antitheses often end with a negative, for example, "The future is best decided by ballots, *not* bullets." Rewritten, it sounds and reads better: "The future is decided best *not* by bullets, but by ballots."

How to Write Memorable Antitheses

To write quotable antitheses, remember these three rules:

1. *Strive for balance.* Try to keep the number of words on both sides of the "seesaw " roughly the same.

2. *Keep them as short and simple as possible.* Long, complex antitheses confuse and befuddle.

3. *Finish on a positive note.* Unless you deliberately want to accentuate the negative, finish with a positive declaration. It is usually much more powerful and memorable.

Every persuader who has ambitions of greatness needs to master antithesis. Communicators who use it with flair, says Carpenter, are seen as "sophisticated," "articulate," and "insightful."[29]

USE REPETITION FOR EFFECT

Communicators who use words in novel and memorable ways are much more persuasive.

When Lincoln spoke of:

> "government of the people, by the people, for the people"

at Gettysburg in 1863, he exploited a technique called stylized repetition. The impact "of the people, by the people, for the people", comes from the repetition of the same phrase at the end of successive phrases or sentences. In rhetoric, parallel like endings are called *antistrophe or epistrophe.*

The use of like beginnings is called *anaphora* or *epanaphora.* The most quoted lines from Abraham Lincoln's second Inaugural Address, delivered in 1865, created impact by repeating the beginnings of successive phrases:

> "With malice toward none,
> with charity for all,
> with firmness in the right."

Parallel repetitions usually sound better in groups of three. When Churchill paid tribute to the pilots of the Royal Air Force for their heroic role in saving England during the Battle of Britain in 1940, he repeated just one tiny word, "so," three times to create one of history's most memorable speeches:

> "Never in the field of human conflict was so much, owed by so many, to so few."

We also remember Roosevelt's famous line, "The only thing we have to fear is fear itself," from his 1933 Inaugural Address because of the way it cleverly uses repetition. Martin Luther King Jr. used four words "I have a dream," and repeated them four times in his famous 1963 March on Washington speech to create this century's most-quoted call for freedom.

Research psychologists confirm what the ancient Greeks believed: Repetition increases persuasiveness. To use repetition effectively, confine your repetitions to key words and phrases. Remember:

Parallel repetitions work best in groups of three. Page 106 lists ten persuasion pointers covered in this chapter.

One of the reasons John F. Kennedy is so often quoted, he was lucky to have the talents of Ted Sorenson, arguably America's most gifted speech-writer.

PERSUASION
POINTERS

1 Persuade with power talk. Talk positively, assertively, and decisively.

2 Avoid intensifiers such as *definitely* and *very*. Avoid hesitations and fillers, disclaimers, hedges, and qualifiers.

3 Sell the sizzle, not the steak; sell benefits, not features.

4 To analyze how your proposition will appeal, ask:

A. What do they stand to gain from my proposal?

B. What do they stand to lose if they don't adopt my proposal?

5 When selling products or ideas, focus on what makes you different or unique. Develop a unique selling proposition for everything you sell.

6 Consider the emotional impact of every word you use. Most words have emotional overtones.

7 Use positive words to support your ideas; use negative words to highlight your opponent's weaknesses.

8 Whenever possible, inject attention-grabbing words, such as *free, new,* and *easy,* into your proposals and presentations.

9 Exploit the power of antithesis when you want to create a memorable, quotable statement.

10 Use stylized repetition in your phrasing to increase the impact of your words.

Winning People's Hearts

The Power of Metaphors, Analogies, and Stories

■ VIVID LANGUAGE

Jaws

When *Jaws* (the film starring a man-eating shark) opened at cinemas across the United States, the number of swimmers visiting California beaches dropped dramatically. Sharks do inhabit the California coast, but the risk of a swimmer actually being attacked by a shark is much less than the risk of being killed in a car accident while driving there.[1]

People are often not influenced by the true facts of a situation; more often, they are influenced by what makes the most vivid impression on their mind.

A Lemon

To demonstrate how vivid words and images play in our mind, slowly read the following description of cutting a lemon:

Imagine you are in the kitchen. You pick up a large, fresh, succulent lemon from the fruit bowl. It is cool in your hand. The yellow dimpled skin feels smooth and waxy. It comes to a small, green, conical point at either end. The lemon is firm and quite heavy for its size as you look at it in the palm of your hand.

You raise the lemon to your nose. It gives off a characteristic, unmistakable citrus smell.

You take a sharp knife and cut the lemon in half. The two halves fall apart, the white pulpy outer skin contrasting with the drops of pale lemon-colored juice that gently ooze out. You raise the lemon toward your mouth. The lemon smell is now slightly stronger.

Now you bite deeply into the lemon and let the juice swirl around in your mouth. That sharp, sour lemon flavour is unmistakable.

Did your mouth produce saliva? Almost everyone's does. Yet the extraordinary thing is that if I had simply instructed you to produce saliva, you couldn't have done it.

The vivid picture worked because your mind cannot distinguish between what is imagined and what is real.

Vivid images work because they stick in our minds and are recalled more quickly. To illustrate this point, fill in the missing letters below. What words do they make?

S_X   SHI_   F_ _K

If your mind is typical, you would have first recalled the more vivid, suggestive, off-color words, yet the words could just as easily be "six," "shin," and "fork."

Emotions Versus Fact

Vivid language works because it taps into our emotions. Emotions are the single most powerful force of persuasion. Without emotions, our words are pallid and lifeless.

The word *emotion* comes from the Latin *emovere*, which means to move away or to move greatly.

As rational human beings, we like to think that logic drives most of our decisions. But the fact is, *in most persuasive situations, people buy on emotion and justify with fact.* People may be persuaded by reason, but they are moved by emotion.

Advantages of Emotion

Emotion has a five advantages over logic:[2]

1. Emotion-arousing arguments cause us to drop our natural defenses and distract us from the speaker's intention to persuade.

2. Emotion requires less effort than logic. Weighing the pros and cons of a logical presentation requires a lot more cognitive effort than an emotional pitch.

3. Emotion-based pitches are usually more interesting. Stories, for example, have plots, characters, and inherent drama.

4. Emotion-based arguments, especially those that use pictures and music, are much easier to recall than factual evidence.

5. Emotion seems to lead more quickly to behavior change than logic does.

Harvard professor and author of *Managing With Power* Jeffrey Pfeffer says, "It's your head that sends you off to check *Consumer Reports* when you are thinking of purchasing a new car. It's your heart that buys the Jaguar, or the Porsche. It's your head that tells you that political campaign speeches cannot be believed or trusted, but it's your heart that responds to the best oratory, and makes you refuse to vote for people who come across as 'dull,' as though that were a reason to vote or not vote for a governmental representative."[3]

Consider a few of the great public events where emotions moved audiences across the world:

- Martin Luther King calling for black equality in August 1963 with his famous "I Have a Dream" speech.

- Teddy Kennedy quoting George Bernard Shaw while paying homage to his assassinated brother Bobby at St. Patrick's Cathedral in June 1968: "Some men see things as they are and say 'why.' I dream things that never were and say 'why not.'"

- Elton John singing his moving tribute to Princess Diana at Westminster Abbey in September 1997: "Goodbye England's rose, from a country lost without your soul."

Emotions, properly managed, can be powerful persuaders. The great example is Churchill's back-to-the-wall speech delivered to the British House of Commons on June 4, 1940, following the evacuation of the British Expeditionary Force from Dunkirk. "We shall fight on the beaches, we shall fight on the landing grounds, we shall fight in the fields and the streets, we shall fight in the hills; we shall never surrender."

Politicians said it was the finest speech they had ever heard. Several MPs cried. So did Churchill.

When Roosevelt heard these words at the White House, he remarked to his aide Harry Hopkins, "As long as that old bastard is in charge, Britain will never surrender. It's not like giving to the French, which is only pouring money down the rathole."

Churchill biographer James C. Humes says, "Because of these words, Roosevelt, the head of a neutral nation, sent aid to a beleaguered Britain."[4]

Because they are more concrete, personal, and image-provoking, vivid messages grab our attention; because vivid messages are more memorable, they linger longer for later recall.

Selling Home Insulation

A powerful example of vivid appeals comes from the work of psychologists Anthony Pratkanis and Elliot Aronson. Pratkanis and Aronson were called upon by a local power company to help sell the advantages of home insulation.

The utility offered homeowners a free energy audit. A trained auditor would go through each consumer's house identifying what was needed to make the home more energy-efficient. The utility even provided an interest-free loan.

The benefits seemed obvious. Energy savings of 40 percent were common, and the power savings following the installation of insulation would quickly pay for the cost of the loan. The puzzle was that while huge numbers of homeowners requested a home audit, only 15 percent of them actually followed the advice of the auditor – even though clearly it made excellent financial sense.

Why? Researchers interviewed several homeowners and discovered that most had a hard time believing that small cracks under a door or lack of insulation in an attic could result in such a large energy loss.

To solve this problem, Pratkanis and Aronson trained the auditors to communicate their findings and recommendations in more vivid and graphic terms. They advised the auditors to tell this to the homeowners:

Look at all the cracks around that door! It may not seem much to you, but if you were to add up all the cracks around each of these doors, you'd have the equivalent of a hole the circumference of a basketball. Suppose someone poked a hole the size of a basketball in your living room wall. Think for a moment about all the heat that you'd be losing from a hole that size – you'd want to patch that hole in your wall, wouldn't you? That's exactly what weather-stripping does.

And your attic totally lacks insulation. We professionals call that a "naked attic." It's as if your home is facing winter not just without an overcoat, but without any clothing at all! You wouldn't let your young kids run outside in the winter time without clothes on, would you? It's the same with your attic.[5]

When homeowners heard this speech, they signed up in droves. Whereas previously only 15 percent had signed up, now 61 percent signed up to have their houses insulated. Vivid language had turned barely visible cracks into holes the size of basketballs. The idea of running around naked in winter also grabs attention and makes you want to take action.

Here is another example. Suppose you were thinking of buying a new Ford and had just read a *Consumer Report* study rating it highly in a sample survey of 1,000 owners. You mention this to a friend, who paints a damning picture of his own experience. He swears the Ford he owns is totally unreliable and that he will never buy another one as long as he lives.

Your friend's experience has increased the statistical sample to 1,001, yet you are unlikely to buy the Ford. Research shows that most people are moved more by one powerful, vivid example than by a mass of statistics.[6]

THE POWER OF METAPHORS

Churchill's Greatest Speech?

In 1946 Churchill was a beaten man. The previous year, he had lost the prime ministership after his Conservative government had suffered an overwhelming election defeat.

Churchill wanted to warn the Western world about the spreading menace of Soviet communism, but he worried that Americans wouldn't listen to someone who was now just the leader of an opposition party, rather than the head of an elected government.

Churchill's opportunity to convince Americans came when he was invited to speak in Fulton, Missouri. He knew he had to paint a vivid, graphic picture of what was happening to countries like Poland and Czechoslovakia.

He toyed with words like "Soviet imperialism," "militarism," and "tyranny," but he rejected these as shapeless abstractions. None of these would paint a vivid enough picture in his listeners' minds.

On the train trip down to Missouri, Churchill scanned his map of Europe. To highlight the spread of communism, he drew a black pen line from the Baltic Sea through Poland down to the Adriatic Sea. He retraced the line, searching his mind for the right image to describe the Soviet threat.

The inspiration came at 2 a.m. during an overnight stop in Salem, Illinois, when the right word picture appeared – which Churchill quickly added to his speech.

The next day, Churchill delivered the words that would mobilize the United States and move it to action:

"From Stettin in the Baltic to Trieste in the Adriatic an *iron curtain* has descended across the continent."

The iron-curtain metaphor became one of the galvanizing images of the Cold War. When China fell to Mao Tse-tung's communists in 1949, the metaphor changed to *bamboo curtain*.

The iron curtain speech was, according to James C. Humes (author of *Churchill: Speaker of the Century*), Churchill's greatest speech. "Why was it the greatest? Because a single speech triggered a change in American feelings about the Soviet Union [America's wartime ally], and started the Americans to rearm."[7]

How Metaphors Work

A metaphor is an imaginative way of describing something by saying it is something else. Think of the metaphor *time is money*. With this as the organizing concept, you can say:[8]

- You're *wasting* my time.
- This will *save* you hours.
- I don't have the time to *give* you.
- How do you *spend* your time?
- That delay *cost* me an hour.
- I've *invested* a lot of time in you.

Metaphors are powerful because they allow us to personify abstract ideas. Look at how these metaphors paint inflation as an enemy that can destroy us and steal from us:[9]

- Our biggest *enemy* now is inflation.
- Inflation has *robbed* us of our savings.
- The dollar has been *destroyed* by inflation.

The Domino Metaphor

One of the most powerful examples of a metaphor shaping a generation's thinking and behavior is the domino theory.

The domino theory, pushed by U.S. President Dwight Eisenhower and Secretary of State John Foster Dulles, portrayed countries threatened by communism as a row of dominoes. The theory was based on a fear that if one country fell to the communists, the others would also fall, one after the other, "like a row of dominoes."

According to the theory, if any single domino was tipped over, all the rest would fall; therefore, every domino was critical. None could be allowed to topple, no matter what the circumstances.

As a result, successive U.S. Presidents felt obliged to prop up all sorts of dubious dictators who claimed to be anti-communist.

By the time Lyndon B. Johnson became President in 1963, his advisers were still pushing the theory. South Vietnam, they argued, was another critical domino that the United States must prop up.

It was foolhardy advice founded on a flawed metaphor. A total of 58,000 Americans died in Vietnam, and the United States suffered its first defeat on foreign soil.

Britain's Iron Lady

Metaphors are one of the most powerful word tools we have to make vivid lasting impressions.

Britain's first woman prime minister, Margaret Thatcher, will go down in history as the *Iron Lady*. For her supporters who admired her strong personality, the nickname became a term of endearment. Ironically, the label came from the Russians, who called her the "Iron Lady" for trying to revive the Cold War.

Over the years, Thatcher's critics attacked her with every form of abusive metaphor: Clement Freud called her Attila the Hen; Richard Holme labeled her the Enid Blyton of economics; Harry

Urwin called her Plunder Woman; one British MP savaged her in Parliament "for behaving with all the sensitivity of a sex-starved boa constrictor."

Thatcher's admirers countered with equally strong language. U.S. President Ronald Reagan called Thatcher "the best man in England." The *New Yorker* praised her tough economic policies by calling her a "handbag economist who believes that you pay as you go."

Churchill and Lady Astor

Churchill loved using zoological metaphors to attack his opponents. He once ridiculed Lady Astor and her pro-German supporters in Parliament saying, "An appeaser is one who feeds the crocodile hoping it will eat him last."

The attack so upset Nancy Astor that when she met Churchill at a dinner party, she said, "Winston, if I were your wife, I'd put poison in your coffee."

In a flash, Churchill countered, "And if I were your husband, Nancy, I'd drink it."

Martin Luther King

Martin Luther King was a master of the metaphor. King's words delivered in his famous "I Have a Dream" speech to a Washington crowd of 200,000 in 1963 continue to inspire: "I have a dream ... that the sons of former slaves and the sons of former slave owners will be able to sit down together at the table of brotherhood; ... that one day, even the state of Mississippi, a state sweltering with the heat of injustice, sweltering with the heat of oppression, will be transformed into an oasis of freedom and justice."

Metaphors Shape Our Actions

We call a metaphor that shapes a view of life or influences the way we act an organizing metaphor.

Organizing metaphors shape our everyday actions. If you understand a person's organizing metaphors, you are well on the
way to understanding how he or she thinks. Shakespeare, hardly
surprisingly, saw the world as "a stage, and all the men and women
merely players."

Using Metaphors to Change Actions and Attitudes

Once you figure out someone's organizing metaphor, you can
influence that person by modifying his or her metaphor or by
substituting a more powerful one.

Internationally acclaimed psycholinguist Suzette Haden Elgin says,
"Metaphors are the most powerful device available for changing
people's attitudes quickly, effectively and lastingly."[10]

From Buffalo to Geese

In the following example, observe how two businessmen, James
Belasco and Ralph Stayer (they write as a single person), used a new
metaphor to change their thinking and the way they managed:

For a long time, I believed the old leadership paradigm that told
me that my job was to plan, organize, command, coordinate, and
control. I saw my organization functioning like a herd of buffalo.

Buffalo are absolutely loyal followers of one leader. They do
whatever the leader wants them to do, go wherever the leader
wants them to go. In my company, I was head buffalo.

I realized eventually that my organization didn't work as well as I'd
like, because buffalo are loyal to one leader; they stand around and
wait for the leader to show them what to do. When the leader isn't
around, they wait for him to show up. That's why the early settlers
could decimate the buffalo herds so easily by killing the lead
buffalo. The rest of the herd stood around, waiting for their leader
to lead them, and were slaughtered.

I found a lot of "waiting around" in my buffalo-like organization. Worse, people did only what I told them to do, nothing more, and then they "waited around" for my next set of instructions.

I also found it was hard work being the lead buffalo. Giving all the orders, doing all the "important" work took 12–14 hours a day. Meanwhile my company was getting slaughtered out there in the marketplace because I couldn't respond quickly enough to changes. All this frustrating work as the leader of the buffalo herd was growing old – and making me old before my time.

Then one day I got it. What I really wanted in the organization was a group of responsible, interdependent workers, similar to a flock of geese. I could see the geese flying in their "V" formation, the leadership changing frequently, with different geese taking the lead. I saw every goose being responsible for getting itself to wherever the gaggle was going, changing roles whenever necessary, alternating as a leader, a follower, or a scout. And when the task changed, the geese would be responsible for changing the structure of the group to accommodate, similar to the geese that fly in a "V" but land in waves. I could see each goose being a leader.

Then I saw clearly that the biggest obstacle to success was my picture of a loyal herd of buffalo waiting for me, the leader, to tell them what to do. I knew I had to *change the pictures* to become a different kind of leader, so everyone could become a leader.[11]

Lee Iacocca Bails Out Chrysler

In 1980 Chrysler Corporation, America's tenth-largest company, was running out of cash and was near bankruptcy. Chief Executive Lee Iacocca's only hope was to convince Congress to grant $2.7 billion in loan guarantees to Chrysler. On the surface, the task seemed hopeless. Few Congressmen believed it was the government's job to save a private corporation. The business media attacked any idea of a government bailout.

Iacocca, a master persuader, understood a big part of the problem was the language.

"Bailout," he wrote in his autobiography, "is a colorful metaphor. It conjures up images of a leaky boat foundering in rough seas. It implies the crew was inadequate."[12]

To change and reframe Congressional thinking, Iacocca used powerful metaphorical language. He argued that if it made sense for the government to provide a safety net for individuals, it made sense to have a *safety net* for their companies.

Iacocca claimed Chrysler's plight was not unique. He framed Chrysler's problems as *America's* problems. Chrysler's problems were merely *"the tip of the iceberg* facing American industry"; Chrysler's bailout was a *"test lab* for everyone else." Congress bought Iacocca's pictures and delivered the financial guarantees Chrysler desperately needed.

Metaphors as Frames

Metaphors frame the way we think. They work like the window frames that architects position to give a desired view. But window frames not only focus what we look at; they also limit what we can view. Metaphors act in the same way: They focus on certain features while obscuring others.

Repositioning *Rolling Stone* Magazine

The way imagery works to frame our perceptions and shape our attitudes was dramatically illustrated in the brilliant award-winning Perception/Reality ad campaign for *Rolling Stone* magazine.

Rolling Stone magazine's problem was disastrously low advertising revenues. The media buyers and advertisers wouldn't buy ads because they thought the magazine was read by poor, counter-culture hippie dropouts. The truth was very different. *Rolling Stone's* provocative articles, written by many of America's top writers, attracted an affluent and articulate readership.

To increase ad revenue, *Rolling Stone* had to get advertisers and their agencies to fundamentally change their attitudes toward the magazine. The Minneapolis-based advertising agency Fallow

McElligott Rice produced an eight-ad campaign titled Perception/ Reality. The launch ad is reproduced in Figure 8.1.

The campaign was a brilliant success; advertising revenues immediately shot up 25 percent. The campaign has now been running for many years, helping *Rolling Stone* become one of the ten hottest magazines in the United States.[13] Along the way, the campaign won a raft of international advertising awards.

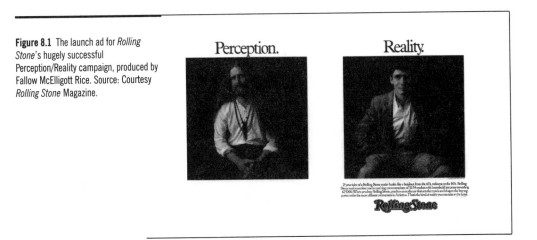

Figure 8.1 The launch ad for *Rolling Stone*'s hugely successful Perception/Reality campaign, produced by Fallow McElligott Rice. Source: Courtesy *Rolling Stone* Magazine.

The Perception/Reality ad campaign provides a perfect example of how imagery frames our perception and how skilled persuaders can use metaphorical images to reframe our thinking and in turn change our attitudes.

The "1984" Macintosh Super Bowl Ad

In 1983, Apple Computers, arguably faced an even bigger perception challenge than *Rolling Stone* magazine. It was planning to launch the Macintosh, a new line of personal computers. The dominant competitor was IBM, which had recently displaced Apple as the leader in personal computers and was virtually the unchallenged king of mainframe computing.

Apple chose a small advertising agency, Chiat Day, to create a sixty-second advertisement to be shown during the 1984 Super Bowl.

Figure 8.2 Here Big Brother, IBM is lecturing customers on what they should do. During the scene, a women athlete charges in and smashes the screen, destroying Big Brother (IBM).

The ad, titled "1984," was based on the Orwellian theme of *1984*. The ad pictured an executive lecturing to an audience of zombie-like listeners from a giant screen. The scene, writes University of Southern California Professor Gerald Tellis, "was a parody of IBM's domination of the computer market with customers at its mercy, reminiscent of the domination of Big Brother in the novel *1984*. In the midst of the scene, a woman athlete ran down the aisle carrying a mallet, and slammed it at the screen destroying Big Brother (see Figure 8.2). As the screen crashed, a voice-over announced, 'Introducing the Apple Macintosh. Why 1984 will not be like 1984.'"[14]

Even though the advertisement was shown just once, the ad (plus the publicity it generated) helped Apple sell 72,000 Macintoshes the first day, almost 50 percent above target. *Advertising Age* rated "1984" the ad of the decade. A recent survey named it the best commercial of all time.

The ad was so powerful that when it was shown at Apple's sales meeting, the sales force stood and clapped solidly for fifteen minutes.

Like the *Rolling Stone* campaign, the "1984" ad was brilliantly successful because it was able to frame the way the product was perceived. Persuaders who tap into power metaphors to influence their audience do exactly the same.

'Advertising may be described as the science of arresting human intelligence to get money from it."
— Stephen Leacock

The Mindshift Process: How to Change a Person's Mind-Set

Mindshift is a three-step process to help you use metaphors to change someone's mind-set.

Step One: *Identify your target's organizing metaphor.*
Your first task is to work out the organizing metaphor that frames your target's thinking. The easiest way to do this is to meet with the person you want to influence a number of times and jot down the common phrases and word pictures he or she uses when speaking about the area you want to influence. In the example that follows, the CEO being influenced constantly uses military talk to describe his attitude toward business.

If you can, try and reduce your target's words, idiomatic expressions, and word pictures to a one-sentence metaphorical statement. This is called the target's organizing metaphor. When you analyze the other person's organizing metaphor, ask:

- What does the metaphor highlight?
- What does the metaphor conceal?
- What does the metaphor distort?

Step Two: *Create a new metaphor to act as a frame for the changes you are proposing.*
The ideal replacement metaphor is one that forces a fundamental "mindshift" without your target ever realizing it.

Step Three: *Challenge and replace your target's organizing metaphor.*
Here you use rhetoric to challenge and shatter your target's mind-set. At the same time, you should try to offer a new way of thinking that offers clear advantages over the old way.

Mindshift Case Study

Here is an example of how one of my clients used the Mindshift process to reframe the thinking of his CEO.

James Campbell (not his real name) was frustrated. As the head of new product development, he couldn't persuade his CEO to invest in new technology and hire the extra staff he felt were needed in research and development. Every time he presented his case for more resources, he ran into the same brick wall: "We can't afford it."

After a series of fruitless meetings, he sat down and, with our help, listed the phrases, word pictures, and idiomatic expressions his CEO commonly used. It was remarkable how often the same phrases cropped up. The CEO's common expressions included:

"We can't afford any unnecessary fat."

"If we don't move quickly, our competitors will blow us out of the water."

"This is a dog-eat-dog business."

"We have to become a lean and mean fighting machine."

"We have to defend our market share."

"We can't concede ground to our competitors."

On the whiteboard in James's office, we drew a large, empty picture frame to represent his CEO's mind-set. Around the outside of the frame, we jotted down all the phrases, word pictures, and idiomatic expressions he commonly used:

James then encapsulated his boss's statements into one metaphor, "Business is war," which he placed in the center of the frame. This appeared to be the organizing metaphor that framed his CEO's thinking.

We played around with his boss's metaphor to see whether it could be adapted to fit what James wanted. James decided it couldn't. His CEO's military metaphor focused the business on the competitor whereas James believed the focus should be on the customer. James's research also showed that the present approach wasn't working. The spending cuts were not resulting in the savings or efficiencies hoped for.

James concluded that the business needed a new organizing metaphor – one that would create purpose and direction and that would support an environment that would encourage increased spending on research and development.

At the next budget meeting, James presented a series of graphs that vividly showed the negative effects of the present approach. He concluded his presentation:

"Our aim has been to create a lean and *mean* organization. I believe the evidence shows we are not just lean and mean – we are suffering from corporate anorexia. The cuts have removed the *muscle* – our people – and left us with *fat* – outdated processes.

"We have to reinvent the way we do business. Imitating our competitors will lead to disaster. Our competitors are much larger than we are and better equipped financially to fight a war of attrition.

"We need to do a Dick Fosbury. Some of you in this room will remember Dick Fosbury – the Olympic high jumper. Until Dick Fosbury came along, all high jumpers used the same approach – the feet first approach called the Western roll. Fosbury competed and won – by turning the conventional wisdom upside down. Fosbury went over the bar headfirst.

"The press called it the Fosbury Flop, and Fosbury went on to win the Olympic gold medal. Today Fosbury's Flop is the standard high-jumping technique.

"Our business has to do a Fosbury Flop: We have to innovate, spend more on research and development, and create new products that will leap-frog the competition."

The speech worked. The CEO latched on to the Fosbury Flop metaphor and asked James which Fosbury Flops he believed were possible. James replied, "There are two exciting product innovations in early development. But they need extra funds and extra staff to take them to the marketplace."

The CEO still required a lot of further convincing, but seven weeks later, James's boss allocated the additional funding and staff James needed. James also noticed his CEO's language change. Twice he heard his CEO urge staff to think outside the square and do a Fosbury Flop. A "mindshift" had begun.

THE POWER OF ANALOGIES

Analogies can have the same impact as metaphors. An analogy allows you to introduce a new idea quickly by comparing it with something familiar and simple. When Benjamin Franklin said, "Fish and visitors start to smell in three days," he was delivering a vivid message of why we tire of visitors who outlive their welcome.

Analogies are particularly useful when you have to produce complex abstract data as part of your presentation. By comparing the complex and abstract with something simple and concrete, your listeners understand by association.[15]

Udder Madness

Look at how a journalist from *The Economist* uses analogy and humor to argue for the need for insolvency reform:

"A firm in financial trouble is sometimes likened to a cow stuck in mud. At its head are the owners trying to haul it out of the mire. At its tail are squabbling lenders dragging it back. And underneath lurk the lawyers and accountants, milking the marooned beast."[16]

Income Statements and Bikinis

Here American investment expert Professor Burton Maikel is arguing why you should never take a firm's accounts at face value:

"A firm's income statement may be linked to a bikini – what it reveals is interesting, but what it conceals is vital."[17]

Quality and Sex

Here is quality guru Phil Crosby likening quality to sex:

"Quality has much in common with sex. Everyone is for it. Everyone feels they understand it. Everyone thinks execution is a matter of following natural inclinations. And everyone feels that all problems are caused by other people."[18]

Medicare and the *Titanic*

When President Clinton proposed expanding the struggling Medicare system to include millions of people below the age of sixty-five, Senator Phil Gramm vividly debunked the idea: "If your mother is on the *Titanic* and the *Titanic* is sinking, the last thing on Earth you want to be preoccupied with is getting more passengers on the *Titanic*."

Forbes magazine noted: "Gramm's response will do more to sink this proposal than will reams of learned, actuarial analyzes."[19]

THE POWER OF STORIES

Stories, like metaphors and analogies, bring presentations alive. Most great persuaders use stories to drive their message home. Socrates and Homer taught with stories; Jesus spoke in parables. Lincoln, Churchill, Roosevelt, Kennedy, and Reagan used anecdotes to make many of their most telling points.

Stories work in four ways:

1. Stories grab listeners' attention. Like a movie, stories have a plot and characters for the audience to relate to.

2. Stories simplify complex ideas and make abstract concepts concrete.

3. Stories tap into listeners' emotions better than dry sets of facts.

4. Stories are memorable. A vivid story stays in listeners' minds long after everything else is forgotten.

Lincoln the Storyteller

Few people have used storytelling as a persuasive tool better than Abraham Lincoln. His father, Thomas Lincoln, was a gifted yarn spinner. After a long day's work as a lawyer, Abe Lincoln perfected his storytelling with friends at the local tavern. There they held storytelling contests, often entertaining large crowds. Over time, Lincoln built up a stock of tales that he drew on at will.

As a lawyer on the Illinois circuit, Lincoln aquired a formidable reputation for his remarkable persuasive skills.

Few peers could match Lincoln's ability to read a jury's mood. Anecdotes and humorous stories were key weapons in his arsenal. In one notable case, Lincoln finished his summing up to the jury by saying, "My learned opponent [the prosecutor] has given you all the facts but has drawn the wrong conclusions."

When the prosecutor lost, he asked Lincoln how he had turned the jury around.

"Well," Abe said, "during the recess I wandered into a café, sat with the jury and told them a story about a farmer who was mending a fence, when his ten-year-old son came running crying, 'Dad, sis is up in the hay loft with a hired hand and he is pulling down his pants and she is pulling up her skirts and I think they are going to pee all over the hay.' "

According to Lincoln, the farmer said to his son, "You got all the facts straight, but you have drawn the wrong conclusion."

The Sound of (No) Music

It's hard to think of a more powerful way to attack downsizing than this outlandish but true story used by Robert S. Miller, Jr., executive vice president of Chrysler Corporation:

A foreign cinema owner decided the movie he was showing was too long, so he decided to cut out what he considered irrelevant. Well, the movie was *The Sound of Music*. And you know what he did? He cut out all the songs. So help me God, believe it or not, he actually shortened *The Sound of Music* by cutting out the songs! I figure his version of the movie must have started with the Nazis chasing the von Trapp family up a mountain and it must have lasted about fifteen minutes.

It was of course an absurd, shortsighted, and unpopular decision, and to you and me, it sounds flat-out, world-class crazy, but when you get right down to it, is cutting the songs out of that musical really all that different from, say, cutting research and development out of a company by crippling it with staggering debt in the name of 'improving shareholder value'?"[20]

Sales researchers Dr. Donald Moine and John Herd say that some top salespeople succeed largely through stories. Compared to their colleagues, they give out little product information, yet they still make lots of sales.[21]

Salespeople use a range of stories to:

- Establish initial credibility
- Grab attention to make customers sit up and listen
- Overcome customer objections
- Create value in their customers' minds
- Prove how their products and services have worked

FEAR AS A MOTIVATOR

Vivid language, metaphors, analogies, and stories work because they tap into our emotions. Of all our emotions, fear is possibly the most powerful human motivator. Fear sells us many things: alarm systems, life insurance, air bags, and condoms.

Politicians everywhere have used fear to win votes. In the 1930s, Hitler whipped up the fear of communism and Judaism to win support for the Nazi Party. In the 1950s, Senator Joseph McCarthy used the fear of communism engendered by the Cold War to help launch government investigations into the daily lives of thousands of loyal Americans whom he labeled communist sympathizers.

Appeals to fear, however, don't always work. We've all watched mass campaigns warning us about the dangers of cigarettes and drug abuse as well as the risk of contracting AIDS, yet huge numbers of people continue to smoke and use drugs, and few practice safe sex.

For a fear appeal to work, it must meet four conditions[22]:

1. The appeal must really *scare* people.

2. The persuader must offer a *specific recommendation* on how to overcome the threat.

3. The receiver must believe the recommended action *will work*.

4. The receiver must believe that he or she can *easily carry out* the recommended action.

Hitler's fear appeals worked for those four reasons:

- Many Germans really believed the propaganda about Jews and communists and were scared.

- Hitler offered a *specific recommendation* – join the Nazi Party.

- Many Germans thought the recommended action – vote the Nazis into office – *would work*.

- It *didn't take much effort* to follow the recommended action. All they had to do was vote for the Nazi Party.

"The greater the lie, the greater the chance that it will be believed."
— *Adolf Hitler*

In contrast, compare the fear appeals parents use to try and stop their teenagers' smoking. Parents often try to scare their children by stressing the long-term health risks of smoking. Yet few teenagers are scared or care about a threat that seems a lifetime away. Few teenagers find it easy to follow their parents' advice to say no to friends who tempt them with cigarettes. It's extremely difficult for most teenagers to resist peer pressure. The result is teenage smoking continues to rise – in spite of the real dangers.

The Fear of Loss

Of the many fear appeals, one of the most powerful is the fear of loss. Psychologists have discovered we have a particular aversion to loss. People are motivated more by the fear of losing something than by the reward of gaining something of equal value. Psychologically, it's much more painful to lose $100 than it is pleasurable to win $100.

Why do losses loom larger than gains in our minds? The world's leading researcher in this area, Stanford University psychologist Amos Tversky, says, "Probably the most significant and pervasive characteristic of the human pleasure machine is that people are much more sensitive to negative than to positive stimuli.... Think about how well you feel today, and then try to imagine how much better you could feel. There are a few things that would make you feel better, but the number of things that would make you feel worse is unbounded."[23]

For the moment, imagine you are a salesperson selling home insulation. You have two approaches. The first approach is to stress to your customers how much they will *lose* if they continue with their present inadequate insulation. The second approach is to stress to your customers how much money they will *save* or gain by insulating their homes.

The first pitch, the one that stresses the potential losses, is the more persuasive. Those who received the first pitch in a research study bought much more insulation.

Similar findings have come from experiments carried out by health researchers. The researchers wanted to find the best way to word a pamphlet urging women to carry out regular breast self-examinations. The first pamphlet they tried emphasized the negative effects of not performing a regular self-examination. It said women who do *not* carry out such examinations have a *decreased* chance of finding a tumor while it is still treatable.

The second pamphlet stressed the positive effects of performing a regular self-examination. It said women who carry out such examinations have an *increased* chance of finding a tumor while it is still treatable.

The researchers found that, four months later, those women who had read the pamphlet stressing the negative consequences were much more likely to be carrying out regular self-examinations.[24]

As a persuader, it's easy to switch the emphasis in most proposals from gain to loss. For example, if you are suggesting that your company have a booth at a national trade show, instead of talking about the extra customers you'll *gain*, emphasize the customers you would *lose* to your competitors who already have booths at the trade show.

A recent direct-mail campaign from American Family publishers was framed to tap into readers' fear of loss. The key message was, "Enter the contest and win $10 million." But the letter was angled to read that if you don't enter the contest, you could be losing $10 million:

"If you return the winning number in time, I'll be personally handing you the first ten million dollars. But, if you decide to ignore this letter and throw your exclusive numbers away, I'll surely be awarding all the money to someone else.

"PREVIOUS WINNERS HAVE THROWN THEIR NUMBERS RIGHT INTO THE TRASH – THEY LITERALLY THREW AWAY MILLIONS."[25]

Writer Robert Ringer claims the best-selling headline he ever composed was to sell Douglas Casey's best-selling book, *Crisis Investing*. The headline: WHY YOU WILL LOSE EVERYTHING IN THE COMING DEPRESSION. The book spent fifteen weeks on the *New York Times* best-seller list and sold 400,000 copies.

THE POWER OF MOOD

It's much easier to exploit an emotional appeal – or for that matter, a logical appeal – if your listener is already in a receptive mood.

The mood of your audience can affect how they will receive your message. Several studies show that positive moods are associated with increased persuasion; conversely, negative moods are associated with less persuasion.

Your listener is much more likely to develop support arguments rather than counterarguments if he or she is in a good mood. It can therefore pay to assess the mood of the person or audience before you start persuading. Research shows music and humor help to arouse positive emotions.

USING HUMOR TO PERSUADE

During a 1993 world tour, Michael Jackson, then a Pepsi spokesman, faced accusations of child molestation. Under siege, Jackson pulled out of shows in Thailand, claiming he was dehydrated. Pepsi's archrival Coke exploited the negative publicity by publishing an ad in Bangkok papers. The ad was a simple question and answer: "Dehydrated? There's always Coke!"[26] The ad had humor and bite – too much, it seems. Coke withdrew the ad after complaints from Pepsi.

Professional persuaders know humor can be a powerful tool. Humor, for example, is used in 36 percent of TV ads in the United Kingdom and 24 percent of TV ads in the United States.[27]

> *"Once you've got people laughing, they're listening and you can tell them almost anything."*
> — *Herbert Gardner*

"Humor is a powerful ... tool," writes humor consultant Malcolm Kushner. "It can gain attention, create rapport and make a message more memorable. It can also relieve tension, enhance relationships and motivate people, if it is used appropriately."[28]

"If I can get you to laugh with me," says actor John Cleese, "you like me better, which makes you more open to my ideas. And if I can *persuade* you to laugh at the particular point I make, by laughing at it you acknowledge its truth."[29]

How to Make Humor Relevant

The cardinal rule when using humor is to add the humor after you've planned your message and made a list of the key points you want to make. Your humor, says Kushner, should "introduce, summarize or highlight" one or more of your points.[30]

When using humor to persuade, be sure it is relevant. The biggest mistake unskilled persuaders make is to use irrelevant humor. To be effective, humor must make a point.

"A basic principle of audience psychology," says Malcolm Kushner, "is that people resist humor if they think someone is *trying* to be funny." On the other hand, humor reduces our resistance to the central message of the pitch. We are less likely to object to or challenge and are more accepting of a message that is laced with humor to make a point. Even if we don't think the speaker is funny, the "humor still makes a point and moves the presentation forward."[31]

PERSUASION
POINTERS

1. Use vivid language to support your presentations. One vivid example is more powerful than a mass of statistics.

2. Use metaphors to personify abstract ideas.

3. Use metaphors to frame the way you want your listener to think.

4. Use analogies when you want to introduce a complex, abstract idea.

5. Bring presentations alive with stories. A vivid story stays in the listener's mind long after everything else is forgotten.

6. Keep your metaphors, analogies, and stories simple – even for well-educated listeners.

7. Fear is the most powerful human motivator. To make fear work, you must really scare your audience and offer a workable, easy-to-follow, specific recommendation on how to overcome the threat.

8. People are motivated more by the fear of losing something than by the reward of gaining something of equal value.

9. Assess your audience's mood before you start to persuade.

10. Use humor to introduce, summarize, or highlight your key points.

Winning People's Minds

How to Structure and Package Your Message

K.I.S.S.: KEEP IT SHORT AND SIMPLE

The Principle of Selective Attention

Most presenters overwhelm their audiences by drowning them in tidal waves of information. Human beings are simply incapable of absorbing, let alone remembering, the masses of data they are bombarded with every day.

Advertisers talk about the principle of selective attention, which says that consumers ignore most messages and focus their attention on a few key messages, usually one at a time. If you want to persuade, the message is: Limit the number of points you want to make; three to five are plenty.

> 'The real message isn't what you say. It's what the other person remembers."
> — Harry Mills

Keep it Short

In our information-saturated world, the greatest mistake we make when persuading is to drown our audience in a sea of words. "It is better to be brief than tedious," wrote Shakespeare. Franklin Roosevelt offered similar advice: "Be sincere. Be brief. Be seated." Consider the great speeches of history. Abraham Lincoln took less than three minutes to read the 269 words of his Gettysburg Address. Churchill took less than two and a half minutes to deliver his "blood, sweat and tears" speech. On the day Nelson Mandela was released from 27 years' imprisonment, the speech he delivered to signal the end of apartheid lasted just five minutes.

Churchill's entire speech to Harrow School, still widely quoted today, was:

> Never give in
> Never give in
> Never, never, never, never –
> in nothing great or small, large or petty –
> Never give in, except to convictions of honor
> and good sense.

People recall most information when you limit the main points to two or three.

The Two-Part Contrast

The simplest and most common chunking technique is the two-part contrast. The mind readily chunks information into two parts:

old	new
young	old
problem	solution
cause	effect
us	them

Some of the most memorable phrases use the two-part contrast: Hamlet's famous soliloquy starts, "To be or not to be, that is the question"; John F. Kennedy inspired us with "Our task is not to fix the blame for the past, but to fix the course for the future"; and George Orwell wrote one of literature's most memorable lines in *Animal Farm:* "All animals are equal, but some are more equal than others."

The Rule of Threes

The second most common organizational pattern is the rule of threes. Although we don't fully understand the psychological reasons behind the rule of threes, information is extraordinarily compelling when it is clustered in groups of three: "three points, three arguments, three phrases."[1]

Here are some of history's most memorable three-part sayings:

The Bible – "Father, Son, and Holy Ghost."

Julius Caesar – "I came, I saw, I conquered."

Robert the Bruce – "Try, try and try again."

Franklin D. Roosevelt – "I see one-third of a nation ill-housed, ill-clad, ill-nourished."

Abraham Lincoln – "of the people, by the people, for the people."

Danton – "to dare, to dare again, ever to dare."

On a more mundane level, we talk about the three-beat conservation slogan: reduce, reuse, recycle; the three-step commands: ready, aim, fire; and the 3Rs of education: reading, writing, and arithmetic. Then there are the three bears, the three stooges, and the three little pigs.

Keep It Simple

Most persuaders are shocked when they discover how often they are misunderstood. This is not surprising when you discover how common miscomprehension is. A remarkable U.S. study on the comprehension of television messages found:[2]

- Of these questioned, 97 percent misunderstood some part of every message they viewed as part of the survey.

- On average, viewers misunderstood about 30 percent of the content they viewed.

When you consider that television messages, especially ads, are packaged by communicators highly skilled in the art of message delivery, these are staggering figures.

To keep the message clear and comprehensible:

- Speak simply, clearly, and to the point.

- Avoid technical jargon. Use simple, commonly used words.

- Use specific, concrete language rather than abstract, ambiguous language.

- Make every word count. Don't litter your speech with redundant words.

- Draw conclusions. Don't make your reader guess what you want.

STRUCTURING YOUR ARGUMENT

Persuasion is built on a foundation of logic and reason. The rational mind looks for structure and order; otherwise, it creates its own. We need facts and structure to make sense out of nonsense and order out of chaos.

Use a Thematic Structure

Facts acquire muscle when they are structured around a theme. The old speaker's adage – "Tell 'em what you're going to tell 'em, then tell 'em, then tell 'em what you just told 'em" – still remains core advice for all persuaders. Themes structure your listeners' thinking.

Let's Put the Honor into the Handshake

Trial lawyers know the success of a case often hangs on their ability to create a powerful case theme. When noted American trial lawyer Gerry Spence's client, a small U.S. ice-cream manufacturer, sued hamburger giant McDonald's for breach of an oral contract, Spence chose the theme, "Let's put the honor back into the handshake." The message was that a "handshake deal should be fully honored by honest business people."[3] The jury agreed and awarded Spence's client $52 million.

"Human Need Versus Corporate Greed"

In another recent case, Spence sued an insurance company for its fraud against a quadriplegic client. Spence created the theme "human need versus corporate greed," seeking damages for emotional pain and suffering. The jury ordered the insurance company to pay damages of $33.5 million plus interest of another $10 million.

Playing the Race Card

When lawyers Robert Shapiro and Johnnie Cochrane came to represent O.J. Simpson, charged with the murders of Nicole Brown Simpson and Ronald Lyle Goldman, they faced, according to Jeffrey Toobin (author of *The Run of His Life*), a dilemma: What to do about a guilty client? The answer, the defense decided, was to build a defense around the theme of race. Toobin claims: Because of the overwhelming evidence of Simpson's guilt, his lawyers could not undertake a defense aimed at proving his innocence....

Almost from the day of Simpson's arrest . . . his lawyers posited that Simpson was the victim of a wide-ranging conspiracy of racist law enforcement officials who had fabricated and planted evidence in order to frame him for a crime he did not commit.

For this effort the defense needed a receptive audience, which it most definitely had in the African-Americans who dominated the jury pool in downtown Los Angeles. The defense strategy played to experiences that were anything but fictional – above all the decade of racism within and by the Los Angeles Police Department. The defense sought to identify the Simpson case as the latest in a series of racial abuses by the LAPD, which featured such celebrated outrages as the Rodney King case.[4]

POSITIONING YOUR MESSAGE

Where you position your message affects your influence as a speaker.

The Primary and Recency Effects

A primary effect occurs when the information you present first has a greater impact; a recency effect occurs when the information presented last has the greater impact. Research shows we remember the first and last parts of any presentation best. Information buried in the middle of a presentation is quickly forgotten.

The Primary Effect and Justice

As part of a trial, the lawyers for both sides are allowed to make opening statements. Even though opening statements are not evidence, they can exert great influence on jurors, occurring as they do at the beginning of the trial. The legal system insists that jurors should not form their decisions on the basis of opening statements. Judges often instruct the juries that "statements and arguments of counsel are not evidence." In theory, they are only intended to assist the jury in understanding the evidence, yet research shows that jurors are heavily influenced by opening statements and often make their minds up very early in a trial.

In one Miami trial, two lawyers disagreed over a point of law, right after the completion of the opening statements and before the introduction of any testimony. The judge asked the jury to leave the courtroom while the legal point was discussed. When, a few minutes later, the jury was brought back, the foreperson announced, "We've arrived at a verdict, Your Honor."[5]

Deliver Good News First

If you have to deliver a mixture of good and bad news – and you are the only speaker – deliver the good news first. Putting the good news first will produce more attitude change than the reverse order. The good news moves the audience toward you and makes them more receptive to any bad news that follows.

Turn Taking and the Primary and Recency Effects

Imagine for the moment you are making an important public presentation. There is one other competitor, also a formidable presenter. If you had a choice, would you go first, make a good first impression, and take advantage of the primary effect? Or would you go last, make a few vivid and easily remembered points, and exploit the recency effect?

The answer depends upon *when* the audience will make their decision. If your audience is going to decide between the two of you virtually immediately after the two presentations, go second.

The recency effect will operate, and your points will still be fresh in your audience's mind.

By contrast, if your audience will take several days to make up their mind, then the primary effect will operate – and you should go first. In these circumstances, the first speaker can set the agenda decision criteria.[6]

DYNAMIC OPENINGS

Creating History at Gettysburg

It was a solemn occasion when President Abraham Lincoln arrived in Gettysburg on November 19, 1863, to dedicate part of the Civil War battlefield as a cemetery. The losses had been horrific: 50,000 were dead, wounded, or missing. Coffins were still piled high at the railway station waiting to be buried.

The gathered crowd numbered 15,000. For two hours, they listened to the classical oratory of the principal speaker, Edward Everett. Lincoln spoke for just three minutes. His opening line – "Four score and seven years ago our fathers brought forth upon this continent a new nation, conceived in Liberty, and dedicated to the proposition that all men are created equal" – is the most remembered and quoted in American history. The Gettysburg Address has, in fact, been called the best short speech since the Sermon on the Mount.

Shakespeares's Persuasive Openings

Like Lincoln, Shakespeare understood the power of a persuasive opening. In *Julius Caesar,* Mark Antony is delivering the eulogy over Caesar's body. The crowd is belligerent; they detested Caesar. They are angry because they believe Mark Antony is about to tell them they should feel guilty for taking delight in Caesar's death, which is exactly what Mark Antony wants them to feel.

First, Mark Antony tests the crowd. "Gentle Romans!" he appeals. The boos of the crowd tell him this is the wrong approach. Again he tries: "Friends, Romans, countrymen, lend me your ears. I come to bury Caesar, not to praise him." This works; the crowd quietens and listens. Now that he has their ear, he can begin his attack on the real villain – Brutus.

All effective openings have to make their audience sit up and listen. Dynamic openings grab attention; they can also serve to introduce your topic and establish your personal credibility.

Get Straight to the Point

The trend in today's business presentations is to leave out the introductory remarks and get straight to the point. Picture this opening delivered by a vice president to the board of a pharmaceutical company:

"In exactly two years from today, the patents on our most profitable product line will expire forever. On that day, generic manufacturers will swamp our market with cheap copies – and eat us alive."[7]

Advertisers know that, in most advertisements, the headline is by far the most important element. Most people read little else. It took David Ogilvy 104 drafts before he came up with this classic headline:

"At 60 miles an hour the loudest noise in this new Rolls-Royce comes from the electric clock."

The advertisement became a model for copywriters everywhere. Legend has it that when David Ogilvy offered it to Rolls-Royce for approval, the executive in charge paused, frowned, and said, "We really must do something to improve our clock."

The simplest openings are often the most powerful. Here is Sir Richard Steele's opening lines written to his wife while he was away from home. The date is September 30, 1710:

"I am very sleepy and tired, but could not think of closing my eyes till I told you I am, dearest creature, your affectionate and faithful husband."[8]

THE CLIMAX COUNTS

Your ending is the last thing people hear. It is your last chance to get through. In persuasion, starting off badly is a setback; finishing badly often signals failure.

Actors love a great exit line because they leave the stage with a bang. One of the great final lines in literature comes from Charles Dickens's *A Tale of Two Cities*. Sidney Carton, the derelict English barrister, says this as he saves another man's life by taking his place on the scaffold:

It is a far, far better thing that I do than I have ever done; it is far, far better rest that I go to, than I have ever known." Carton, in one final line, has redeemed his wasted life.

Blood, Sweat, and Tears

Churchill was the master of the great ending. On May 8, 1940, the Chamberlain's government fell and King George VI asked Churchill to lead a new coalition government. In his first speech as prime minister, Churchill set out his plans:

> I would say to the House, as I said to those who have joined this Government: I have nothing to offer but blood, toil, tears and sweat. ...
>
> You ask what is our policy? I will say: It is to wage war, by sea, land and air, with all our might and with all the strength God can give us. ...
>
> You ask, what is our aim? I answer in one word: Victory – victory at all costs. ... I say, come then, let us go forward together with our united strength.

AAFTO

The most effective endings call for action. If possible, use your last line to ask for a commitment. Salespeople call this the AAFTO – "Always ask for the order." Advertisers know a coupon placed at the end of an advertisement increases orders by ten times or more.

And in the field of direct mail, "time limit offers, particularly those with a specific date, outpull offers with no time limit practically every time."[9]

Again Churchill provides a classic illustration of how to do it. It is 1941 and Churchill is calling on President Roosevelt to provide military and economic aid to Britain. Churchill concludes his broadcast by quoting from the poet Longfellow, whose poem Roosevelt himself had sent him in January 1941. Then comes the punch line:

"We shall not fail or falter; we shall not weaken or tire."

Then comes the last sentence – short, specific, and asking for action:

"Give us the tools and we will finish the job."

In general, it pays to state your conclusions as clearly as possible. Facts do not speak for themselves; be specific. If you are too subtle in your conclusions, your audience often draws different conclusions from those you intend.

A Dollar a Rape

Kim Pring, a former National Baton Twirling Champion and Miss Wyoming, sued *Penthouse* magazine for defamation.

In 1978, Kim Pring won the title of National Baton Twirling Champion. She then went on to capture the Miss Wyoming crown and represent Wyoming at the Miss America Pageant.

There, a *Penthouse* writer watched Kim perform her baton twirling act. According to Kim, the *Penthouse* article that followed "transformed her from the greatest baton twirler in the nation to the greatest blow-job artist in the history of the world." The story claimed Miss Wyoming was so good at oral sex she could actually levitate a man – all this without her permission and without even bothering to label the story as fiction.

The indecent calls, obscenities shouted at her in public, and messages on her car left Kim devastated.

Gerry Spence, Kim's attorney, painted a powerful analogy to make a picture of the effect the article had on Kim.

"It was as if she had been raped," Spence pleaded, "because rape is when someone takes from you what you don't want to give, and what *Penthouse* had done to Kim was to take her privacy and her good name ... and sold it to the twenty-five million men who, according to *Penthouse,* constitute the readership of the month's edition." Spence argued "that every time someone read that article, Kim was raped and that the jury should punish Penthouse by charging them a *mere dollar a rape.* One dollar for each of the twenty-five million subscribers to that month's edition."[10]

The jury awarded Kim $26.5 million: $1.5 million as damages for Kim and $25 million to punish *Penthouse.*

How much is a woman's name worth? It's virtually impossible to calculate. Moreover, most juries wouldn't have the skills or the motivation to spend the time calculating a figure based on logic. Gerry Spence helped the jurors calculate a price by *explicitly calling for* a dollar a rape.

MARSHALL YOUR FACTS

Evidence Enhances Persuasion

The right evidence can strengthen your arguments; poorly chosen evidence can destroy your case. Research shows:[11]

- Using evidence from highly credible sources increases your credibility; citing irrelevant evidence from poorly qualified sources destroys credibility.
- Evidence supported by an independent expert is more convincing than facts presented alone.

- Individual case studies are more persuasive than statistical evidence. When vivid examples are backed by statistics, the examples become more powerful.

- Specific facts are more persuasive than general facts.

- It pays to clearly document the sources of any testimonials you use. Sourced testimonials are much more persuasive.

- It pays to use novel evidence; fresh information is more convincing.

- People interpret evidence from the perspective of their own attitudes, regardless of the quality of your evidence. Evidence that is consistent with the other side's beliefs is much more persuasive.

- Finally, you should involve the other side when presenting your case. Lectures are far less persuasive than two-way discussions.

Expert Testimony

"Information is giving out; communication is getting through."
— *Sydney J. Harris*

If your topic is controversial or if your audience doesn't consider it important enough, use expert testimony.

For the moment, imagine you are delivering a presentation calling for more spending on speech recognition software. You cite Microsoft as proof of where the market is moving. "Microsoft," you say, "is already spending millions to make future editions of Windows speech compatible." You continue, *"Business Week* quotes Bill Gates as saying, 'Speech is not just the future of Windows. It is the future of computing itself.' "[12] You conclude, "I believe it is also our future."

When you have few hard facts to support a case, expert opinions from respected gurus such as Bill Gates are likely to be your most convincing support.

Persuaders often make the mistake of citing experts without first establishing their credentials. Even if you think your audience knows your source or you think a person's title or an institution's name suggests authority, it still pays to briefly highlight the expertise of your source.

Examples as Evidence

Examples turn vague generalizations and abstractions into specific, concrete proof. Here is Jean L. Farinelli, CEO of Creamer Dickson Basford, addressing a Boston audience of female entrepreneurs on how to overcome the obstacles they will face in business:

"So what about external barriers? Here's an example. Many years ago, an entrepreneur had a very big dream. He needed capital. He went to 301 banks, and 301 banks said 'no' to his dream. Then the 302nd bank said, 'OK, we'll help to build your theme park, Mr Disney.' "[13]

Farinelli then goes on to cite an example that her female audience will more easily relate to:

Recently, I talked with Sandie Tillotson, co-founder of Nu Skin International, the skin care products company that grew from nothing in 1984 to $500 million in annual sales today. I asked Sandie about barriers. Her story is inspiring. Picture this: Sandie lives in Utah. In Utah, 98 percent of women are at home. Only two percent are career women – not exactly the best environment for businesswomen role models.

Sandie was a teacher when she co-founded Nu Skin in Provo. Almost everyone around her said it was a dumb idea. Sandie calls these people "dream stealers," or people who say your dreams cannot come true. Some do it out of envy, of course, but many do it in a misguided effort to protect women like Sandie from disappointment.[14]

Relevant examples, especially when combined with statistics, can be extraordinarily compelling.

MESSAGE REPETITION

It's amazing how many people give up trying to persuade when they don't succeed the first time. Advertisers know message repetition is essential for successful persuasion.

Some advertisers claim three exposures to an ad are enough to make advertising work. Advertising theorist Herbert Krugman argues that the first exposure creates interest, the second makes people think about the message, and the third acts as a reminder or closure.

How far apart should you deliver your messages? Research on ads shows five exposures delivered a day apart work better than five exposures delivered on the same day.[15]

All persuaders should pay heed to these findings on message repetition. The lesson is: Don't expect your message to get through the first time; try to give your message at least three exposures, and, if possible, spread the messages out.

The trick with face-to-face persuasion is to keep repackaging the message. Each time you deliver the message, use fresh evidence; otherwise, you'll sound like a broken record.

ARGUMENT STRATEGY

How do you win arguments? How do you deal with attacks from rivals? How do you protect yourself from criticism?

Refuting Attacks

"The fellow that agrees with everything you say is either a fool or he is getting ready to skin you."
— *Kin Hubbard*

Don't ignore attacks from rivals. If you don't deal with criticism, people will start to believe your rival's claims. Early in the 1988 U.S. presidential campaign, Democratic candidate Michael Dukakis held a 51 to 34 percent lead over Republican rival George Bush. Bush launched a no-holds-barred campaign claiming Dukakis was soft on criminals. Dukakis naïvely ignored the attacks and watched while his lead disappeared. The failure to rebut turned out to be a fatal error. Dukakis thought rebuttal and counterrebuttal would lead to increasingly negative ads and turn off voters. In this sense, he was probably right.

What Dukakis should have done was what Clinton did in 1992 when campaigning against Bush. Clinton used his assistants, through the press, to actively rebut every one of Bush's attacks. Meanwhile, Clinton's own ad campaign continued to focus on his strengths.

Author and PR investigator David Michie says, "The most impressive example of Rapid Response [rapid rebuttal] in action was during the Republican Convention. As Bush made his speech, the War Room was packed with researchers recording every claim Bush made, and providing a fact to counteract it. Before Bush had finished speaking, the Democrat team was ready to release a long list of Bush "lies" followed by the fact to back up the accusation. [Campaign Director] Stephanopoulos was ringing or paging the journalists before Bush sat down. Remarkably, as the cheering stopped, some of the TV commentators began by listing the false claims in the speech and outlining the counter-claims."[16]

Britain's Labour Party was so impressed by the success of rapid response that they used Clinton's communications war machine as a model to help Tony Blair become Britain's prime minister in 1997.

One-Sided Versus Two-Sided Messages

You have to announce to the staff that management has decided to restructure, and that means layoffs. Should you present a one-sided case biased in favor of restructuring, or should you present a case that covers both sides of the issue?

The correct answer depends on the composition and attitude of your audience. Two-sided messages are more persuasive with audience members who start out disagreeing with your proposition. Giving both sides works better with audience members who already know something about the opposition's case. By presenting both sides, you increase the strength of your credibility by first acknowledging the opposition's case and then concluding that the weight of evidence supports your argument.

Two-sided messages work better with knowledgeable opponents because they communicate respect for your opponents' intelligence. A two-sided message also allows you to refute your opponents' case point by point.

On the other hand, if your audience is full of committed believers, you win few points by acknowledging there is another position. Those at meetings of staunch political activists don't want to hear the merits of the opposition's policies. They want the speaker to rally them by reinforcing their values and beliefs. However, in most situations, people possess information on opposing position so it usually pays to present both sides of the case.

Inoculate Yourself Against Attack

In ancient times, doctors discovered that by injecting a mild dose of a disease into a patient, they could inoculate the patient against a subsequent attack by a much more virulent form of the disease.

A similar principle applies in persuasion. Persuaders protect themselves from attacks by alerting their audience to an impending attack by a rival. Generally, this involves anticipating what the opponent is likely to say.

Imagine your political rival is about to announce an ambitious welfare package. You tell your supporters what the package will contain; you undersell its effects and hit back with strong counterarguments. Your supporters are now inoculated. When your opponent releases his or her promotional campaign, your supporters are already immune to those arguments. When they see or hear the campaign, they use the arguments you planted to reject the message.

Inoculative arguments work. Don't be naïve and ignore what your rivals are saying about you. Protect yourself by inoculating your supporters or customers with defensive arguments.

STRATEGIES FOR ORGANIZING PERSUASIVE PRESENTATIONS

There are a number of ways to organize a persuasive presentation. Here are four useful organizational patterns:

1. Problem-solution
2. Refutation
3. Cause and effect
4. Motivated sequence

Problem-Solution

The most basic of all organizational patterns for a persuasive speech is to create a problem for your audience and then solve it by presenting a convincing solution.

If you are working with an apathetic audience, or your listeners seem unaware that a problem exists, then a problem-solution pattern works well.

Refutation

A second way to persuade an audience is to refute your opponents' points by challenging their evidence in your speech and disproving their arguments.

Refutation works best as a persuasion strategy when you know your position is under attack. Refutation also works well when you know in advance what your listeners' chief objections to your proposal are likely to be.

When you use a refutation strategy in a presentation, allow time for a follow-up question-and-answer session. Use it to deal with any remaining objections. The question-and-answer forum will also increase your credibility and enhance your persuasiveness.

Cause and Effect

The cause-and-effect persuasion pattern is similar to the problem-solution pattern. If you want to emphasize the causes, discuss the effect first and then examine the causes.

If, by contrast, you wish to highlight the effects of a situation, first present the problem as your central idea and then spell out its effects.

Motivated Sequence

The motivated sequence is a five-step sequence – attention, need, satisfaction, visualization, action – developed by Alan Monroe, based on the way we think when we are being persuaded:

1. *Attention*. First, you must capture your audience's attention. There are dozens of ways to do this. You can start with a startling statistic or use a joke or anecdote.

2. *Need*. Second, your audience must feel they have a definite need. Here you have to convince your audience why your topic or issue should concern them directly.

3. *Satisfaction*. After creating a need, you need to explain how you plan to satisfy the need you've created.

4. *Visualization*. Now you need to paint a picture with words of how bright the future will be if they adopt your solution. Alternatively, you could paint a negative visualization and tell your listeners how terrible the future will be if they don't adopt your solution.

5. *Action*. Finally, you tell your audience what specific action you want them to take.

INFLUENCING WITH STATISTICS

When the news leaked out in 1994 that Intel's Pentium computer chip was faulty, two statistics hit the press to describe how computer users would be affected.

IBM calculated it would affect an average spreadsheet user every 24 days; Intel claimed it would happen every 27,000 years. Since these two estimates differ by approximately 32,400,000 percent, it is no wonder cynics claim there are "three kinds of lies: lies, damned lies and statistics."[17]

Nevertheless, we can't ignore the fact that statistics are often portrayed as the ultimate in hard evidence.

Use Credible Sources

Statisticians say, "Figures don't lie, but liars figure." Since skeptics know figures can be used to support any argument, make your statistics credible by citing reputable, authoritative, unbiased sources.

Sampling. As you evaluate your sources, find out how the statistics were gathered. If a statistic relies on a sample, find out how the sample was gathered.

Magazines and newspapers are notorious for announcing biased results based on responses to questionnaires appearing in the periodical.

Historians love to cite the 1936 *Literacy Digest* poll, which predicted Republican presidential hopeful Alf Langdon would trounce Democrat contender Franklin Roosevelt by a margin of three to two, when in fact Roosevelt went on to win by a landslide. The reason the poll was so wrong was that only 23 percent of the people who were sent questionnaires returned them, and these came mostly from wealthier Republican-leaning respondents.

Interpret Statistics Accurately

People are often influenced by statistics that sound impressive but that have been distorted through selection.

Let's imagine you have just completed a customer satisfaction survey for your business. The figures read:

Very dissatisfied	12 percent
Somewhat dissatisfied	28 percent
Satisfied	30 percent
Very satisfied	14 percent
Extremely satisfied	16 percent.

You could claim that 60 percent of your clients think you are doing a reasonable job or better. You could also claim that 70 percent of your clients thought your company was just adequate or worse. Either interpretation would be true, but the slant in each case is entirely different.[18]

Averages. Statistical concepts are often deceptively labeled. Take the concepts of mean, median, and mode. All three are called averages; however, they describe vastly different things. If you don't know which average is being used, it's very easy to be deceived.

Suppose we want to know the average income of the employees of ACME Trucking. Here is a list of the salaries:

$470,000 (earned by the chief executive officer)

$100,000 (earned by his wife)

$ 80,000 (earned by his wife's three brothers)

$ 50,000 (earned by his wife's best friend)

$ 30,000 (earned by the plant manager)

$ 25,000 (earned by each of the six production worker)

The mean is the arithmetical average, the one we're most familiar with. The average employee earns a whopping $80,000. (The total payroll of $1,040,000 divided by thirteen employees equals $80,000.)

The chief executive's wife can claim her brothers earn no more than the average employee.

The median is the second type of average. For ACME Trucking, the median income is $30,000, that is, six employees earn more than $30,000, and six employees earn less.

The mode is a third kind of average that can easily be manipulated; the mode is the most common of the numbers listed. In ACME Trucking's case, the mode is $25,000.

Thus, for ACME Trucking, we have three very different averages: The mean income is $80,000, the median income is $30,000, and the mode income is $25,000.[19] The average you pick depends on the interpretation you want to make.

Risks. Risks are another area of ignorance that professional persuaders love to exploit. Few of us can visualize what it means when we read the risk of dying this year from pesticide poisoning is 1 in 200,000 (worldwide). Research also shows there is a huge gap between the average person's guess about the magnitude of a given risk and its true threat.

In January 1993, the U.S. Environmental Protection Agency (EPA) announced its calculation that exposure to secondary, or passive, tobacco smoke was a "dangerous and major health risk." The EPA estimated the chances of contracting fatal lung cancer from exposure to secondary smoke as 1 in 30,000 each year.

The EPA announcement caused numerous city councils to ban smoking in public places and employers to place or expand bans on smoking in the workplace.

Yet no one in the EPA ever publicly compared the risk of secondary-smoke exposure with other risks of ordinary life. If they had, the public would have found out that drinking two glasses of milk a day poses a greater threat of death than a lifetime of exposure to secondary smoke. Also, eating a smoked pork chop once a week is twice as likely to kill you as secondary smoke is.[20]

Percent and Percentage Points. Since much of the population is mathematically illiterate, it is very easy for spin doctors to manipulate statistics.

Few people, for example, understand the difference between percent and percentage points. If your profit margin has fallen from 10 percent to 5 percent, you might say that it's fallen 5 percentage points. This doesn't sound nearly as bad as saying it has fallen by 50 percent.

Whenever percentages are used, it pays to examine the raw data. A company's claim that over 30 percent of its researchers have a Ph.D. is much less impressive when you know the company only employs three researchers.

Margin of Error. Imagine you're reading your favorite magazine. An article on the remake of the movie *Grease* says that in a scientifically selected sampling of 500 adults, with a margin of error of 5 percentage points, 55 percent of whites said they preferred the remake of *Grease* to the original while only 40 percent of African-Americans did. By comparison, a huge 75 percent of Asians said they liked the remake better.

What's wrong with these figures? The odds are that none of the generalizations is statistically significant.

Let's look at the figures for whites: 55 percent liked the new; 45 percent liked the original. The margin for error is 5 points. Statistically, this could mean that a range from 50 percent to 60 percent liked the original better while a range from 40 percent to 50 percent liked the remake better. In other words, the result could be split 50–50.

Now let's look at the African-American and Asian figures. Few polls reveal that when you break data down by subgroups, the error margin rockets upward. While the pollsters may have surveyed 500 people, only 80 of them may have been black while only 4 were Asian.[21] The error margin for such tiny subgroups is huge.

Loaded Phrases. Most audiences are naturally suspicious when persuaders use loaded words to interpret figures. Comments such as sales rose an "incredible two-thirds" invite scepticism. However, more subtle interpretations are often absorbed subconsciously. If persuaders want to emphasize that a number is large, they say:

- More than two-thirds
- Nearly seven out of ten
- More than two out of three

If they want to play down the number, they say:

- Less than three-quarters
- Fewer than two out of three
- Under two-thirds

Make Your Numbers Understandable and Memorable

Large Numbers. Large numbers are especially difficult to understand. Few of us, for example, can intuitively grasp the difference between 1 million (1,000,000), 1 billion (1,000,000,000), and 1 trillion (1,000,000,000,000).

If you want someone to grasp the enormity of a large number, you have to put it in context and make it meaningful. If you want to stress the enormity of $1 trillion, you could say: "If you were to count a trillion $1 bills, one per second, 24 hours a day, it would take 32 years."

If you want your audience to grasp the relative magnitude of a million and a billion, you might say that it takes only eleven and a half days for a million seconds to pass, whereas it takes 32 years for a billion seconds to pass.[22]

Comparisons. Comparing a statistic with another will often heighten its impact. Compare the speed of the supersonic *Concorde*, which travels 2,000 miles per hour, with that of a snail, which travels at 25 feet per hour, a pace equivalent to about .005 mile per hour. The *Concorde's* velocity is 400,000 times that of the snail.[23]

Personalization. The more personal and fun you can make a statistic, the more it will be remembered. Imagine starting a speech on our sexual habits with, "Of the half of us who have pets at home, 45.5 percent allow them in the room during sex."

To personalize a speech on tax avoidance, you could say, "Four out of ten of us admit to claiming more than we should. A third of us exaggerate our expenses or deductions, and 21 percent don't report all the income we make."[24]

Rounded-Off Numbers

It's much easier to visualize and remember 3 million than 3,168,758. Percentages, too, are much more easily recalled if they are rounded off. About 30 percent is easier to remember than 31.69 percent, and about one-third is even easier to understand and remember.[25]

PERSUASION
POINTERS

1. Be brief – limit the main points in any presentation to two, three, or five.

2. Use the two-part contrast for maximum impact: old/new, problem/solution.

3. Information is extraordinarily compelling when it is clustered in groups of three.

4. Structure your argument around a single theme.

5. Position your main message at the beginning or end of your presentation. Information in the middle is quickly forgotten.

6. Try to speak first if the audience is to make up their mind at a later date. Speak last if the decision is immediate.

7. Grab your audience's attention with a dynamic opening.

8. End strongly – call for action and spell out exactly what you want.

9. Choose the right evidence carefully, using highly credible sources, independent experts, individual case studies, specific facts and fresh information.

10. Don't expect to persuade the first time you deliver a message. Repeated exposures – at least three – are usually essential. To prevent boredom, use fresh evidence and different packaging, but keep stressing the same central point.

11. Don't ignore attacks from rivals. Rebut all attacks immediately.

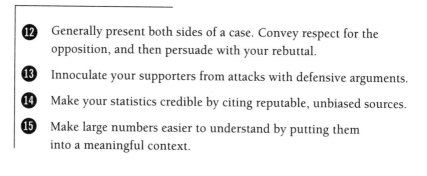

12 Generally present both sides of a case. Convey respect for the opposition, and then persuade with your rebuttal.

13 Innoculate your supporters from attacks with defensive arguments.

14 Make your statistics credible by citing reputable, unbiased sources.

15 Make large numbers easier to understand by putting them into a meaningful context.

Power Pitches

How to Persuade with Graphs, Charts, and Videos

THE POWER OF A VISUAL

A powerful visual leaves an indelible impression we never forget. When I picture the Vietnam War, I still see a naked girl, burnt by napalm, running toward the camera. When I recall John Kennedy's assassination, I still see vividly the details in a news picture showing Jack Ruby shooting Lee Harvey Oswald.

Visuals Increase Persuasiveness

Of what we learn, 75 percent comes to us visually, 13 percent comes through hearing, and 12 percent comes through smell, taste, and touch.[1] Visuals come in many forms and include slides, overheads, audiotapes, flipcharts, props, product samples, and brochures. When used well, all enhance persuasion.

A 1986 study by the University of Minnesota and 3M found that presenters who use slides and overhead transparencies are 43 percent more persuasive than those who don't.

The study also found that presenters using computer-generated slides were seen as more professional, more interesting, and more effective.[2]

The research showed that the more skilled a presenter you are, the more your audience will expect you to use visual aids.

HOW TO CREATE AND USE PERSUASIVE VISUAL AIDS

In just a few years, we've moved from flipcharts, overheads, and slides to videos. With the latest technology and computer graphics, we can produce stunning images. But in the rush to dazzle, many presenters forget the prime purpose of a visual aid: to *aid* comprehension through *visual* means.

Determine Your Message First

The prime purpose of a presentation is to communicate a persuasive message – not to dazzle your audience with elaborate graphics, videos, and sound effects. So, start by writing down your presentation goal and the central message you want to communicate.

Think KISS (Keep It Short and Simple)

Remember architect Mies van der Rohe's paradoxical rule: "Less is more." *Business Week* magazine reports there are 33 million business presentations given every day. Most are too long and too complex; an effective visual is simple, clear, and visible.

Stick to One Thought, Concept, or Idea per Visual

Organize all visuals around one specific point. Keep your visuals simple and uncluttered. Ask yourself, What is the central point I want to communicate? Then design your visual around that point.

Each visual should have a headline or caption that clearly states what it shows. It should be simple and brief and should communicate the purpose of the visual.

Avoid trying to summarize several points with one visual; try to give each point its own visual. If you leave one visual on the screen and go through several points, the presentation soon becomes static. Successive visuals, instead of one, heighten interest and involvement, and they improve retention. Successive visuals also give the presentation a dynamic sense of movement.

Organize Your Content Around Three to Five Main Points

Most audiences and decision makers struggle to remember more than three key points. The biggest mistake high-tech persuaders make is to overwhelm their audience with too much information.

Watch for Visual Overkill

Analyze each slide or overhead to make sure it adds value to your presentation. If it doesn't, drop it. As a guide, don't present more than one slide or overhead every two minutes. A twenty-minute presentation should therefore contain no more than ten slides.

Use as Few Word Lists as Possible

Most presenters use far too many text frames. They bore their audiences with endless lists of bullet points. Bulleted lists presented on overheads or text slides are much less powerful than an excellent visual.

Visuals grab our attention, simplify concepts, and are much more memorable than text. The mind stores information visually. Visuals work better because our minds find it easier to process and store symbols than to decode text. Bulleted lists presented on overheads or text slides are much less powerful than an excellent visual. So wherever possible, turn your word lists into graphics (see Figure 10.1).

Figure 10.1 Wherever possible, turn word lists into graphics.

Think Visually

Readers of graphics fall into two groups: those who are personally affected by an issue and those who aren't. Those who are personally affected by an issue will spend much more time actively searching a graphic for all the information they need. If you want to hook members in an audience who are uninterested, your graphics have to be vivid and dramatic (see Figure 10.2).

Figure 10.2 Here a music retailer uses notes to add visual impact to a presentation.

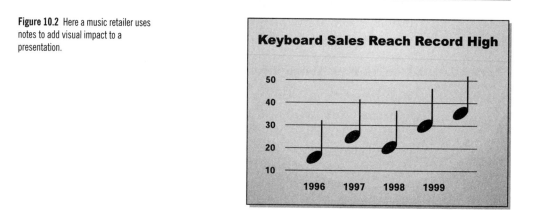

Keep the Text Brief, Simple, and Readable

Use a maximum of six lines per visual and six words per line. Use short, simple words. Jargon, "bureaucratese," and pompous language are presentation killers.

Make Your Letters and Text Large and Readable

Words have to be readable from anywhere in the room. To guarantee readability, make sure your smallest letters are in at least 14-point typeface. If you can read the text on a slide while holding it in your hand, it will probably pass the visibility test (see page 166).

Recommended Minimum Type Sizes		
	Overheads	Slides
Titles	36 point	24 point
Subtitles	24 point	18 point
Text	18 point	14 point

For text, use upper- and lowercase type. Capitalize only the first word in a line; don't use all caps because they are difficult to read.

Avoid using multiple typefaces. One typeface is usually sufficient to support an entire presentation. However, many designers like to use two typefaces for variety and contrast: one for headlines and a second for body copy.

Remember, type has to be read. Choose a face that is clean, is easy to read, and looks good in a variety of sizes and weights. The world's most popular typeface is Helvetica, probably because it has a bold, clean look and looks good in all sizes. Helvetica is also available in a huge selection of fonts – extended, condensed, and italic.

If you're looking for a standard typeface around which to build your presentations, also look at Optima, Futura, Century, and Times Roman (see Figure 10.3).

Figure 10.3 In the text frame, Arial Black, a sans serif font, is used for the headline. Garamond, a serif font, is used for the body text.

Never Read Your Visual to Your Audience

Nothing turns an audience off more than someone who reads out loud word for word what the audience can read on a visual. Paraphrase the key message, and be sure to sustain eye contact with your audience.

Don't Talk to Your Visual

Look at your audience when speaking. Don't look at your slide or overhead while you are explaining what's on your visual. Also, be careful not to talk while your eyes are focused downward on your notes; talk only when your eyes are focused on your audience.

USE COLOR

Color dramatically improves comprehension and retention.

The 3M study found color was one of the prime reasons presentation visuals have such a big impact compared to black-and-white. Color advertisements attract up to 80 percent more readers. Sales of advertised products increase by over 50 percent when color is used, and the retention of ad content increases 55 percent to 80 percent with color.

Colors stimulate an emotional response. Reds and yellows tend to be evocative, greens and blues calming.

Don't Use Too Many Colors

Too many colors cause confusion. Two different colors of text with one background color usually work best. To unify your presentation, use the same background color for all of your visuals.

The best color combinations vary from media to media (see page 168).

Selecting Colors for Different Media			
	Overheads	**Slides**	**Video**
General rule	Dark text on a light background	Light text on a dark background	Light text on a dark background
Best color combinations	Dark blue and dark red text on a white, light gray, or light yellow background	White or yellow text on a dark blue, black, or dark green background	Same as slides but contrast range and color saturation need to be reduced to 80%

Tailor Your Colors to Your Audience's Biases

Colors have the power to influence viewers' emotional state of mind. However, different colors mean different things to different audiences.

A skilled presenter will tailor the presentation colors to cater to the biases of the audience. To an accountant, green represents money and has positive connotations; red ink represents losses and has negative associations. For a surgeon, red (blood) is positive; green (necrosis) is negative. In business presentations, most persuaders play it safe by using conservative corporate blue (see below).

How Different Audiences Interpret Colors				
	Movie-goers	**Financial Managers**	**Health Care Professionals**	**Control Engineers**
Blue	Tender	Corporate, reliable	Dead	Cold, water
Cyan	Leisurely	Cool, subdued	Cyanotic, deprived of oxygen	Steam
Green	Playful	Profitable	Infected, bilious	Nominal, safe
Yellow	Happy	Highlighted item, important	Jaundiced	Caution
Red	Exciting	Unprofitable	Healthy	Danger
Magenta	Sad	Wealthy	Cause for concern	Hot, radioactive

Source: Gerald E. Jones, *How to Lie With Charts,* Sybex 1995, p. 205

Some People Are Color-Blind

Color blindness and color perception problems are not uncommon. It is therefore best to avoid red/green, brown/green, blue/black, and blue/purple in combination.

HOW TO CREATE PERSUASIVE CHARTS

There are three steps to creating persuasive charts:

1. Make the message the title of your chart

To help readers, make the title the one message you want to be remembered. Most graphs are headed by topic titles that leave the reader searching for the central message. A graph labeled "Sales by Product" is much less informative than "Beer accounts for 60% of our sales." A graph headed "Company Sales Trend" is much less informative than "Company sales have tripled since July."

2. Interpret the chart for your audience

Whenever possible, interpret the graph for your audience. Look at the chart in Figure 10.4; it could be interpreted four different ways:

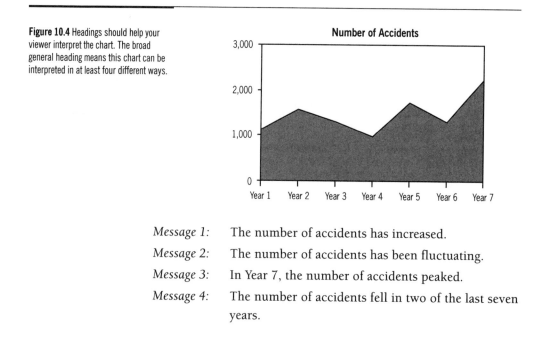

Figure 10.4 Headings should help your viewer interpret the chart. The broad general heading means this chart can be interpreted in at least four different ways.

Message 1:   The number of accidents has increased.

Message 2:   The number of accidents has been fluctuating.

Message 3:   In Year 7, the number of accidents peaked.

Message 4:   The number of accidents fell in two of the last seven years.

3. Select the appropriate chart

There are six common chart types. They are:

1. Pie charts
2. Horizontal bar charts
3. Vertical (or column) bar charts
4. Line charts
5. Area charts
6. Scatter (or dot) charts

To choose the best graph form, pinpoint the relationship you want to emphasize:

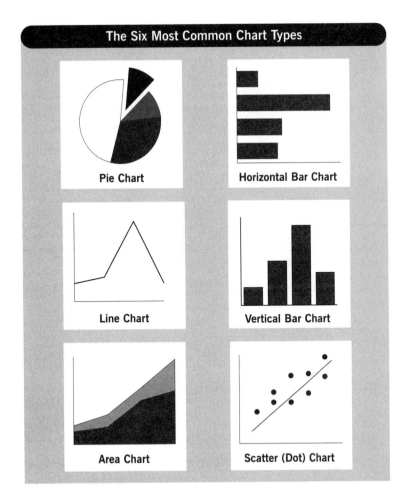

The Six Most Common Chart Types

Pie Chart · Horizontal Bar Chart · Line Chart · Vertical Bar Chart · Area Chart · Scatter (Dot) Chart

1. PIE CHARTS

A pie chart is essentially a circle sliced up into segments. Keep in mind, pies are for percentages. However, you can also use a pie graph to illustrate any proportional relationship between a segment and a whole pie. This can be expressed as a percentage (10%), a fraction ($^1/_{10}$), or a decimal (0.1).

Tips

- If you have more than six slices, choose the five most important and put the rest in an "other" slice. Pie graphs with more than six slices are difficult to read.

- Position the most important slice in the top right-hand position starting at one o'clock. Most people read the data in a pie graph in clockwise order.

- The importance of a slice can be emphasized further either by using a contrasting shade or by exploding the slice out from the rest of the pie.

- Regardless of position, any segment that gets exploded will be viewed as the most important slice.

- Use rounded numbers when labeling your pie.

- Keep your labels short and place them next to the slices (see Figure 10.5).

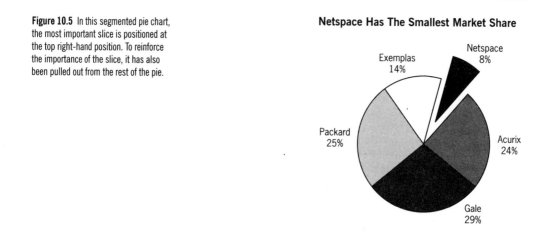

Figure 10.5 In this segmented pie chart, the most important slice is positioned at the top right-hand position. To reinforce the importance of the slice, it has also been pulled out from the rest of the pie.

Netspace Has The Smallest Market Share

Netspace 8%
Exemplas 14%
Packard 25%
Acurix 24%
Gale 29%

2. HORIZONTAL BAR CHARTS

Horizontal bar charts are useful when you want to compare the size or magnitude of a group of items.

Tips

- Arrange the bars in the order that best suits the message you want to send.

- Use a contrasting color or shade to highlight the most important bar, and reinforce the message title (see Figure 10.6).

Figure 10.6 In this bar graph, the bars have been ranked from best (highest) to worst (lowest) sales. The key Rathbone bar has been shaded differently to reinforce the central message.

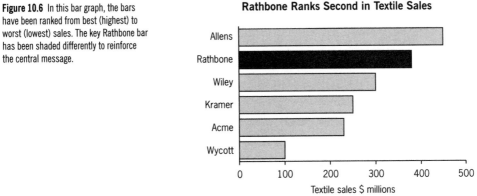

3. VERTICAL (OR COLUMN) BAR CHARTS

Vertical (or column) bar charts are ideal when you want to compare changes in data over time.

Tips

- If practical, keep the number of bars to five or less.
- Make sure the labels read horizontally rather than vertically.
- Use shadings, color, arrows, or other graphical devices when you want to stress a particular point (see Figures 10.7 and 10.8).

Figure 10.7 In this column graph, the arrow helps highlight the central message.

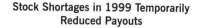

Company Payouts Have Multiplied Seven Times Since 1996

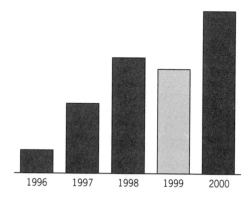

Figure 10.8 This column graph, uses lighter shading for 1999 to help focus the eye of the viewer on the key message.

Stock Shortages in 1999 Temporarily Reduced Payouts

Power Pitches **171**

4. LINE CHARTS

Line charts are the most popular of all chart forms and are ideal when you want to plot or highlight a trend in the data. Line graphs are particularly useful when you have lots of figures that you want to plot over multiple or extended periods of time. Line charts are also useful when you want to compare several trends at once.

Tips

- Make sure the trend line is bolder than the baseline of the graph.

- When possible, limit the number of trend lines to two or three. Multiple line graphs can easily degenerate into visual spaghetti.

- In a multiple-line chart, use the most contrasting color or the boldest solid line to highlight the most important line (see Figure 10.9).

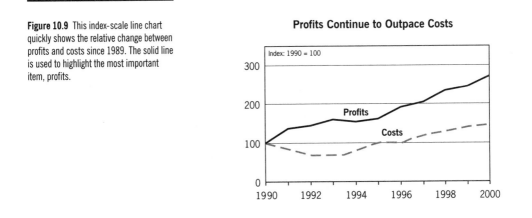

Figure 10.9 This index-scale line chart quickly shows the relative change between profits and costs since 1989. The solid line is used to highlight the most important item, profits.

Profits Continue to Outpace Costs

Index: 1990 = 100

5. AREA CHARTS

Area charts are essentially filled-in line graphs. They are useful when you want to compare a change in volumes or quantities over time.

Tips

- Make sure the bottom layer takes up the largest share of the graph.

- Use your darkest color to show your base.

- Area charts are more difficult to interpret than pie and bar charts, so give your audience extra time for comprehension (see Figure 10.10).

Figure 10.10 The thick bold line keeps the primary emphasis on the total, while the dark bottom layer highlights the huge contribution consulting makes to profits.

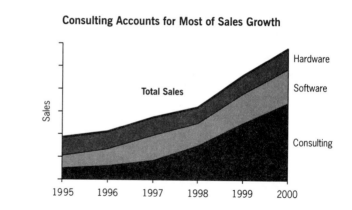

Consulting Accounts for Most of Sales Growth

6. SCATTER (OR DOT) CHARTS

Scatter charts or dot graphs show whether or not the relationship between two variables follows an expected pattern.

Tips

- Keep the message as simple as possible. Scatter charts can easily confuse unsophisticated audiences.

- Give your audience extra time to view dot graphs. A dot graph takes twice as long as a bar or pie graph to comprehend (see Figure 10.11).

Figure 10.11 In this scatter chart, the dots cluster around the expected pattern, showing there is a relationship between spending on research and profit levels.

There is a Link Between Spending on Research and Profits

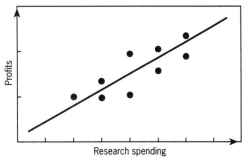

HOW TO LIE WITH CHARTS

Charts are commonly misused and distorted by persuaders to mislead. Here are seven common tricks used by unscrupulous persuaders to confuse, mislead, and distort.

Trick 1: Distort the 3-D pie

The popular pie chart is the most misused of all chart forms. A 3-D pie can be used to distort the size of the bottom slice: The thick edge makes it look much larger than it really is (or would look in a two-dimensional pie).

To take advantage of this, you place the segment you want to highlight at the bottom of a 3-D pie. To increase the impact even further, you can thicken the base of the pie and tilt it back. The effect is remarkable (see Figure 10.12).

Another trick with a 3-D pie is to vary the heights of the slices. Unethical persuaders love this trick because it's virtually impossible for someone in the audience to accurately assess the different sizes of the segments.

Trick 2: Use Scale Manipulation

Unscrupulous presenters are experts in scale manipulation. A different scale can dramatically change the impression you want to make. Compare the two charts in Figures 10.13 and 10.14. Which one would you choose? The answer depends on your professional judgment. It should be the one that best reflects the significance of the changes you want to highlight.

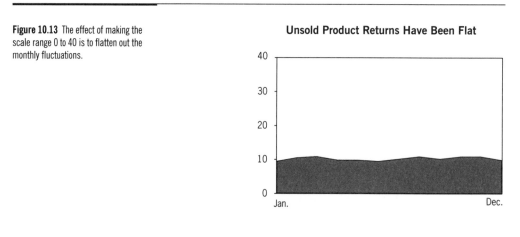

Figure 10.13 The effect of making the scale range 0 to 40 is to flatten out the monthly fluctuations.

Figure 10.14 The effect of compressing the scale range from 9 to 11 is to magnify the monthly fluctuations and present a picture of volatility.

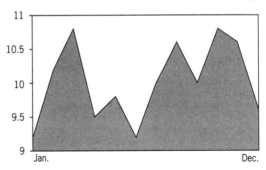

Figure 10.15 By compressing the left-hand scale line, the presenter creates the misleading impression that sales are healthy and rising. Source: Gene Zelazny, *Say It With Charts*, Dow Jones-Irwin, 1985, p. 77

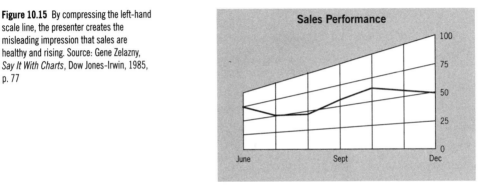

Figure 10.16 This accurate chart shows that sales have actually declined. Source: Gene Zelazny, *Say It With Charts*, Dow Jones-Irwin, 1985, p. 77.

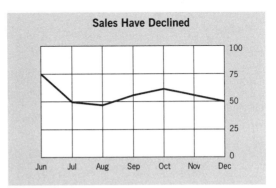

Trick 3: Change the Scale

If manipulating the scale is too obvious, you can always use a different scale altogether.

In the graph headed Pay Increases in Figure 10.17, the facts seem undeniable: The chief executive's hourly rate has risen much faster than the employees' pay. If trade union members were fighting for a big pay rise, this graph would provide all the proof they would need to make a strong case for a catch-up pay increase.

Figure 10.17 This chart shows that the chief executive's hourly rate has risen much faster than the employees' income.

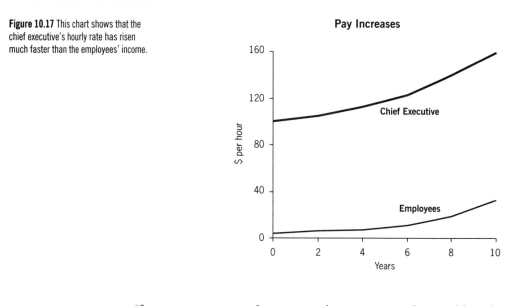

If management wanted to contest the union case, they could easily counter with the chart in Figure 10.18. This uses an index scale, which puts both sets of hourly rates at 100 in Year 1 and reveals that the chief executive's pay increases have trailed well behind those of the employees.

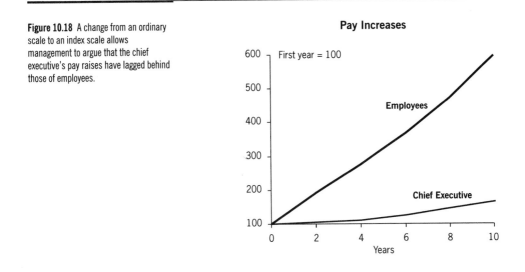

Figure 10.18 A change from an ordinary scale to an index scale allows management to argue that the chief executive's pay raises have lagged behind those of employees.

Trick 4: Change the time periods

If you feel the pattern suggested by a chart doesn't fit the message you want to present, you can always try changing the time periods.

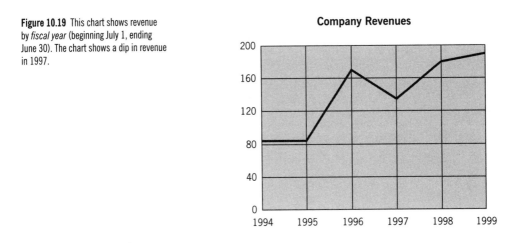

Figure 10.19 This chart shows revenue by *fiscal year* (beginning July 1, ending June 30). The chart shows a dip in revenue in 1997.

The previous chart in Figure 10.19 paints a picture of uneven yearly earnings. If you want to paint a picture of uninterrupted growth, you could change the time periods into calendar years. The result is shown in Figure 10.20. By changing the time periods from fiscal year to calendar year, you have been able to paint a picture of continual revenue increases.

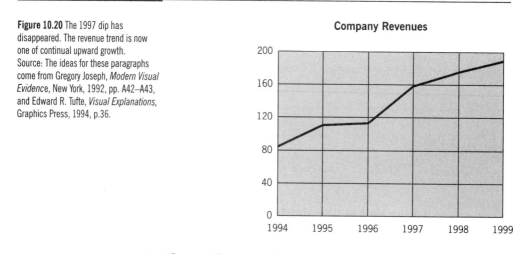

Figure 10.20 The 1997 dip has disappeared. The revenue trend is now one of continual upward growth. Source: The ideas for these paragraphs come from Gregory Joseph, *Modern Visual Evidence*, New York, 1992, pp. A42–A43, and Edward R. Tufte, *Visual Explanations*, Graphics Press, 1994, p.36.

Trick 5: Change the perspective

A common trick of persuaders is to use 3-D to exaggerate the size of all the bars in the chart. The tops of the bars in the 3-D graph in Figure 10.21 have been angled upward: This makes all the bars appear taller than they really are.

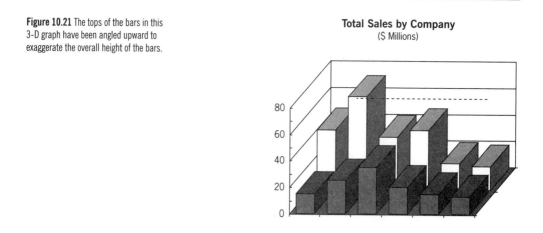

Figure 10.21 The tops of the bars in this 3-D graph have been angled upward to exaggerate the overall height of the bars.

Trick 6: Mix proportional and quantity time relationships in the same chart

This trick takes advantage of the fact that audiences find it much more difficult to accurately estimate the areas of objects than the areas of bars. In Figure 10.22, the satellite on the right is 20 percent taller than the satellite on the left. However, the satellite on the right – which has increased in width as well as height – is actually *twice* as large by area. In other words, the increase now looks much larger than it really is: 200 percent instead of 20 percent.

Figure 10.22 A careful reading of this graph shows satellite dish sales will only increase by 20 percent in the next five years. However, the satellite on the right is twice as large by area, which makes the projected sales increase look much greater than it really is.

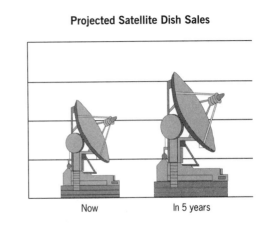

Projected Satellite Dish Sales

Now   In 5 years

Trick 7: Use a visually misleading image

Look at the pyramid chart in Figure 10.23. Try to accurately estimate the percentages of the various segments; most people find it impossible. Unethical persuaders take advantage of this fact. A simple pie graph would convey a much more accurate impression.

Figure 10.23 Although this pyramid chart is visually appealing, it is difficult to interpret accurately.

Age of Clients

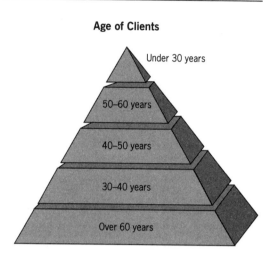

Under 30 years

50–60 years

40–50 years

30–40 years

Over 60 years

THE POWER OF VIDEO

Rodney King and the Los Angeles riots

When most people recall the name of Rodney King, they automatically recall a videotape of King being brutally beaten up by white officers of the Los Angeles Police Department. The video tape was recorded by an amateur cameraman who had been waked up by police sirens and a police helicopter in the early hours of March 3, 1991.

Played over and over again on television, the video shows uniformed officers surrounding a large black man, who "writhed on the ground and attempts to rise, but is clubbed and kicked into submission while other policemen watch with folded arms."[4]

Because King is black and the police officers are white, the videotape portrayed a vivid picture of racism and police brutality. This picture was reinforced when, in April 1992, an all-white jury "exonerated three of the officers of using excessive force against King and acquitted another officer of all but one charge."[5]

That verdict triggered the worst urban riots in this century. Fifty-four people were killed and 800 buildings were burned, turning South-Central Los Angeles into an urban desert.

The persuasive power of video comes from the multiple ways we can combine words, music, images, and narrative into a powerful, compelling message. According to Scott Heimes, editor of *Presentations Magazine*, "Nothing beats the pure communication power of video. . . . When video is used in a presentation, it appeals to our entertainment sensibilities. We've become a visually orientated society used to processing information through video as opposed to text."[6]

Bush, Dukakis, and Willie Horton

Few Americans remember much about the 1988 presidential campaign when George Bush overwhelmed Democrat Michael Dukakis. What memories do linger center around the Willie Horton ad campaign run by Bush to convince voters that Dukakis was "soft on crime."

The ad was deliberately designed to link Michael Dukakis to a convicted murderer, Willie Horton, who (while on furlough from prison) had raped a Maryland woman and assaulted her fiancé.

The opening picture of the ad shows Dukakis and Bush side by side. Dukakis is somber, set against a black background. Bush, by contrast, is smiling, set against a background bathed in light (see Figure 10.24).
Voice-over: Bush and Dukakis on crime.

[Bush's picture flashes on screen.]
Voice-over: "Bush supports the death penalty for first-degree murderers."

[Dukakis's picture is on screen.]
Voice-over: "Dukakis not only opposes the death penalty, he allowed first-degree murderers to have weekend passes from prison."

[A close-up mug shot of Willie Horton appears.]
Voice-over: "One was Willie Horton who murdered a boy in a robbery, stabbing him nineteen times."

[A sinister-looking black-and-white photo of Horton flashes.]
Voice-over: "Despite a life sentence, Horton received ten weekend passes from prison."

[The words "kidnapping," "stabbing," and "raping" flash below Horton's scowling picture.]
Voice-over: "Horton fled, kidnapping a young couple, stabbing the man and repeatedly raping his girlfriend."

[Michael Dukakis is on screen for a final shot.]
Voice-over: "Weekend prison passes. Dukakis on crime."

Figure 10.24 Willie Horton ad used by George Bush to discredit Democrat candidate Michael Dukakis during the 1988 U.S. Presidential campaign. *Source:* Kathleen Hall Jamieson, *Dirty Politics*, Oxford, New York, 1992 p. 18–19.

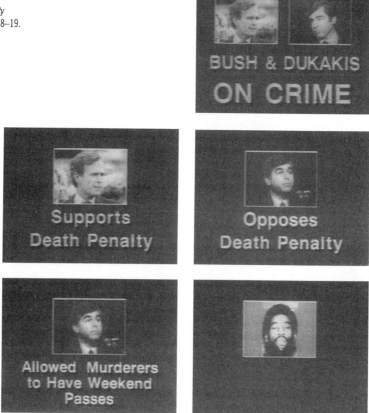

The video was an incredible success. The numbers of voters who thought Dukakis was "soft on crime" soared. The percentage of those polled who thought Bush was "tough enough" on crime shot from 23 percent in July 1988 to 61 percent in October 1988. In the meantime, the perception that Dukakis was tough enough dropped 13 points.[7]

The ad campaign was successful because it perfectly exploited the persuasive potential of video[8].

- The ad was structured as a story with a protagonist and antagonist – in this instance, a villain and a victim.
- The story focused on a single vivid incident.

- The evidence was dramatic and personalized. The producers cleverly avoided using lifeless statistics.

- The scowling images of Horton, sound, and vivid language were cleverly juxtaposed for maximum impact.

- The central message rang true with most voters. Bush's tough talk on crime worked because it fit in with what most Americans viewed nightly on their TV news programs.

- The negative ads unashamedly exploited voters' fears of uncontrolled violence. Negative information carries more weight and is more easily remembered than positive information. Messages that arouse fear are also much less likely to be analyzed for logic and honesty.

THE POWER OF A SIMPLE PROP

Sometimes a simple $5 prop can prove as dramatic and persuasive as a $20,000 video.

On 28 January 1986 the space shuttle *Challenger* exploded, killing seven astronauts. The cause: Two rubber O-rings leaked. The rubber rings had lost their resiliency because the shuttle was launched in icy conditions.

At the presidential commission set up to investigate the crash, much of the testimony presented was highly technical, confusing, and often evasive. Most of the experts used standard overheads – usually crammed full of numbers, formulas, and calculations to support their cases.

Then the late Richard P. Feynman, the Nobel Prize-winning laureate, cut through the confusion with a compelling visual demonstration.

Preparing for the moment when a piece of the rubber O-ring would be passed around, that morning Feynman had gone to a hardware store and purchased a simple C-clamp. He squeezed the O-ring piece tight with the C-clamp and then dramatically placed it in a glass of water containing icecubes. After waiting a few moments, he pulled the O-ring piece from the ice water and released the clamp. The rubber remained compressed; it didn't spring back. Holding up the distorted rubber O-ring before the commission and onlookers, Feynman graphically showed that the freezing temperatures at the crash site had caused the O-ring failures.

The simple physics experiment made front-page news across America. Memorable high-impact visual aids don't have to be high-tech or expensive (see below). You just have to make sure that, they're *visual* and that they *aid*.

Media Choices for Visual Persuasion					
Flipcharts	**Boards and Props**	**Overheads**	**Computers**	**Slides**	**Videos**
Advantages					
■ Are low cost ■ Are flexible ■ Are easy to prepare ■ Facilitate eye contact and discussion ■ Are great to record ideas from audience	■ Are usually low cost ■ Are flexible ■ Use with room lights on ■ Facilitate good eye contact ■ Encourage audience participation	■ Are easy to create on computer ■ Are low cost ■ Are flexible ■ Use with room lights on ■ Facilitate discussion	■ Use multimedia ■ Visual effects can be stunning ■ Animation and sound effects are available ■ Are flexible and easy to change ■ Are portable	■ Look very professional ■ Multiple slide projectors create stunning presentations ■ Work well with large audiences (over 100) ■ Display anything that can be photographed	■ Can be used with any size group ■ Are most powerful medium of all ■ Are ideal for emotion-based pitches ■ Are excellent instructional tool ■ Are excellent for transmitting complex ideas ■ Are good image enhancers ■ Are easy to use
Flipcharts	**Boards and Props**	**Overheads**	**Computer**	**Slides**	**Video**
Disadvantages					
■ Are effective only with small groups (under 20) ■ Can appear unprofessional	■ Are effective only with small groups (under 20) ■ Props have to be large to be seen ■ Boards are cumbersome ■ Boards are difficult to change	■ Lose impact with large groups (over 100) ■ Are less professional than slides ■ It is tricky to get rid of keyhole effect	■ Require good technical skills ■ Technical hitches reflect badly on speaker	■ Are expensive ■ Darkened room removes eye contact and limits discussion	■ Are expensive to produce well ■ Low-budget videos look amateurish

CHAPTER 10

PERSUASION
POINTERS

1. Determine your central message before you design your visuals.

2. Stick to one idea per visual.

3. Organize your presentation around three to five main points.

4. Think visually. Use as few word lists as possible.

5. Keep text brief, simple, and readable.

6. Wherever possible, add color. Two contrasting colors usually work best.

7. Tailor your colors to the audiences' biases.

8. When using charts, first pinpoint the key relationship you want to emphasize.

9. Check all your charts for distortion.

10. Use video when you want to combine words, music, and images in one seamless compelling message.

11. Choose the media that best suit your message. A simple prop used effectively can be just as powerful as an expensive video.

Ask, Don't Tell!

The Gentle Art of Self-Persuasion

HOW SELF-PERSUASION WORKS

Overcoming Food Taboos

Most Westerners are disgusted at the mere thought of eating insects, worms, toads, and caterpillars – even though these are highly nutritious and are consumed by many people throughout the world. During World War II, American pilots went hungry rather than eat the toads and insects they had been taught were safe and nutritious.

Even when it comes to animal meats we are highly selective. Many Americans only eat the skeletal muscle of cattle, chicken, and pigs, as well as some fish.[1] Other parts, such as kidneys, hearts, eyes, brains, and guts, are thrown away or end up as pet food.

This was the problem that faced members of the Committee on Food Habits set up by the U.S. government during World War II to overcome the shortages of popular high-protein foods. How could they overcome the traditional American aversion to eating intestinal meats?

To solve the problem, they called on social psychologist Kurt Lewin, who devised an ingenious program to get Americans to persuade themselves to eat intestinal meats.

To show how participatory, self-generated persuasion works, Lewin set up a simple experiment with two groups of housewives. The first group was lectured on the advantages of eating intestinal meats and what that meant for the U.S. war effort. Recipes were handed out, and the lecture ended with an enthusiastic testimonial from one housewife on how her family loved the taste of intestinal meats.

The second group spent their time in a group discussion persuading themselves. A group leader began the discussion with a brief talk on the problem of maintaining the nation's health during wartime. The leader then asked the group members how they thought "housewives like themselves could be persuaded to participate in the intestinal meat program." The discussion covered the same issues as the lecture but proved much more effective.

The results: A mere 3 percent of housewives who had been lectured to served intestines to their families, but 32 percent who had participated in the self-persuasion group went on to feed their families intestinal meats.[2]

It was a remarkable result, and later research confirms that self-persuasion is one of the most powerful persuasion tactics ever discovered.

Role-playing and Visualizing

Getting the customer to role-play and visualize using a product has much the same impact as group discussion. Researchers Larry Gregory, Robert Cialdini, and Kathleen Carpenter went door-to-door selling cable television subscriptions. Some of the potential customers were given a straight pitch stressing the benefits of cable TV; others were invited to "imagine how cable television will provide you with broader entertainment."

The results: Only 19.5 percent receiving the straight information pitch signed up; in stark contrast, a huge 47.4 percent bought when asked to imagine using the service.[3]

In other words, self-persuasion using visualization was two-and-a-half times more effective than the straight pitch.

Television and Self-Sell

As consumers have become more cynical and disillusioned "from years of ad abuse," advertisers are finding the traditional pushy, hard-sell messages are no longer working. Ad-weary consumers switch on their advertising radar shields to screen out incoming messages.[4]

The problem of consumer resistance is magnified when the market is already saturated with competing brands. This was the challenge the Cossette Advertising Agency faced when asked to help launch a new beer, Molson Grand Nord, in the Canadian beer market. Canadian beer drinkers already had the choice of over 1,000 beers, so the ad campaign had to be high impact to stand any chance. Cosette's idea was simple but powerful: Create a huge media campaign that would get buyers involved and tap into the power of self-persuasion.

Cosette created a series of episode commercials based on the adventures of two heroes. At the end of the first episode, Molson proposed two different endings and asked viewers to vote for the one they preferred. A total of 992,000 people voted – that's 15 percent of all Canadians.

Two months later, the agency called for another vote to choose the ending of a second commercial. To everyone's surprise, there were 1.1 million calls. People wrongly feared that without the novelty value the first vote had enjoyed, the number of voters would plunge.[5]

This was a brilliant example of what you can achieve when you actively involve people in the persuasion process.

The Power of Questions

Questions are among the most potent communication tools persuaders can use. All persuaders must know how and when to ask questions and be able to use them to control the direction and pace of a meeting, negotiation, or sale.

Neil Rackham (of the Huthwaite Research Group) and John Carlisle observed hundreds of negotiators in action to discover what it takes to become a top negotiator. A key finding: "Skilled negotiators ask more than twice as many questions as average negotiators."[6]

Questions Elicit Answers

Russian novelist Leo Tolstoy wrote, "There is no such thing as a right answer, only good and bad questions." Most of us love answering questions.

A large part of our schooling consists of learning how to answer questions. A question triggers an automatic response inside us; when we hear a question, we feel an urge to answer.

We look down on those who avoid or can't answer questions. Watch how uncomfortable a politician appears when he or she answers "No comment" to a reporter's question. Persuaders who face their counterpart with a list of well-thought-out questions, therefore, always start with an advantage.

Questions Keep You in Control

Successful influencers use questions to plant ideas in the other party's mind and then get him or her to nurture their ideas as if they were his or her own. Whereas questions move meetings, sales, and negotiations forward, statements often create roadblocks that need to be cleared away.

Questions give you power to control the content, tone, pace, and direction of a meeting. With questions, you can control the issues you want to discuss – and also what you want to avoid. Using questions, you can set the mood and tone of a meeting, slow down or force the pace of a discussion, and bring a meeting back on track after losing direction. Because the other party feels compelled to answer, the initiative invariably lies with the asker.[7]

Questions Persuade

Most of us try to persuade others to accept our point of view with reasons, yet people are often highly resistant to this form of persuasion. Neil Rackham and the Huthwaite Research Group found in their negotiating research "that reasons will only work successfully in persuading people who are already on your side.... If we're both in favour of a particular political policy, you'll be very receptive to any reasons I give for supporting it. But ... if you're against the policy, the longer my list of reasons, the more you'll find counter arguments to support your existing opinion."[8] Hence, successful negotiators use questions, rather than reasons, as their main persuasive tool.

Types of Questions

Open Questions

What type of question is the most persuasive? For years, the most common answer has been open questions. Most sales trainers, for example, teach that open questions are the key to successful selling.

Open questions are those that cannot be answered with a one-word answer. They typically start with *what, how,* or *why.* Examples of open questions include:

- *What* problems are you having with your business?

- *How* do you calculate the cost of rejects?

- *Why* are your sales declining?

The proponents of open questions argue that open questions are powerful because they get the customer talking and often reveal unknown information.

The problem is that while open questions do promote an open dialog, *they don't persuade or convert.* All open questions do is get people talking, and they don't even guarantee that. In a huge study by Neil Rackham of 10,000 sales calls in 33 countries, he found there was no relationship between open questions and sales success.[9] Moreover, when you do ask people open questions, they often give you a one-word answer; when you ask them a closed question, they may talk for half an hour. In other words, people don't always behave the way the theory suggests they should.

Closed Questions

Once you have a customer responding to open questions, you can then narrow the focus of the conversation with closed questions and eventually pin the client to a commitment. Closed questions require a specific answer. Examples of closed questions include:

- Do you prefer the white or the red model?
- Would a June 28 delivery meet your deadline?

Disturbing Questions

The real problem with most open or closed questions is they don't disturb. They don't move people to change.

The world's greatest life insurance salesperson was the late Ben Feldman; in his lifetime, he sold over $1 billion in life insurance. *The Guinness Book of the Business World* called Ben Feldman "the most outstanding salesman in history." Feldman believed the key to a successful sales interview was "disturbing questions."

When he was selling, Ben would first locate a client's problem. Typically this would be a lack of insurance to cover a major emergency. Ben would then frighten or disturb a prospect: "What would you do if you died tomorrow? Could your business survive?" Questions such as these made prospects sit up and think about the consequences of not carrying enough insurance.

Feldman's advice to new salespeople was simple: "Get the prospect fired up. There's nothing like a disturbing question to build a fire under a person."[10]

What Feldman knew was that prospects don't move in their mind from "I have a problem" to "I have a need for your service" without being first made to think about the effect and consequences of the problem.

Neil Rackham's study of 10,000 sales calls came to much the same conclusion. He found that once top salespeople locate a prospect's problem, they disturb the client by making the customer uncomfortable with what Rackham called implication questions.[11]

For the moment, imagine you own a courier company. You are having problems with your parcel-tracking system; customers are complaining about lost and delayed parcels. You are talking to a salesperson of a parcel-tracking software system who gets you to admit that you have a problem in this area. The issue is the high cost of his parcel-tracking software system. He's asking more than $250,000 for the base system. In other words, you know you have a *problem*, but you're not sure whether you have a *need* for his expensive system.

The skilled salesperson will use Rackham's implication questions. These could include:

- What *effect* is this problem having on your reputation with your key clients?
- Could this problem *slow* down your proposed expansion into new markets?
- What *impact* is this having on your sales team's credibility?
- How much *unproductive time* is your staff spending locating lost parcels?

Questions like these will increase the size of the problem in your mind and make the $250,000 price that much more palatable.

Leading Questions

Smart persuaders are skilled in using leading questions. The best trial lawyers are experts at using leading questions to cross-examine and influence witnesses.

Elizabeth Loftus researched how leading questions influence eye-witness testimony. In one of her projects, Loftus's subjects watched a one-minute film of a multiple automobile accident. After the film, one group was asked, "About how fast were the cars going when they *smashed* into each other?" A second group was asked how fast the cars were going when they *hit,* and third group was asked how fast they were going when they *contacted.*

The results: The subjects who were asked about *smashing* cars estimated the cars were traveling at 40.8 miles per hour; the subjects who were asked about the cars *hitting* estimated 34.0 miles per hour; and the subjects who were told about contacting cars estimated 31.8 miles per hour.[12]

Leading questions not only alter the way we interpret facts but also influence what we remember. In another ingenious study, Loftus showed subjects a film of an automobile accident. Subjects who were asked "Do you see *the* broken headlight?" were two to three times more likely to answer "Yes" than subjects who were asked, "Did you see *a* broken headlight?" There was in fact no broken headlight in the film.[13] A simple question had distorted the subject's memory.

Rhetorical Questions

A rhetorical question is one that you give the answer to after asking the question. Compare this to most questions – you expect the listener to answer your questions directly. Because rhetorical questions engage your listeners' minds, they are much more persuasive than direct statements.

Summaries of speeches and addresses are ideal places to use rhetorical questions. In his book *Outrage,* author and former prosecutor Vincent Bugliosi attacks the prosecution for their weak summation in the O.J. Simpson trial. He then rewrites the prosecution's closing arguments, filling his address with rhetorical questions. Notice when you read Bugliosi's address how your mind locks onto his questions:

If Mr. Simpson didn't commit these murders, then who? Who else would have had any reason to commit these murders? We know Mr. Simpson beat his wife severely, to the point where she had to call the police nine times during their marriage ... who else could have had the motive to kill these two young people [Ron Goldman and Nicole Simpson]? ...

What is the likelihood that someone they knew would have had a reason to kill either one of them, much less both of them, and particularly in such a savage and brutal way? ... Who in the lives of these young people would have had any reason to hire someone to kill either one of them? ... I ask you once again to ask yourself this question back in the jury room – who else had any reason at all to kill Ron and Nicole, particularly in this way? This is simply no one except O.J. Simpson, the defendant in this case.[14]

THE ART OF GIVING FEEDBACK

Whichever type of question they use, smart persuaders listen intently to the other side. They are active listeners and don't get distracted by emotion-laden words. They withhold judgment and try to understand the other person's point of view. They look behind the spoken words for the emotional content of the message transmitted by the subtleties of voice and body language. They appreciate that what is not said can be just as important as what is said.

Reflective Listening

One of the best ways to show you've heard and understood the other person is to *reflect or paraphrase* the content of what the other person has said and/or the feelings of the speaker.

Reflecting Content

Your desktop publishing supervisor is in your office, obviously annoyed. "We can't keep up with all the demands on the new system," she says. "Nobody, particularly the departmental managers, is using the booking system. They all want everything yesterday. I don't know how I'm going to get your monthly performance review done."

You say, "It sounds like you're having trouble keeping some of the managers in line. Is that what you're saying?" That brief exchange shows the essentials of reflective listening.

An effective reflection is concise, simple, and easily understood. If you get too wordy, you can easily derail the speaker's train of thought. An effective reflection gives the essence of the speaker's message and cuts through the verbal clutter; it mirrors the speaker's own words. Above all, effective reflection demonstrates understanding.

> *"The Golden Rule of Persuasion – Listen to others as you would have them listen to you."*
> — *Harry Mills*

Don't fall into the trap of simply parroting the other person's words; reflecting is not parroting. Parroting stunts conversations, whereas reflecting encourages discussion. So don't make the mistake of repeating the speaker's exact words.

Reflect content with phrases such as:

- It sounds like
- In other words
- So
- So, you're saying
- It seems that
- You mean
- I guess

Notice that an effective reflection signals tentativeness. You don't know whether your interpretation is correct until the other person replies, "Yes, that's it!" or uses some similar statement.

Reflecting Feelings

Effective listeners not only paraphrase facts; they reflect feelings as well. Anyone who speaks to you with an emotional overtone first wants his or her feelings understood and acknowledged.

Your office manager has begun a discussion with you about her career. She says, "I've been here four years, and I'm still doing the same old job. I could do it in my sleep. I had hoped I might have been able to do some of the accountant's work, but it's never happened."

You respond, "Seems like you're feeling bored and frustrated. Is that it?"

By acknowledging the feelings, labeling them, and accepting them, you are laying the foundation for a productive discussion.[15]

Reflective listening is an essential part of win-win persuasion. Good reflecting:

Listening, not imitation may be the sincerest form of flattery."
– Joyce Brothers

- Encourages the other person to keep talking
- Corrects misunderstandings, false assumptions, and misinterpretations
- Reassures the speaker that you are listening
- Gives you a much deeper insight into the needs of the other party
- Helps you remember what was said
- Builds rapport and mutual respect

Summarizing

Sometimes meetings wander off course. To get the meeting back on track, summarize the points made.

A summary refocuses attention on the issues. Summaries should be short – no one wants to hear a long, drawn-out account. Summaries should be balanced and cover both sides' viewpoints and proposals. If the other party thinks your summary is inaccurate, then ask him or her to summarize until you both agree. A one-sided summary will simply spark more arguments, whereas a balanced summary can markedly improve the climate of the negotiation:

"I'm concerned, Peter, that we seem to have wandered off track. Let me see if I can summarize the main points we've covered."

"To prevent any misunderstanding, I would just like to summarize the main points of our last meeting."

"Let me summarize the key issues as I see them."

Summarize during all phases of the meeting, but especially:[16]:

- Whenever emotion and argument are clouding the issues
- Whenever you feel your views are not being properly recognized, appreciated, or understood
- Whenever you feel it's time to conclude an agreement
- After reaching agreement, to make sure your understanding of what has been agreed to is exactly the same as the other party's understanding

PERSUASION
POINTERS

1. Use group discussions rather than lectures to persuade your audience. Self-persuasion outscores hard sell.

2. Use role-plays and visualization for greater impact and involvement.

3. Use questions rather than statements to control the content, tone, pace, and direction of a meeting. Questions plant ideas in the other party's mind.

4. Use open questions when you want to get the other person talking.

5. Ask closed questions to narrow the focus of the conversation, to seek specific details, to shift direction, or to force commitment.

6. Ask disturbing questions when you want the other person to really think about the implications or effects of an issue or problem.

7. Ask leading questions when you want to plant specific information in your listener's mind.

8. Use rhetorical questions when you want to influence a person to accept a narrowly predetermined conclusion.

9. Be an active listener. Show you understand the other person's needs by reflecting the content and feelings of what he or she has said, and continually summarize the points that have been made.

Different Groups, Different Messages

How to Target and Influence Different Groups

TAILOR YOUR STRATEGY TO YOUR AUDIENCE

One of the biggest mistakes amateur persuaders make is to treat all audiences the same. There are at least six different types of audiences and each one requires a different persuasion strategy.

Six Audience Types

1. *The hostile audience.* This group disagrees with you and may even be working actively against you.

2. *The neutral audience.* They understand your position but still need convincing.

3. *The uninterested audience.* These people are informed about the issues you want to discuss but couldn't care less.

4. *The uninformed audience.* They lack the information they need to be convinced.

5. *The supportive audience.* This group already agrees with you.

6. *The mixed audience.* This group has a cross-section of differing attitudes and views.

Analyzing Your Audience

There are three areas and three critical questions you need to address when analyzing an audience before choosing a persuasion strategy.

1. *Knowledge:* What does my audience know about the topic I want to talk about?
2. *Interest:* How interested is the audience in my subject?
3. *Support:* How much support already exists for my views?

Your answers to these three questions will allow you to classify your audience into one of the above six categories and determine your strategy.

Persuading Different Audiences

Persuading the six different types of audiences requires six different approaches:

1. *Persuading the hostile audiences.* The hostile audience disagrees with your proposals. They feel just as strongly as you do, but they hold opposing opinions. Because of your differences, they will question your credibility and openmindedness. Since we also tend to dislike people who hold viewpoints opposing our own, there may also be some personal antagonism you have to overcome.

First, a hostile audience has to be warmed up to the point where they will listen to you and consider your points. Using humor or a story is often a good way to build initial rapport.

Focus on the areas you agree on and have in common. Stress these before dealing with the areas of conflict.

Don't start your presentation with a direct attack. You will lose your audience and very likely increase their hostility. Credibility is critical with a hostile audience, so take every opportunity to demonstrate your expertise. Cite experts the audience respects, even if they are not your first choice. Be scrupulously fair when citing facts and statistics, and mention your sources and references to prove your fairness.

> "A jury consists of twelve persons chosen to decide who has the best lawyer."
> — *Robert Frost*

Don't make any statements you can't support with solid evidence, and don't exaggerate. When there is doubt, understate your claims. Avoid using hypothetical examples; make sure all your case studies and stories are representative and are drawn from real life.

Don't tell the audience you plan to change their minds. That will simply antagonize them and add to their resistance.

Stress you are looking for a win-win outcome rather than a win-lose solution. Don't expect major shifts in attitude; ask for a little and get it rather than ask for a lot and face rejection. If you neutralize a hostile audience, you've made progress. They are no longer working against you, which is often the difference between success and failure when dealing with groups.

"Use soft words and hard arguments."
— *English Proverb*

2. Persuading the neutral audience. Neutral audiences neither support nor oppose you. They understand the issue but have yet to be converted.

Since they are wavering in their commitment, start by spelling out the benefits of your proposition by linking these benefits to the interests of your audience.

Limit your points to three clear, compelling messages. Back them up with expert testimony, quotes, statistics, and case studies. Draw heavily on concrete examples that are familiar to them.

Use stories, personal experiences, and analogies to appeal to your listeners' emotions.

Don't forget to point out the downside of not accepting your proposals. Alert your audience to any competitor or common enemies who might take advantage of their inaction.

Demonstrate your fairness and expertise by acknowledging other points of view.

3. *Persuading the uninterested audience.* Facing an uninterested audience is much tougher than facing a neutral one. The uninterested audience knows about your topic but couldn't care less. The issues either bore them or are seen as irrelevant.

The uninterested audience needs motivating and energizing. The first task is therefore to grab their attention by using a story, a headline, or a heart-stopping fact. The second task is to make them care by showing them how the topic affects or will affect them. Finally, support your case with three to five compelling facts supported by expert testimony or statistics.

4. *Persuading the uninformed audience.* The uninformed audience simply lacks information. They don't know enough to act, so they need educating.

Start by establishing your credibility. Showcase your expertise, experience, or qualifications.

Don't bury your audience in data. Limit your presentation to three easy-to-follow, logical points. Back these up with statistics and solid, concrete examples. Don't confuse your audience by discussing the pros and cons of each issue; keep your structure simple and straightforward.

Use one or two anecdotes and analogies to create an emotional link. Use an interactive style; encourage the audience to ask questions throughout the presentation, and leave time for extended discussion at the end.

5. *Persuading the supportive audience.* The supportive audience is the easiest to persuade. Since they already agree with you, your task is to recharge them and then make sure they are committed to a plan of action.

Your first task is to refire the group's enthusiasm with an inspirational address. Reinforce their commitment with success stories and vivid testimonials.

You don't have to prove your case so there is no need to present a balanced view.

Remind everyone what you share as a group. Stress T.E.A.M. (Together Everyone Achieves More).

Inoculate your audience against future attacks by anticipating your opponents' possible arguments. Refute their likely points, one by one. Finally, hand out a detailed plan of action with clear deadlines.

6. *Persuading the mixed audience.* Very few audiences are all neutral or all supportive. Most audiences are mixed, representing a spectrum of viewpoints.

First, identify who in the audience you really have to win over. Identify which subgroup has the most power; identify which subgroup has the numbers. Then concentrate your efforts on the groups that count.

Second, where possible, appeal to the different groups in your audience with different parts of your message. Look for creative ways to influence each subgroup by offering each of them a different reward. Look at a typical snack food commercial: It promises kids a great taste while reassuring parents that the snack is healthy and nutritious.

Third, don't promise "everything to everyone." If there are groups in your audience with competing subagendas, you may end up alienating everyone. One of the easiest ways to discredit a politician is to show that he or she is making conflicting promises to different groups. The politician who one day tells farmers she supports farm subsidies and the next day tells factory workers she supports lower food prices can easily lose the trust of *both* groups.[1]

Setting Realistic and Achievable Goals

Many persuaders make the mistake of trying to achieve too much. For example, they try to convert an actively hostile opponent into a believer and think they have failed when the person fails to turn into a born-again zealot.

Full-scale conversions from active opposition to active support are relatively rare. If you neutralize someone who is hostile, you have been successful. They may not ever become a supporter, but the fact they are no longer working against you must still be chalked up as a victory.

Achieving Cognitive Consistency

One of the reasons we are resistant to making radical attitude changes is our psychological need to stay cognitively consistent. Cognitive consistency refers to our need to have consistency between any new information and our existing attitudes, beliefs, and behaviors.

If we hear a new message that clashes with our existing beliefs, we can argue against it and reject it or we can reinterpret it and accept it. Normally, if the message is clear and threatening, we reject it. For example, cigarette smokers tend to reject clear evidence that cigarette smoking causes lung cancer and other diseases.

New information that challenges our existing beliefs causes stress. The easiest way to get rid of that stress is to reject the new information or selectively reinterpret it.

The O.J. Simpson Verdict

When the jury in the criminal trial of O.J. Simpson found him not guilty, white Americans were outraged; a poll found 65 percent of whites disagreed with the verdict. Yet, the same poll found 77 percent of African-Americans agreed.

How could two groups who had listened to the same saturation media coverage hold such conflicting views?

Interviews showed both races interpreted the same evidence very differently. African-Americans (75 percent) believed the defense argument that police had planted evidence. Whites rejected the same evidence.

However, when you consider the negative dealings most African-Americans have had with the police, this is hardly surprising. Many more African-Americans than whites can point to personal experiences of police harassment. All of us interpret new information in the light of our prior experiences.

Knowing Zones

Before you attempt to persuade any individuals or groups, it is useful to note which zone they fit in: Rejection (red zone), noncommitment (yellow zone), or acceptance (green zone) (see below). *Note:* It usually takes time and a number of meetings to move someone who holds strong opinions on a subject to move from rejection (red zone) to acceptance (green zone).

The Zones of Acceptance and Rejection

Red Zone
Rejection – Negative attitude

Yellow Zone
Noncommitment – Neutral attitude

Green Zone
Acceptance – Positive attitude

Roosevelt and Step-by-Step Persuasion

If ever there was a politician who understood how to move an audience from hostility to support in a series of moves – often over a long period of time – it has to be President Franklin D. Roosevelt.

Unlike Presidents today, Roosevelt was involved in the crafting of all his major speeches. Each month, Roosevelt put aside five or six evenings to work on what he would say.

Roosevelt understood that great Presidents must be great persuaders. Using brilliantly spun speeches, he slowly but progressively won over the American public to his own radical New Deal program.

The most brilliant example of Roosevelt's step-by-step persuasion was his success in moving U.S. public opinion on foreign affairs from isolation, neutrality, and resistance to involvement in European affairs (1937), to a position where the United States was prepared to support and provide aid to Britain in its fight against Hitler (1940).

In October 1937, Roosevelt warned Americans about international lawlessness. He labeled the lawlessness an epidemic that needed to be quarantined. Here the language was deliberately vague; there was no talk of becoming involved in European affairs or taking sides. In 1938 and 1939, Roosevelt further softened up public opinion with stronger words.[2]

With the Nazi invasion of Poland in September 1939, Roosevelt was able to sell a cash-and-carry arms policy. The United States would sell arms to the Allies but not get involved in the war. Roosevelt understood the current mood of the country perfectly: Support the Allies but stay out of the war.

By the end of 1940, Britain was flat broke. By now, however, U.S. public opinion was ready for Roosevelt's next proposal: Lend-Lease, a plan for the United States to send Britain arms without charge, to be repaid in kind after the war. Even so, there was still some measure of strong hostile opinion in America, citizens who believed the fight in Europe was hopeless and Roosevelt should keep all the weapons at home to defend the United States.

On December 29, 1940, Roosevelt delivered what he regarded his most important speech since his first speech as President in March 1933.[3]

Roosevelt and his team of four writers worked day and night to get the words right. In his address to the nation, Roosevelt said it was impossible to appease Hitler: "No man can tame a tiger into a kitten by stroking it." An Allied victory was essential for U.S. security. The peoples of free Europe needed arms. America, he said, "must be the great arsenal of democracy."[4]

The speech was a triumph. In London, citizens huddled around their radios openly cheered when they heard Roosevelt's words.[5] The arsenal of democracy speech, as it became known, raised the number of Americans willing to consider aid to Britain from barely 50 percent to 60 percent.

Seventy-six percent of Americans listened to Roosevelt's arsenal of democracy speech – a record for a presidential speech. Theatres even reported a drop in attendance that day.

In three years of sustained step-by-step persuasion, Roosevelt had moved the American people from hostility to willingness to aid Britain to strong support for the war.

PERSUASION
POINTERS

1 Neutralize a hostile audience by establishing your credibility with solid evidence and expert testimony.

2 Convert a neutral audience by selling the benefits of your proposal.

3 Motivate and energize an uninterested audience with stories, compelling facts, and highly relevant information.

4 Educate the uninformed audience with a credible, logical, easy-to-follow presentation supported by one or two memorable anecdotes.

5 Refire a supportive audience with an inspirational address that will galvanize them to action.

6 With a mixed audience, focus your pitch on the subgroup who has the most power.

7 Don't promise all things to people – you will lose credibility.

8 Set realistic, achievable goals. Full-scale conversions are rare; if you neutralize someone who is hostile, you've been successful.

9 Use the model of the red, yellow, and green zones to quickly gauge the attitude of an individual or group you want to persuade.

10 If you want to achieve a major change, plan a series of gradual step-by-step changes.

Strategy Pure and Simple

13

How to Outthink and Outwit Your Opponents

THE INTENSIFY/DOWNPLAY STRATEGY

Given the hundreds of tactics used by professional persuaders, it's often easy to lose sight of your overall goal or persuasion strategy.

Persuasion researcher Hugh Rank has developed a simple but highly practical model that explains how professional persuaders think strategically. Rank developed the model to help people become critical receivers of persuasion. However, it is also a highly practical planning tool.

Rank calls his model the intensify/downplay schema. Persuaders use two broad strategies to achieve their aims. They can *intensify* or highlight particular features of what they want to promote – be it a product, a politician, or an idea – or they can *downplay* the points they want to make. Often, they can do both. Like a skilled conjurer, successful persuaders can shift our attention away from what they want to conceal and focus our eyes on what they want us to see.[1]

Think of it this way. Persuaders can:

1. Intensify their strong points
2. Intensify their opponent's weaknesses

3. Downplay their own weaknesses

4. Downplay their opponent's strengths

Intensification

When we intensify our own good points or intensify our opponent's weaknesses, we can choose from a variety of tactics. The three most common are repetition, association, and composition.

1. Repetition. The simplest and often the most effective way to intensify the good or bad points about a product, politician, or idea is to repeat the same idea over and over again.

The effectiveness of most advertising is based on the continual repetition of a single point.

Selling Expensive Hypertension Drugs. When it comes to treating high blood pressure with anti-hypertension drugs, medical opinion overwhelmingly favors the prescription of low-cost beta-blockers and diuretics. In 1997, a panel of cardiologists gathered by the National Institute of Health said that in the absence of complications the low-cost beta-blockers and diuretics should be prescribed.

Yet the prescriptions and sales for the cheapest drugs – beta-blockers and diuretics – have dropped dramatically. In the meantime, sales for the newer, more costly calcium blockers and ACE inhibitors have sky-rocketed – in spite of the evidence that the new products aren't any better.

Why are the sales of the more expensive and as yet unproven medications soaring? Heavy repetitive advertising is the reason. The expensive and much more profitable calcium channel blockers are by far the most heavily advertised. In contrast, advertisements for the cheaper, less profitable diuretics and beta-blockers have virtually disappeared.

The drug companies back up their advertising with sales blitzes. Drug reps give general practitioners masses of free samples, hoping the doctors will give them to a patient. *Business Week* reports that

> *"Advertising is the art of making whole lies out of half truths."*
> — *Edgar A. Shoaff*

once a patient is on a medication and it seems to be working he or she is reluctant to switch to other drugs even if they are cheaper.[2]

2. *Association.* Association is another powerful intensification tactic. Opponents of medical tests on animals, for example, try to discredit their opponents by associating them with cruelty and brutality.

Sport stars are associated with a whole variety of products from sports shoes to breakfast cereals. The associations are designed to intensify the good aspects of the products.

3. *Composition.* One of the easiest ways to intensify a message is to change the physical makeup of the message.

One of the experts, when it comes to message composition, has to be former President Ronald Reagan. More than any President before him, Reagan knew how to visually choreograph a message for television.

Each presidential action was designed as a one- or two-minute spot on the evening network news. "We would go through the president's schedule day by day and hour by hour," said Michael Deaver, Reagan's deputy chief of staff, "and figure out what we wanted the story to be at the end of each day and at the end of each week, and that worked 90% of the time."[3]

Downplaying

Persuaders rarely want to focus attention on their weaknesses. For similar reasons, they rarely want to promote the strong points of a competitor. What the persuader wants to do is *downplay* his or her weaknesses and *downplay* his or her competitor's good points.

The three most common tactics of downplaying are omission, diversion, and confusion.

1. *Omission.* Omission is simply leaving out damaging information. The result is we are presented with half-truths or biased evidence. Politicians try to do it all the time. During the 1992 presidential

> *"You can fool all the people some of the time, and some of the people all of the time, and that's good enough."*
> — *Laurence J. Peter*

campaign, it was never revealed that Bill Clinton had avoided fighting in the Vietnam War.

2. *Diversion*. Diversion consists of shifting the focus of attention away from your weaknesses or away from your opponent's strengths. In 1998, President Clinton was able to shift some of the media's focus away from his sex scandals by going on a successful tour of Africa.

3. *Confusion*. The final way to downplay your own limitations or your competitor's strengths is to create confusion. Persuaders typically can create confusion by complicating a simple issue, using jargon instead of everyday language, and engaging in faulty logic.

> *"If you can't convince 'em, confuse 'em."*
> — *Harry S. Truman*

For years, the tobacco industry has spent millions on downplaying, indeed strongly denying, the harmful effects of cigarette smoking. To downplay the link between cigarettes and cancer and create confusion, the industry sponsored research on "other causes of cancer including stress and genetics."[4] A confused public would be much less likely to focus their anger on the cigarette industry.

Page 218 contains an intensify/downplay scorecard with the tactics listed for each strategy.

Intensify/Downplay Scorecard

Tactics
- Repetition
- Association
- Composition

Tactics
- Omission
- Diversion
- Confusion

Intensify own good
1. _____
2. _____
3. _____
4. _____
5. _____

Intensify others' bad
1. _____
2. _____
3. _____
4. _____
5. _____

Downplay own bad
1. _____
2. _____
3. _____
4. _____
5. _____

Downplay others' good
1. _____
2. _____
3. _____
4. _____
5. _____

PERSUASION
POINTERS

1 Use the intensify/downplay model to plan your strategy or analyze an opponent's strategy.

2 Intensify your strong points.

3 Intensify your opponent's weaknesses.

4 Downplay your weaknesses.

5 Downplay your opponent's strengths.

Part 3

MINDLESS INFLUENCE

"The advantage of the emotions is that they lead us astray."

OSCAR WILDE

CHAPTER 14

Mindless Persuasion

The Seven Persuasion Triggers of Automatic Influence

MINDLESS BEHAVIOR

Programmed Thinking

Humans spend much of their lives with their minds locked unthinkingly on automatic pilot. Most of the decisions we make are made mindlessly, with little thought at all. Our minds are programmed with persuasion triggers that activate when we receive an appropriate cue.

To show how minds are preprogrammed to mindlessly say yes or no to persuasive requests, Harvard psychologist Ellen Langer tried a simple experiment on students queuing up to use a library photocopier.

When students were asked, "Excuse me, I have five pages, may I use the Xerox?" 60 percent agreed to the request; 40 percent, however, said no and continued with their own copying.

When a reason was added – "Excuse me, I have five pages, may I use the photocopier, I'm in a rush" – 94 percent agreed to the request.

This makes sense. Since childhood, most of us have been taught to say yes to someone who asks a favor and backs up that request with a sound reason.

However, what doesn't make sense is why the same number agreed when the request was changed to "Excuse me, may I use the Xerox because I want to make copies." This reasoning is just plain stupid. Why would you use a photocopier if you were not planning to make copies? It is the same as no reason at all.

Langer's conclusion: Most of the people did not think about the request at all. They mindlessly complied.[1]

Searching for Familiar Patterns

The way the mind searches for familiar patterns and locks onto automatic pilot is shown in this word-trap game, which most of us played as children:

Q. What do we call the tree that grows from acorns?

A. Oak.

Q. What do we call a funny story?

A. Joke.

Q. What do we call the sound made by a frog?

A. Croak.

Q. What do we call the white of an egg?

A. Yoke. (*sic!*)

Humans Are Mental Misers

Humans are, in fact, mental misers. We are always trying to conserve our cognitive energy. Active thinking – *mindfulness* – requires effort. When we can, we often shortcircuit the process by using heuristics or simple rules of thumb.

Of course, there are limits to this. If the requests are outrageous, we are likely to stop and think about what was said. It is not that we don't hear the request; we simply don't bother to process it actively.

The Mintzberg Findings

Whether we like it or not, most of us live and work in a world where we think, decide, and act on the run – with little reflective, rational thought. Some recent research by Henry Mintzberg found that most managers he studied in the working world shun formal reports, skim magazines, and merely scan the mail. They pick up their intelligence from meetings, telephone calls, gossip, and hearsay. Agreements are commonly made during chance encounters in corridors. They form impressions and make judgments about peers, subordinates, and superiors based on a very limited number of interpersonal cues – dress style, voice, sex, and age.[2]

The Two Routes to Persuasion

As stated earlier, psychologists Richard Petty and John Cacioppo believe there are two routes to persuasion – central and peripheral.

In the central route, the message receiver actively thinks about the message and rationally analyzes all the logic and evidence presented.

In the peripheral route, the message receiver spends little time processing the content. The mind activates a persuasion trigger that tells the receiver to say yes or no. The triggers are largely emotionally driven, and the receiver relies on simple cues or heuristics.

We tend to short-cut the central or rational decision-making paths and switch to automatic pilot when:[3]

1. We don't have time to think about an issue

2. We are suffering from information overload

3. We believe the decision is not that important

4. We don't have enough information to make a decision based on fact and logic

5. A given heuristic readily springs to mind as we are challenged by an issue

Seven Persuasion Triggers

Psychologists have identified seven persuasion triggers that compliance professionals exploit to take advantage of us when we are in a state of mindlessness. The seven persuasion triggers are:

1. Contrast
2. Reciprocation
3. Commitment
4. Authority
5. Scarcity
6. Social proof
7. Liking

In the remainder of Part 3, we look at how the seven persuasion triggers that underpin the process of instant influence work.

PERSUASION
POINTERS

1 Our minds are programmed to mindlessly say yes or no to many persuasive requests.

2 Humans are mental misers. When we are rushed or pressured, we like to conserve our energies by using simple rules of thumb to make decisions.

3 There are seven persuasion triggers that underpin the process of instant influence:

- Contrast
- Reciprocation
- Commitment and consistency
- Authority
- Scarcity
- Social proof
- Liking

Persuasion Trigger One: Contrast

The Power of a Benchmark

◼ CONTRAST – JUDGMENT IS RELATIVE

Rating Beauty

Two researchers, Douglas Kenrick and Sara Gutierres, showed male students photographs of potential blind dates and asked students to rate the potential dates' attractiveness before and after viewing the television show *Charlie's Angels*.

Watching the television show affected their opinions. The males rated their potential dates as far *less* physically attractive after they viewed the show than before. The students contrasted the blind dates' beauty with the stunning beauties from *Charlie's Angels* and consequently rated the former less attractive.[1]

Judgment of beauty, like most things, is relative, not absolute. Having television beauties as a benchmark made the blind dates seem much less attractive than they actually were.

The contrast principle shapes our perceptions in all sorts of different ways. You open your pay check and are overjoyed to find you've been given a 7.5 percent pay raise – until you discover your coworkers have been given a 10 percent raise.

Selling Real Estate

Real estate salespeople commonly exploit the contrast principle to sell more houses. First, they show you a run-down shack, which fills you with horror. Then, they take you to the house they know will be much more appealing. Sure, the second house has faults and is still far from ideal, but compared to the last one, it's magnificent! This one has a view, the kitchen is larger, and the carpets will last for at least three more years. While the price is slightly higher compared to the last one, it's a bargain. The real estate agent stresses the shortage of good houses like this – and before you know it, you've signed a contract.

Selling Cars

Used-car dealers play the same game. They first show you a barely roadworthy clunker in an effort to improve the look of another car on their lot. After you do buy the second car, a salesperson will use the contrast principle to sell you a very profitable extended warranty. After all, you've just spent thousands of dollars on the vehicle. Doesn't it make sense to spend just a few hundred dollars more to service it?

Selling Clothes

Clothing stores train their staff to exploit the contrast effect. If a customer walks in looking for a suit and shoes, the salesperson is instructed, "Always sell the suit first." If you have just paid $1,000 for a suit, $200 for a pair of shoes seems reasonable. And if you've spent $1,200, you might as well buy a new tie and belt.

Selling Appliances

Two neighbors are watching a salesperson demonstrate a revolutionary new vacuum cleaner. When he finishes, one asks for the price. "This machine," he says, "is priced less than $800." Both look at each other aghast and prepare to show him the door, when the salesperson adds, "This particular machine's price is only $379." They both buy one. The $379 is, of course, a bargain when compared to the outrageously high $800.

Raising Prices

When raising prices, most companies know a series of small price increases is more palatable than one big increase. Because of the contrast effect, each new small price increase seems tiny compared to the benchmark price.

Winning a Budget Increase

A client of mine had a problem: getting approval for a new computer system. The required sum of $2.3 million was well over budget. To win approval, she invoked the contrast principle. She contrasted the 700 percent to 1,100 percent performance improvement the new system offered over the old one, which had cost $4.9 million. Her proposal was approved.

Contrasting Agenda Items

Another way to use the contrast effect to win approval for capital projects is to have your proposal placed on an agenda following a request to approve a much larger project. Compared to the much larger proposal (ideally costing millions), your request will seem eminently reasonable.

Contrasting Political Images

Politicians and political issues are always being compared and contrasted by the media (see Figure 15.1). The personal charisma of British Labour Party leader Tony Blair was often contrasted against the "gray" Conservative leader, John Major.

Television pictures of President Clinton jogging always project a much more positive image when contrasted with the infamous TV image of President Carter collapsing from exhaustion after a run.[2]

Figure 15.1 This conscience-stabbing British ad vividly exploits the contrast effect to deliver its message.
Source: Bainsfair Sharkey Trott, Courtesy: Christian Aid.

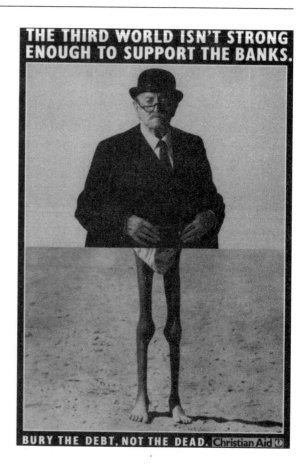

THE THIRD WORLD ISN'T STRONG ENOUGH TO SUPPORT THE BANKS.

BURY THE DEBT, NOT THE DEAD. Christian Aid

Winning Extra Tips

People place more tip money in a bartender's tip jar when it is seeded with $5 bills rather than with mere coins. To tip someone 50 cents when everyone else is tipping $5 seems mean-spirited.

Hiring Employees

The contrast effect plays a huge role in influencing judgments in job interviews. If a selection committee first interviews an exceptional candidate (who becomes a benchmark), they are likely to underrate the next candidate interviewed.

The effect also works in reverse. If a candidate who performs very poorly is followed by an average candidate, the selection committee will rate the average candidate much better than he or she is.

Contrasting Caskets

When muckraking journalist Jessica Mitford investigated the U.S. funeral business in 1963, she found an industry full of sharp sales practices. In her book *The American Way of Death,* she revealed how funeral directors exploited the contrast principle to get families of the deceased to spend more money.

For example, when choosing a casket, the funeral director will show the bereaved family a very expensive model. If they ask to see a less expensive one, they are then shown a very plain, cheap casket. The funeral director knows from experience that the bereaved family members are often shocked by the contrast and "rebound" back to the more expensive model.

In the thirty-five years since Mitford's book, the problem seems to have gotten worse. A 1998 *U.S. News & World Report* exposé revealed, "At a seminar sponsored by an industry newsletter, one speaker advised funeral directors 'how to add $1400 to each cremation call' by requiring an 'identification viewing' of the loved one. If the family has not opted for an expensive container, make sure you show them Mom's body in a cardboard box. Someone in the family is bound to say, 'Maybe we should get something nicer.'"[3]

Manipulating the Contrast Effect

Watch a skilled property developer. Typically the developer looks for quality properties that have been on the market for some months, often because of the ridiculously high price asked by the seller – say, $585,000 when $480,000 would be reasonable.

To drive down the seller's expectation, the property developer employs an agent who, acting anonymously, displays great enthusiasm for the property and then makes a very low, aggressive offer – say, $350,000 – which the seller usually angrily rejects as outrageous. The developer then moves in and offers a much more reasonable price – say, $430,000 – which, after some negotiating, is accepted. It's amazing how often this tactic works because the seller contrasts the developer's offer with the previous lower offer.

The developer also uses the contrast effect when asking for quotations for renovations. When soliciting quotations the developer always suggests a very low-budget figure and finds that suppliers drop their prices to come closer to that budget estimate than they might have done independently.

When it comes to selling, the developer prices property at the high end of the market. In practice, this means pricing the property high enough to make potential customers think it's expensive – but not so high as to drive them and competing buyers away. The developer then displays some flexibility by negotiating down from the high initial price. The buyer feels happy about getting a good deal by driving the price down because he or she judges success by contrasting the selling price with the opening offer.

The developer goes away delighted, knowing he or she has maximized profit on the property. What makes a good deal in most buyers' minds is relative, not absolute. The contrast principle has worked again.

PERSUASION
POINTERS

1 Judgment is relative, not absolute. To judge the value of an offer, the quality of a product, or the fairness of a request, we automatically look for a benchmark to base our decision on.

2 Create a benchmark to anchor the judgments of the person you are trying to persuade.

3 When selling, start with a high but credible opening price.

4 When buying, start with a low but credible opening offer.

Persuasion Trigger Two: Reciprocation

The Law of
Give-and-Take

RECIPROCATION – GIVE-AND-TAKE

The Influence of a Single Flower

How can you be successful as a salesperson yet break virtually every rule taught in basic sales training? That's what the Hare Krishna salesforce did in the 1960s, and in less than a decade they built up a global network of Hare Krishna temples and communes.

For the Krishnas, the chief source of income for expansion came largely from public donations. The Hare Krishnas' first attempts to win donations were singularly unsuccessful. The reason seemed obvious: Most Hare Krishna salespeople were chanting, shaven-headed teenagers clad in orange saffron robes and beads. Many U.S. towns even passed laws banning Krishnas from begging and soliciting. Occasionally scuffles broke out between Krishnas and townspeople.

All this changed when the Krishnas discovered one of society's most powerful persuasion techniques – a weapon that was able to overcome the Krishnas' appalling negative image and induce the public to make generous donations. The persuasion weapon was the reciprocation rule.

The Reciprocation Rule

The reciprocation rule states that we should repay in kind what someone has given us: If a friend does us a favor, we feel obligated to pay him or her back; if someone sends us a Christmas card, we should send one in return; if someone invites us to a party, we should return the invitation.

The Krishnas exploited the reciprocation rule by giving potential targets a gift of a flower. Psychology professor Robert Cialdini spent many days at airports watching the Krishnas work. The sect member would single out a target, rush up to him or her, and without warning press a flower into his or her hand. When the target protested and tried to return the flower, the Krishna refused, saying, "It is our gift to you." Only then did the Krishna ask for a donation. The gift of a flower created a feeling of obligation and indebtedness. Often the target repaid the debt by providing the Krishna with a donation or purchasing an overpriced copy of the Krishnas' teachings, the *Bhagavad Gita*.[1]

The Power of Reciprocation

The reciprocation rule is so powerful it can make us accept requests from people we dislike. In one experiment carried out by researcher Dennis Regan, two students were trained to sell raffle tickets to unsuspecting workers. Before attempting to sell any tickets, one deliberately went out of his way to make himself likable by being kind and considerate to his workmates; by contrast, the other went out of his way to be unlikable by being rude and inconsiderate.

During a work break, the rude and inconsiderate one purchased bottles of Coke for his work colleagues. A little later, the students asked their work colleagues for a favor: "Would you purchase a raffle ticket?"

The finding showed that the unlikable student who exploited the reciprocation rule sold twice as many raffle tickets compared to the other, regardless of how likable he was perceived to be.[2]

Think of what this means. People whom we dislike, whose requests we would normally refuse, can greatly increase their odds that we will do what they ask merely by granting us a small favor prior to their request.

In *Human Universals*, anthropologist Donald Brown shows that reciprocity is practiced in all human cultures.[3] The biologist Richard Trivers claims the "demands of reciprocity are probably the source of many emotions."

Liking is the emotion that triggers the willingness to do people a favor. *Anger* protects you when you have been cheated by someone who has taken advantage of your generosity. *Gratitude* makes us grateful to people who have done us a big favor, and *sympathy* for other people encourages us to grant favors in the first place. *Guilt* is designed to stop us from taking advantage of another person's generosity.[4]

Reciprocation and Political Power

Few politicians have understood this fact better than President Lyndon Johnson. Political analysts were amazed at how easily Johnson was able to get his legislation through Congress compared to his much more charismatic predecessor, John F. Kennedy. Johnson simply called in the scores of favors he was owed from his years as Senate Majority Leader.

Reciprocation and Free Gifts

Mass merchandisers have employed the reciprocation rule since at least the 1930s on a mass scale. The door-knocking Fuller Brush salesmen gave householders a small, cheap brush as a gift before beginning their sales pitch.

Tupperware parties, which first blossomed in the 1950s, started with the presenter giving away an inexpensive Tupperware item. The party host reinforced the power of reciprocation by providing free refreshments, thereby obligating the partygoers to both company and host (who received a gift from the company if she and her friends bought enough).[5]

As a marketing ploy, free samples have a long, successful track record. Vance Packard's *The Hidden Persuaders*, written in 1957, found a supermarket operator who sold an amazing 1,000 pounds of cheese in just a few hours by giving away free samples.

The giant AMWAY company is happy to get one of their sales-people to drop off a free sample kit of AMWAY household products at your home for you to try at no cost. The free kits, called BUGs, are amazingly successful. Customers often purchase half the total number of items contained in the BUG when it is collected.[6]

Numerous direct-mail offers build the reciprocation rule into their offers with great success. For example, the U.S. Disabled American Veterans group found that a typical mailing asking for donations gives a response rate of 18 percent, but if they add an unsolicited gift of gummed, personalized address labels, the hit rate virtually doubles to 35 percent. "It is not at all unusual for the right gift to increase response by 25 percent or more," says Bob Stone, professor of direct marketing at Northwestern University.[7]

Free gifts come in all sorts of guises. One Greenpeace mailing includes a gift of twelve attractive stickers of endangered animals such as dolphins and penguins. They are free for you to keep – but the real purpose, of course, is to invoke the reciprocation rule.

Reciprocation and Negotiation

"You don't get what you deserve in life, you get what you negotiate."

— Anonymous

The reciprocation rule controls the compromise process that is central to most negotiations. The great majority of books on negotiation urge their readers to start with a small concession – and *then wait* for the other side to reciprocate. The implicit request is, "I've made a concession; now it's your turn."

In car-selling situations, the dealer typically pads the sticker price by a few thousand dollars before making that first generous concession.

The Rejection-Then-Retreat Strategy

To test how initial concessions influence persuasion, psychologists Robert Cialdini and Karen Ascani devised an ingenious experiment.

"An actor, negotiating a contract with movie mogul Sam Goldwyn, demanded fifteen hundred a week. 'You're not asking fifteen hundred a week,' snapped back Goldwyn, 'you're asking twelve hundred and I'm giving you a thousand.'"

— Anon

Posing as workers for a local blood bank, they asked students at the University of Wisconsin to (1) either give a single pint of blood sometime tomorrow or (2) give a pint of blood every six weeks for the next three years.

When the students rejected the extreme request, the three-year commitment, the request was dramatically scaled down. If they couldn't commit to a three-year program, the students were asked if they could possibly donate just one pint of blood the next day.

The results: Many more students showed up to give blood, and gave more blood, if they had received the extreme request first.[8]

The rejection-then-retreat strategy works for two reasons. First, the large request sets up a contrast effect. Giving a single pint of blood isn't nearly as onerous as having to turn up and make regular donations over the next three years. Second, the immediate concession by the requester triggers the reciprocation rule.

Negotiating with Dad

My daughter Amy mastered the rejection-then-retreat strategy at the age of three. She quickly learned that I would typically limit her expectations on our trips to McDonald's by telling her she could order one item, and one item only. Generally she chose a burger. She didn't think this was at all fair, so on later visits she tried negotiation. It usually started, "Daddy, I'm really hungry today. I would really love a burger, chips, and a Coke." I would reply, "No, Amy. You can't have three items. You can have two."

I later learned that when she stayed at her grandparents, she opened negotiations at an even higher level, asking for four items – adding an apple pie to her request. Grandparents, I've discovered, are much more gullible.

Selling the Opening Position

Skilled negotiators know there are limits to the rejection-then-retreat strategy. If a negotiator's opening set of demands is too extreme, then the tactic backfires. Since the opening offer lacks credibility, any subsequent concession is not seen as a genuine concession and is therefore not reciprocated.

Skilled negotiators, therefore, plan their opening offer very carefully. Before they even start conceding and trading, they use their selling skills to convince the party of the legitimacy of the opening position. In other words, they sell the value of their position before they ever start trading concessions.

PERSUASION
POINTERS

 Be the first to give service, share information, or give concessions.

 In negotiations, be the first to make a concession, but keep it small and make sure the other side reciprocates before you concede again.

 At home and at work, be the first to offer help to neighbors and colleagues. The goodwill created will enable you to enlist their support later when you really need it.

 When appropriate, use the rejection-then-retreat strategy by asking for more than you expect to receive. Your apparent concession calls for reciprocation.

17

Persuasion Trigger Three: Commitment and Consistency

Getting One Foot in the Door

■ COMMITMENT – ONE FOOT IN THE DOOR

Would you agree to a request by a community worker to erect a large, ugly billboard on your front lawn with the words "Drive Carefully" in huge print? I wouldn't.

But this was the question two researchers, Jonathan Freedman and Scott Fraser, put to two groups of California residents. When asked, 83 percent of the first group refused to put the sign up, saying it was too large and ugly.

Yet the same researchers were able to persuade 76 percent of a second group to agree to the installation of the same "Drive Carefully" billboard in their front yards.

What did the researchers do? A few weeks earlier, another researcher had visited members of the second group of residents to ask them to display a tiny three-inch-square sign that read "Be a safe driver." This seemed such an innocuous request that virtually everyone agreed, but the consequences of accepting were amazing. Because they had first agreed to a tiny request, they were later willing to comply with a similar but much larger one.[1]

This technique, following a small request with a much larger one, is called the foot-in-the-door technique. It works because, having agreed to the smaller favor, we feel committed to agreeing to the larger favor.

The Importance of Commitment and Consistency

Psychologists have found that, having made a commitment, we experience a powerful urge to behave consistently.

In another similar example, people who were first persuaded to wear a small lapel pin promoting the American Cancer Society were twice as likely to donate money later as were those who were merely asked to make a donation. Having made an initial commitment to wear a lapel pin, the call to behave consistently meant they felt they had to make a financial contribution.[2]

The research on commitment and consistency has highlighted four key discoveries:

1. Small initial concessions can lead to huge later commitments.
2. Written commitments are usually more powerful than verbal promises.
3. Public commitments are much stronger than private commitments.
4. The greater our effort, the more committed we become.

1. Small initial concessions can lead to huge later commitments. The Freedman and Fraser "Drive Carefully" study worked because it started with a trivial request. Salespeople are often advised to get an order – any size order, it doesn't matter how small. The profit on the first sale may be minute, but the key is, the prospect has been turned into a *committed* customer. That means the customer will be much more likely to buy again and again.

2. Written commitments are usually more powerful than promises. Compliance professionals have long understood the power of written commitments. Once we make a commitment on paper, we become that much more committed. Lawyers love reminding us that "a verbal contract is not worth the paper it's written on." But the power of a written contract does not come simply because legally written agreements are much easier to enforce. Written commitments exert a powerful psychological hold on the writer.

When several states introduced "cooling off" laws to give customers time to think about purchases made through high-pressure, door-to-door salespeople, masses of customers began canceling their contracts. To fight back, many salespeople used a simple technique: This technique had the customer, rather than the salesperson, complete the sales contract. This written commitment, made voluntarily by the prospect, dramatically reduced the number of customers backing out of their contracts.[3]

3. Public commitments are much stronger than private commitments. When we make a public stand that is witnessed by others, we are driven to hold fast to that stand, so that we may be seen as consistent and trustworthy.

Weight-loss clinics know that the temptations faced by dieters soon destroy their clients' best intentions. To increase their clients' fortitude, they often get them to write their weight-reduction goals down – and then show them to their fellow dieters, friends, neighbors, and workmates. This public commitment significantly increases the success of most diet programs.

4. The greater our effort, the more committed we became. The key here is, the effort has to be voluntary; forced efforts do not result in lasting commitments. In one study, overweight women were asked to participate in a new experimental program for losing weight. They were required to carry out all sorts of bizarre and unpleasant tasks.

The study involved two groups. The first group spent five hours performing the bizarre activities; a second group spent less than half an hour doing the same things. When they were all weighed one year later, the first group who had put in all the effort had lost on average 6.7 pounds, while the second group had lost a mere 0.3 pound.

The so-called treatment, of course, had nothing to do with weight loss, but the group who had put in all the time and effort had to justify the effort to themselves. They therefore proceeded to lose weight.[4]

Stock Losses

When buying and selling share of stock, investors commonly stick with shares that have slumped in price with no prospects of recovery. Rationally, the best decision is to cut losses and invest elsewhere.; irrationally, investors hang on, entrapped by their initial commitment.

Once sacrifices have been made in time, money, or effort, we persist with the initial commitment – even when it no longer makes sense.

The Battle of the Somme

Generals in wartime have a terrible reputation of remaining committed to strategies that have been proved to be totally futile. In World War I's Battle of the Somme, General Haig continued to assault impregnable German positions for five months despite losing 57,000 men on the first day. When he finally called off the attack, the Allies had 600,000 casualties for a gain of just eleven kilometers of ground.

Commitment and Consistency and the Entrapment Trap

Entrapment occurs when, once committed, we blindly follow a losing course of action. Rather than admit defeat, we escalate our commitment, in effect throwing good money after bad even when it doesn't make sense.

The Vietnam War

The Vietnam War is probably the best case of entrapment in recent times.[5] Despite early warnings from advisers that the United States had no business in Vietnam, the U.S. government continued to escalate its commitment.

"Creeping escalation," writes historian Barbara Tuchman in *The March of Folly,* "began under Kennedy. Under Johnson U.S. troops spiralled rapidly to over 500,000. It is not as though Johnson didn't realize that Vietnam could turn into a disaster. In May 1964 Johnson confided to McGeorge Bundy, '... looks like to me that we're getting into another Korea. It just worries the hell out of me. I don't see what we can ever hope to get out of this.'"[6] According to author McMaster's *Dereliction of Duty,* "It was, Johnson observed, 'the biggest damn mess that I ever saw. ... It's damn easy to get into a war, but ... it's going to be harder to ever extricate yourself if you get in.'"[7]

Having made a huge public commitment, Johnson's reputation was now on the line. " 'I am not,' Johnson said, 'going to be the first president of the United States to lose a war.' For a chief of state," writes Tuchman, "admitting error is almost out of the question. The American misfortune during the Vietnam period was to have had presidents who lacked the self confidence for the grand withdrawal."[8] As a result, the war turned into the longest one Americans ever fought in – and ended in a humiliating withdrawal in 1973.

Nixon and Watergate

In November 1996, 200 hours of tapes recording President Nixon's private conversations during the Watergate crisis were released. In his introduction to the written transcripts of the tapes in *Abuse of Power,* historian Stanley Kutler notes, "The recorded revelations offer irrefutable evidence of impeachable instances of abuse of power and obstruction of justice." Kutler continues, "Nixon's scheming, lying and worrying about what truths might be discovered or what must be covered up is at the heart of these tapes."

Even so, Nixon could have saved his presidency. In the tapes, he admits that the decision to break into, burglarize, and wiretap the Democratic national headquarters at the Watergate complex was "stupid." Nixon could have let the "burglars" take the blame and

"Watergate might well have been consigned to the ash can of history as merely a 'third-rate' burglary."[9] Yet Nixon made a fatal mistake to engage in a cover-up, and later on to try and cover up the cover-up. Why? According to Kutler, "Nixon had carefully nourished an image through a quarter-century of public life as an upstanding law and order advocate. Maintaining that image required distance from what he knew of past activities, as well as what he knew of the cover-up."[10]

In other words, Nixon felt entrapped by the need to remain consistent to public commitments he had given. In the end, it was his undoing.

The McLibel Trial

In 1990, McDonald's slapped summonses on five London activists for libeling it in a leaflet entitled "What's Wrong With McDonald's?"

The pamphlets claimed that McDonald's sold food that was unhealthy, exploited its workers, promoted rain-forest destruction through cattle ranching, added to the litter problem, and aimed advertisements at children.

While three of the activists backed down and apologized, two of them – Helen Steel and David Morris (both unemployed) – chose to fight the corporation in court.

The McLibel trial, as it became known, turned into the longest case in British legal history. A total of twenty-eight pretrial hearings plus two-and-a-half years in court turned it into an exercise in endurance. It ended up costing £10 million and generated 40,000 pages of documents and 20,000 pages of transcripts and testimony.

Although the defendants were ordered to pay McDonald's £60,000, the judge found that some of the pamphlet claims, such as the poor dietary value of McDonald's hamburgers, were true. The public verdict on the trial was encapsulated in newspaper headlines: "McDonald's wins pyrrhic victory" said the *Guardian*; *The Daily*

Telegraph declared: "McLibel victory with little relish."[11]

For McDonald's, the trial was a public relations disaster. According to England's Channel 4 news, "Observers believe [the McLibel trial] will go down in history as the most expensive and disastrous public relations exercise ever mounted by a multinational company."[12] Author and public relations commentator David Michie called it "one of the most extended, *self-inflicted* PR disasters of recent corporate times."[13]

The trial had generated enormous negative publicity worldwide. During the trial, 2 million copies of the "What's Wrong With McDonald's?" pamphlet had been circulated by a growing band of supporters. A McSpotlight Internet site set up to publicize the case was accessed over 7 million times in its first year.

Early in the lengthy pretrial period, it had become clear that the case was not turning out at all as McDonald's had hoped. The McLibel Support Campaign had taken off in a dozen countries. "Days of Action" protest marches and mass leafleting were publicizing the struggle as a David and Goliath contest. "The act of taking two people to court," says John Vidal, author of *McLibel*, "was having the exact opposite of the desired effect. Instead of stopping McDonald's critics, it was exacerbating the situation. Instead of just a few people leafleting its stores, the corporation now had hundreds to contend with."[14]

McDonald's had also blundered. In April 1994, McDonald's started distributing its own pamphlets stating the action was "about the right to stop people telling lies." To be called "liars" by McDonald's was just the good fortune the defendants needed.

Steel and Morris immediately counterclaimed for libel against McDonald's. "With the counterclaim," says Vidal, "McDonald's would now have to prove what it was saying in the original Factsheet was lies, indeed it now had to prove that its business practices were not as described in the Factsheet. Effectively McDonald's was on trial ... for its business practices."[15]

> *"Consistency requires you to be as ignorant today as you were a year ago."*
> — *Bernard Berenson*

Why did the largest food retailer in the world, with an annual marketing budget of $2 billion, embark on a legal marathon against two committed activists? What made McDonald's go through with the trial once it became clear that it had everything to lose and nothing to gain? Having made a public commitment to challenge the activists, McDonald's became entrapped. To remain consistent to its stated public position, McDonald's continued to fight to a bitter, unsatisfactory end.

Author John Vidal believes, "It is unimaginable that any company will be so arrogant or so stupid to go through the same experience again." I disagree. The entrapment trap will continue to operate as it always has. History shows we won't have to wait very long at all for another case of corporate or individual arrogance and stupidity.

CHAPTER 17

PERSUASION
POINTERS

1 When asking for commitments, start small. Small initial commitments can turn into huge later commitments.

2 Written commitments are much more powerful than verbal commitments.

3 Where possible, get the person to make a commitment in public. Commitments made in public are much stronger than those made in private.

4 The greater the initial effort we put in, the more committed we become.

5 Having made commitments, people often get caught in the entrapment trap.

Persuasion Trigger Four: Authority

The Influence of Position

AUTHORITY – ITS DANGER AND POWER

The Milgram Studies

Imagine you've volunteered to take part in an experiment on the study of memory with Professor Stanley Milgram at Yale University. When you arrive at the laboratory suite, you are met by a stern-faced researcher dressed in a grey lab coat. The other person you meet is a likable, mild-mannered, middle-age accountant.

The researcher explains the experiment is about how punishment affects learning. After drawing lots, you end up playing the part of the teacher; the accountant will play the learner. The accountant is given a long list of pairs of words to memorize.

You then go into a neighboring room. The learner is strapped into an "electric chair" type of construction. An electrode is attached to the learner's wrist. Electrode paste is also applied to "avoid blisters and burns." The researcher tells you the electrode connects to a shock generator unit located in an adjacent room.

By now, you're feeling nervous. You go into the room with the shock generator. It has thirty lever switches, each marked between 15 and 450 volts. The switches are grouped under the labels Slight

Shock, Moderate Shock, Strong Shock, Very Strong Shock, Intense Shock, Extreme Intensity Shock, and Danger: Severe Shock. The last two switches are simply labeled XXX.

The researcher instructs you, "Administer a shock to the learner every time he gives a wrong answer to a question. And if he gives another wrong answer, move one notch higher on the shock generator." The shocks, the researcher tells you, can be very painful; he demonstrates it by inflicting a 45-volt shock on you – just to prove the equipment is working.

The first part of the test seems relatively harmless. There is the odd mistake, but the shocks seem tolerable. Then the mistakes begin piling up, and the voltages rise sharply. At 120 volts, the learner shouts, "Experimenter, get me out of here! I don't want to be in the experiment anymore! I refuse to go on!" At 180 volts, he screams, "I can't stand the pain!" By 270 volts, the scream is of agonizing pain. When the 300-volt barrier is passed, the learner pounds on the wall.

Whenever you declare you want to stop the shocks, the experimenter commands you to continue.

What would you really do faced with this situation? Would you defy the experimenter and refuse to continue inflicting the shocks? How high would you go before stopping?

Before the experiment started, Milgram asked groups of psychiatrists, students, and middle-class adults how many subjects would administer the maximum shock of 450 volts. The vast majority predicted between 1 and 4 percent. In stark contrast, Milgram found huge numbers – 62 percent, in fact – of the volunteer "teachers" were prepared to administer the maximum shock of 450 volts. (*Note:* The shocks were never actually administered. Milgram's learners were actors.)

What explains these alarming findings? Were the volunteer teachers an unrepresentative bunch of twisted sadists? No. Personality tests and repeat experiments confirmed that Milgram's subjects were a typical group of ordinary citizens. What, then, caused them to behave in such horrifying ways? "It has to do," Milgram says, "with a deep-seated sense of duty to authority within us all." Despite the fact that virtually all the subjects wanted to defy the wishes of the experimenter, when it came to crunch time, they couldn't bring themselves to defy the wishes of the boss of the study – the lab-coated researcher. The lab coat and all the surrounding circumstances vested the experimenter with legitimate authority.

Adults will go to extraordinary lengths to obey a command from a legitimate authority. We shouldn't be too surprised by this finding. If we didn't go along most of the time with those who hold authority – police, judges, bosses – society would collapse into chaos.[1]

There are many other documented instances of the influence of position.

Gross Overprescription of an Unauthorized Drug

In another frightening example, researchers wanted to test whether nurses would overprescribe an unauthorized drug to a patient when requested to do so by a doctor.

In the experiment, one of the researchers telephoned a nurse saying he was a doctor and told her to give a 20-mg dose of a drug called Astrogen to a particular patient. He told her she had to give it right away as he wanted the drug to take effect before he came to the hospital to see the patient. He added he would sign the prescription then.[2]

The experiment was set up to make the nurses cautious on four counts: Hospital policy forbade phone prescriptions; Astrogen was an unauthorized drug; the prescribed dosage was dangerously excessive, twice what was specified on the drug bottle; and the order was given by a man the nurse had never met. Yet 95 percent of the nurses carried out the order unquestioningly and unthinkingly. As soon as they heard the request was from a doctor, they complied.[3]

Blind Obedience in Aircraft

The respect for authority crosses all occupations. There have been a number of commercial aircraft crashes in which the copilot believed that the pilot was in error but did not say so.[4]

When a Korean Airlines 747 went down on August 6, 1997, over Guam killing 228 people, the National Transportation Safety Board's investigation found the crew was reluctant to question the pilot about whether a vital ground-based navigation aide – a glidescope beacon – was out of order. Officials further suggested that Korean culture, in which subordinates are reluctant to question the decisions of superiors, may have contributed to the crash. One Safety Board member described the relationship between the pilot and his flight crew as "autocratic."

Korean Airlines official Jung Tack Lee said that since the disaster KAL flight crews have been instructed that if the nonflying pilot's advice is ignored, then the nonflying pilot is under orders to "aggressively take over the controls."[5]

The Power of a Uniform

The appropriate clothes dramatically increase the chance of blind obedience. In one experiment, a man stopped pedestrians on the street and pointed to a man standing by a parking meter. The requester said, "See that man by the meter. He's overparked and doesn't have any change. Give him a dime!"

When the requester wore the uniform of a security guard, 92 percent went along with the request; when the requester wore street clothes, only 50 percent complied.[6]

The Power of Pinstripe

Business suits act as authority symbols in the same way as uniforms. In one experiment, a thirty-one-year-old man broke the law, deliberately crossing the street against the traffic light. When he was wearing a pinstripe business suit and a tie, three-and-a-half times as many people followed him – like the Pied Piper – across the street than when he was just wearing a work shirt and pants.[7]

The Influence of Trappings

Jewelry and cars carry an aura of status in the same way as expensive clothes. In one San Francisco study, observers found motorists wait much longer before honking their horns at drivers in new luxury cars stopped in front of a green light. Indeed, some 50 percent of motorists waited patiently, never once beeping their horns.

The poor driver of the old economy car received much rougher treatment. Nearly everyone hit their horns impatiently – most more than once. Two impatient drivers even rammed the older economy car's bumper.[8]

PERSUASION
POINTERS

1 Challenge authority when it is used arbitrarily or dangerously.

2 Reinforce the authority that comes from your position with credentials based on expertise and competence.

3 Wear appropriate dress to support your position. In most business situations, you will look more authoritative and come across as more persuasive in a business suit.

Persuasion Trigger Five: Scarcity

The Rule of the Rare

THE SCARCITY PRINCIPLE

In essence, the scarcity principle says we value what is scarce. When we discover that something is scarce or may be unavailable, one of our first thoughts is that it must also be valuable.

The Great Potato Sale

Potatoes haven't always been a popular food staple: In the late 1700s, the French associated potatoes with leprosy; the Germans considered potatoes were only good as cattle fodder; the Russian peasants believed they were poisonous.

It took the guile of Catherine the Great, the Empress of Russia, to turn this negative perception around. She ordered her men to enclose the potato fields with high fences. Her soldiers then posted large notices throughout the countryside warning the populace not to steal potatoes.

It was a brilliant psychological ploy. As soon as the potatoes became unavailable, the scarcity principle took hold and the popularity of potatoes suddenly soared.

Think what must have gone through a Russian peasant's mind as he watched the potato fields being roped off: "Why are they fencing off those potatoes? They must be worth a lot. Once again, the rich are keeping all the best food for themselves. Why should we peasants be restricted to beef soup day in, day out? We deserve potatoes. We need potatoes."[1]

The Tickle Me Elmo Frenzy

In the Christmas shopping frenzy of 1996, the U.S. media were full of tales of parents going crazy over the hottest stuffed toy – Tickle Me Elmo. Reports included:

- New York moms running alongside delivery trucks asking drivers what was on board
- Police arresting two Chicago women fighting over a Tickle Me Elmo
- A Tickle Me Elmo selling for $7,100 in Denver
- A Canadian salesclerk being trampled and sent to the hospital after being caught in a stampede when she opened the store's doors to parents

USA Today quoted University of California, Santa Cruz, psychologist Anthony Pratkanis: "As consumers we have a rule of thumb: If it is rare or scarce, it must be valuable and good."

Advertisers routinely play to the phenomenon, claiming such-and-such an item is available "for a limited time only" or stating that "We've only made 50,000 of these and the molds have been destroyed."

Beanie Baby Hysteria

In 1998, the new toy craze in the United States was Beanies. Toy shops were crowded with kids fighting each other to seize as many of the cuddly Beanie Babies as they could lay their hands on.

However, the Beanie craze differs from toy fads of the past such as Tickle Me Elmo. Beanies, first launched in 1994, developed a huge secondary market as collectibles. Some older-style Beanies sell for 1,000 times the original $5 price.

Beanies were developed by a shrewd marketer, Ty Warner. To exploit the scarcity factor, Warner deliberately kept the market in short supply by retiring certain Beanies. He discontinued their production while continuing to bring out new versions. Almost immediately, the prices of the preowned Beanies soared as collectors and speculators chased after the ones they thought would become rare and valuable. "Struck by the potential for profit," reports Margaret Mannix in *U.S. News & World Report*, "people started trying to guess which one would be retired next. Others, fearful of missing out, started scooping up every Beanie."[2]

Fischer Travel and Exclusivity

Fischer Travel, a small, exclusive New York travel company uses the scarcity principle to build up its highly lucrative business of providing luxury and exotic travel to the rich and famous.

Fischer Travel's select list of 500 business and entertainment "big names" includes record mogul Quincy Jones, basketball legend Magic Johnson, and fashion designer Donna Karan, plus members of the super-rich Vanderbilt and Rockefeller families.

To support its claim to exclusivity, Fischer Travel never advertises, has an unlisted phone number, and distributes business cards that carry only the agency's name and address – no phone number. Clients come in by personal referrals.[3]

De Beers – the Sorcerers of Scarcity

No one understands the power of the scarcity principle better than giant diamond mining conglomerate De Beers of South Africa. Diamonds really were scarce and therefore expensive 200 years ago.

Today diamonds are no longer scarce. Since the 1960s, the world's output of diamonds has grown from 15 million carats to 100 million carats a year. Demand has been much more stable; it's largely driven by the number of people becoming engaged. Even so, between 1986 and 1996, the average price of diamonds increased by 50 percent.

So why is the price so high? The answer is the De Beers monopoly. Nearly all the world's diamonds are sold through the De Beers sales network. De Beers holds back the supply; it doesn't fill all its retailers' orders. It runs ten sales a year, to which only a select 150 diamond merchants are invited. De Beers decides on the supply and the price. There is no negotiation.

Each merchant is issued a plain brown shoebox full of stones. The dealers have no choice; they can take it or leave it. They usually take it or they don't get invited back the next year – and there are plenty of dealers who would love to take their place.

As well as controlling supply, De Beers has used its advertising to manage the perception of scarcity and sustain demand.

De Beers discouraged people from selling their diamonds with its "Diamonds are forever" campaign. This was designed to stop the growing competition in secondhand diamonds. The clever slogan, first used in 1947, sells two dreams in one: "that diamonds bring eternal love and romance and that diamonds never lose their value."[4]

Each year, De Beers spends nearly $200 million on advertising worldwide, mostly in women's magazines, featuring a shadowy female figure and her lover, a glittering diamond, and (at the bottom of the page) the "Diamonds are forever" slogan.

De Beers's advertising tells its male readers to choose a diamond that truly reflects how they feel about the woman they love and, as a guide, to spend at least two months' salary on a diamond. After all, the woman of their dreams is going to wear her diamond ring for the rest of her life as a symbol of their love. [5]

Diamond king Harry Oppenheimer takes the credit for turning diamonds into an essential middle-class accessory. Oppenheimer focused De Beers's advertising by instantly associating diamonds with weddings, anniversaries, and engagements. In the two years from 1939 to 1941, U.S. diamond sales jumped 55 percent.[6]

De Beers's advertising has turned buying a diamond engagement ring into a Japanese tradition. In 1967, only one in twenty Japanese brides received a diamond ring. Now it's virtually compulsory, and Japan is the world's largest customer of diamond jewelery.

When huge numbers of lower-quality, medium-grade Russian diamonds began appearing on the market, De Beers popularized the "eternity ring," an anniversary ring studded with these lower-grade stones – to be bought on a couple's tenth wedding anniversary. The De Beers slogan was "Show her you would marry her all over again." Since the start of the campaign, sales of eternity rings have jumped 400 percent.

With this track record of manipulating desire, it's no wonder *The Economist* says the De Beers personnel "have proved to be among the greatest salespeople of the century." The De Beers sales march continues relentlessly forward. De Beers recently persuaded "Baywatch" to devote an entire episode to a story about the purchase of an engagement ring.[7]

Nevertheless, supply is still racing ahead of demand. Industry watchers are asking if DeBeers can continue to monopolize the diamond market and sustain the myth of scarcity.[8]

Nintendo's Less Is More

Whenever possible, Japanese videogame producer Nintendo exploits the scarcity principle. In 1988, Nintendo let severe shortages of game cartridges develop. Retailers ordered 110 million cartridges; Nintendo supplied 33 million units. (*Note:* Retailers usually order more than they can sell.)

Shortages made the game cartridges even more desirable. News of the shortages generated valuable media exposure for Nintendo – a company that traditionally allowed a tiny 2 percent of sales for promotion.

Shortages – especially at Christmas – helped retailers sell out of the slower-moving Nintendo games because parents would rather buy a less popular title than leave their child with nothing.

After Christmas, kids badgered their parents to go back to the game stores to see if fresh supplies of the sold-out titles had come in. So Nintendo ended up selling two game cartridges instead of one. It truly was a case of less equaling more.

Scarcity and Demand

Have you ever wondered why some "in" restaurants continue to have waiting lines outside? Long lines seem to make the restaurants even more fashionable, further increasing the length of the queues. Why don't restaurants eliminate the waiting line by increasing their prices? They don't because removing the queue would eliminate the scarcity factor, and demand could collapse.

Scarcity and Fashion/Beauty

The world's fashion empires have been built on an understanding of the principle of scarcity. Virtually all of today's established designers are remembered for designing a uniquely different look.

Once established, a designer's reputation acquires value. Designers then earn potentially huge royalties by allowing their name to be imprinted on items such as ties, sunglasses, and watches.

Many prominent fashion labels, however, failed to understand that their image and reputation depended on their relative scarcity. In the late 1980s, Gucci had allowed its logo to appear on over 22,000 items; By 1989, overexposure had so tarnished the Gucci name that its U.S. sales fell 25 percent.[9]

To revitalize the brand, Gucci slashed the number of items carrying its name from 10,000 to 5,000 and the number of retail outlets carrying Gucci from 2,580 to 300. These actions restored Gucci's exclusive image. The scarcity principle locked in again, and once more Gucci is in style.

To restore its tarnished image, Chanel followed a similar strategy, cutting outlets, raising prices, and selling through exclusive Chanel boutiques.[10]

The scarcity principle can even affect our perceptions of beauty. The country-and-western song "The Girls All Look Prettier at Closing Time" is based on sound psychology and is backed up by research.[11]

Scarcity and the Phantom Trap

The scarcity principle can be invoked by creating phantom alternatives. Consider what the computer companies are doing when they announce, sometimes years in advance, their upcoming products.

Suddenly buyers have a phantom alternative. The products you are currently considering look less attractive because you compare them to the phantom alternative. You worry, "If what they say is really a breakthrough, I'll be stuck with a dinosaur. Maybe I should wait."

In many instances, these products don't exist or they are still very much in the early stages of development. This practice is so common in the software industry that commentators label preannounced but unavailable products "vaporware."

Given the way professional persuaders use phantoms to influence, it's not surprising that some persuasion academics call this the phantom trap.[12]

Scarcity and Information

The scarcity principle doesn't apply only to physical commodities. It applies just as strongly to information, messages, communications, and knowledge.

In one experiment, a beef importer's customers (supermarkets and retail food outlets) were split into three groups. The first set of customers was telephoned as usual by the salesperson with the usual sales pitch and then asked for the order.

The second group was given the usual sales pitch plus information that the supply of beef was likely to be scarce in the next few months. This second group purchased twice as much as the first group, who got only the standard sales pitch.

The third group received the usual sales pitch plus scarce-supply news; only this time they were told the information had come from some exclusive connections the company had.

This third group of customers, who found out about the upcoming scarcity via "exclusive connections," purchased six times more than the customers who received only the standard sales pitch.

"The point," says professor of psychology Robert Cialdini, "is that the news carrying the scarcity of information was itself scarce made it especially persuasive."[13]

Juries and Inadmissible Information

The impact of the scarcity principle on the availability of information was tested in a remarkable piece of research carried out by the University of Chicago Law School on how juries reach their decisions.

They found when judges ruled that information a jury had just heard was inadmissible and should be ignored, the juries reacted to the information restriction by valuing the information more than ever. Once the information was banned (i.e., made scarce), it suddenly became more valuable. [14]

Censorship

Similar results have been found in studies on the impact of censorship on human behavior. In one experiment, college students read a description of a book that sounded much like the normal copy found on most dust jackets.

Half the students were told that the book had a "21-year-old age restriction." The students given the restricted message rated the book as more desirable, and many more said they would like to

"The secret of business is to know something that nobody else knows."
— *Aristotle Onassis*

read it than the group given the unrestricted edition. People react the same way to X-rated movies and restricted adult magazines.[15]

The Optimum Conditions for Scarcity

The scarcity principle works best when things we have and value suddenly become scarce. Moreover, we want things most when we have to compete for them.

Competing for Resources

Anyone who has stood in line when department stores hold a sale should understand how these retailers create a competitive frenzy. Usually they offer some phenomenal deals on a few prominently advertised loss leaders. Caught up by the promotion, shoppers rush to buy items they would usually ignore.

In 1985, the most popular toy on the market was the Cabbage Patch doll. The doll was unique (therefore scarce), which shoppers loved. Each doll had its own adoption papers.

However, Coleco kept demand at fever pitch by undersupplying shops. With shops often out of stock, they ran lotteries to see who would win the opportunity to buy the doll. Some owners auctioned dolls off for over $200. In 1985, Cabbage Patch sales rocketed to $600 million.[16]

The knowledge that you are having to compete for a scarce resource is a powerful motivator. Salespeople often create mystery competitors to lure reluctant buyers.

A realtor who is trying to sell a house suddenly rings a prospect with the news that a professional business couple with plenty of money who has just moved into town is about to make an offer. The prospect then feels pressured to confirm or raise his or her offer.

Auctions and the Winner's Curse

An auction is a particularly dangerous place since scarcity and competition combine to create an emotional cocktail that can lead to overbidding. To show how easy it is to use the competition generated by an auction to entrap others, I sometimes like to play a game called the Dollar Bill Auction. The game's inventor, Martin Shubik (a Yale economist), allegedly tested it on the Yale University cocktail party circuit. Try it. You'll make some money, but be prepared to lose a few friends.

Take a $10 bill from your pocket and announce you're prepared to auction it off to the highest bidder. There are three simple rules:

1. Bidding must be in multiples of $1.

2. The highest bidder will win the $10 bill. However, the *second-highest bidder* must pay the auctioneer the amount of his or her losing bid. For example, if Penny bids $5 and Jerry bid $4, and the bidding stops at this point, the auctioneer will pay Penny $5 ($10 minus the amount bid) and Jerry, as the second-highest bidder, pays the auctioneer $4.

3. The auction ends when one minute passes without any new bids.

In a typical auction, everyone bids furiously until they reach $5 or $6. At this point, everyone except the two highest bidders drop out. The two remaining bidders now typically escalate their bids until they reach $10 and $9. At this point, they ponder whether to go on. Often the one who bids $9 will bid $11, and bidding erupts again. Then the bidding typically climbs to $14 or more.

The game often ends when one of the bidders sharply escalates the bidding by offering $20 to top a bid of, say, $15. The auctioneer then proceeds to collect $15 from the loser and $10 from the "winner." Of course, there is no winner. The point of the game, once bidding passes $10, is to avoid losing – to save face. What starts out as a friendly contest quickly turns into a psychological struggle.[17]

That's what happened when former Australian tycoon Alan Bond paid over $50 million for *The Irises* by Vincent Van Gogh. *The Irises* was unique and therefore very difficult to value objectively, and Bond had to have it. Most professional buyers observing from the sidelines said Bond had overpaid. However, overbidding is so common at auctions that scholars call it the "winner's curse." When Bond's empire collapsed, he was forced to sell *The Irises* at a massive discount.

In 1996, Sotherby's put Jackie Kennedy's personal belongings up for auction. Everyone knew Jackie's belongings would fetch a premium. Sotherby's sold more than 100,000 catalogs prior to the auction (at $90 hardback, $45 soft cover). During the week, the objects were on public display; some 40,000 people viewed them.

But the hype and anticipated prices fell far short of what the bidding finally achieved: Such was the competitive frenzy that a brooch with an estimated worth of $6,000 to $8,000 sold for $415,000; John F. Kennedy's set of McGregor golf clubs, with an estimated worth of $700 to $900, sold for $772,500; a wooden cigar box, with an estimated worth of $2,000 to $2,500, sold for $547,500; and a cigarette lighter with an inscribed J, worth $300 to $400, brought in $85,000.[18]

The winner's curse had struck again.

PERSUASION
POINTERS

1 Emphasize scarcity by promoting the unique features of what you have to offer.

2 When you possess exclusive information, sell its scarcity value and promote the benefits that come from being one of a select group who can benefit from the information.

3 If you want to build an image or brand based on exclusivity:

- Maintain premium pricing.
- Don't discount.
- Sell through selected outlets.
- Keep the market undersupplied.

4 In auctions, beware of the "winner's curse." Establish an upper limit before you start bidding and stick to it.

Persuasion Trigger Six: Conformity

Everyone Is Doing It

CONFORMITY – FOLLOWING THE CROWD

The Power of Conformity

Being one of the in-group or following the crowd is a powerful motivator. Let me illustrate with a simple example. Look at the line labeled A on Card 1 in Figure 20.1. Picture its length.

Figure 20.1 The Asch Test

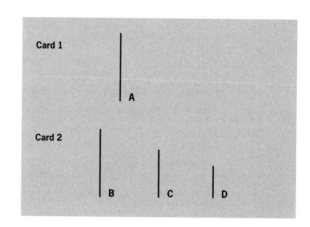

Now compare the length of line A with lines B, C, and D. Before reading on, answer which line is closest in length to line A? It's obvious – line B, of course. In fact, it seems so obvious it's hard to imagine anyone – unless he or she has a sight problem – ever giving any other answer. If you think this, you are wrong.

In the mid-1950s, the brilliant psychologist Solomon Asch invited a small group of people to come to the same room. All *except one* were stooges planted by Asch. All the stooges were instructed to say that line C was the same length as line A. Now imagine you as the subject. Everyone is telling you what you believe is the wrong answer. Your senses are screaming that line B is the correct answer, but everyone around you is convinced line C is the right one.

Would you resist the group pressure to conform? Few people do. Asch found that 75 percent of people faced with this dilemma go against their perception and follow the crowd.

The thought process is familiar to anyone who has gone to a business meeting. Do you back your own views, or do you conform to those of the group?[1]

The Bandwagon Effect

"The only man who can change his mind is a man that's got one."
— Edward Noyes Westcott

People will often go with what they believe is the popular view. We laugh and clap when we are guests on television shows even when we know the initial clapping has been created electronically.

Opinion Polls

Opinion polls tell us what other people are thinking and influence how we react. It's the power of conformity.

Saving Souls

Arizona State University researchers secretly penetrated the Billy Graham organization. They found that before Graham ever arrived in town to preach, a local army of 6,000 volunteers had been primed to "come forth at varying intervals to create the impression of a spontaneous mass outpouring."[2]

Telethons

If you've ever watched a telethon, you may wonder why huge amounts of time and money are spent reading out the names of people who have donated money. The message is: Everyone else has given – so why shouldn't you?

Street hustlers often place a few bills in their "tip boxes" to suggest to other donors that paper money is "standard." Similarly, some church ushers salt their collection plates to guide their congregation in what is an appropriate offering.

Overcoming Insecurity

> "Public opinion is like the castle ghost; no one has ever seen it, but everyone is scared of it."
>
> — Sigmund Graf

Going with the crowd helps us overcome our insecurities. A multimillion-dollar investment in new computers seems much less risky if we know that others have made the same choice.

When IBM totally dominated the computer industry, it was able to exploit these insecurities. Hence the expression: Nobody ever got fired for buying an IBM!

Advertising and Popularity

A prime purpose behind advertising is to increase a product's popularity. According to marketing professor Dr. Max Sutherland, "The more a brand is advertised the more popular and familiar it is perceived to be. Popularity is like a magnet. Advertising can enhance its power to attract. We as consumers somehow infer that something is popular simply because it is advertised."[3]

Advertising Themes

Many advertisers tap into our need for social comformity. Advertisers tell us their product is the number one brand, the largest selling, or the fastest growing. Books are advertised as bestsellers. These advertisements don't push the product; they simply emphasize that everyone else is buying the product.

Dangers of Groupthink

Going with the crowd, when making critical decisions, can lead to terrible situations.

The Bay of Pigs Fiasco

Two days after John Kennedy assumed office as President, the CIA briefed him on a plan for a clandestine army of Cuban exiles to invade Cuba. Then, for a period of eighty days, a small band of presidential advisers discussed the details. On April 17, 1961, 1,400 Cuban exiles invaded the Cuban mainland.

The attack was an absolute fiasco; nothing went right. By the third day, Castro's troops had killed or imprisoned all the invaders. When the attack failed, Kennedy was stunned. "How," he asked, "could I have been so stupid to let them go ahead?"

Irving Janis's research believes the fundamental cause of the disaster was groupthink.[4] At the meetings preceding the invasion, all of Kennedy's advisers possessed different pieces of critical information, which, if presented, could have made Kennedy call off the invasion.

Most of the group assumed that the invasion would trigger armed uprisings by a local Cuban underground. These uprisings were crucial for the campaign's success since the invasion force of 1,400 was too small to smash the 20,000-strong Cuban army on its own. Yet not one of Kennedy's advisers brought up the results of a secret opinion poll showing the vast majority of Cubans supported Castro.

Looking back, Kennedy's adviser Theodore Sorenson remarked, "Our meetings took place in a curious atmosphere of assumed consensus." In the key meetings, no one opposed the venture; no one proposed alternative plans. Yet Sorensen believes, "Had one senior adviser opposed the adventure, I believe that Kennedy would have canceled it."[5]

PERSUASION
POINTERS

 Stress that what you want to sell is popular, standard practice, or part of a trend.

Associate yourself or your product with people or companies the person you want to persuade admires or would like to emulate.

Highlight the failures of people or organizations that have refused to keep up with the trends.

Persuasion Trigger Seven: Liking

Friends Won't Let You Down

■ LIKING: THE MAGIC BULLET

Likable communicators are more persuasive. We try to please the people we like and find attractive.

Communication's expert Roger Ailes, who advised both Presidents Reagan and Bush, argues: "If you could master one element of personal communications that is more powerful than anything we've discussed, it is the quality of being likable. I call it the magic bullet, because if your audience likes you, they'll forgive just about everything else you do wrong. If they don't like you, you can hit every rule right on target and it doesn't matter."[1]

Friendship and Persuasion

If you've ever been to a Tupperware party, you'll understand how compliance professionals exploit our natural desire to say yes to those we like most.

Although a Tupperware representative entertains and demonstrates, the real influence to buy the goods at the party comes from a friend playing the role of party hostess. What chance do you stand? You're in your friend's home, and you've enjoyed your

> "There are three kinds of friends: best friends, guest friends, and pest friends."
> — *Henry Adams*

friend's hospitality. You've played games with the other partygoers – who often happen to be friends.

Even though you know your friend is receiving a commission, the pressure to buy is enormous. The remarkable thing is, you know your friendship is being taken advantage of, yet you still buy. After all, what can you do?

Two researchers, Frenzer and Davis, investigated the power of what influences people to buy in home party-plan settings. They found the strength of the friendship tie "is twice as likely to influence the purchase as is preference for the product itself."[2]

The sale results are undeniable. Party-plan is a multibillion-dollar industry. Tupperware sales alone total over $2.5 million a day.

Sales Organizations. Insurance companies, for example, advise their new salespeople to compile their initial list of prospects from friends. These, they are told, are the "easy sales"; they're right. It is not uncommon for insurance salespeople to give up as soon as their network of friends runs out.

It's very common for salespeople to ask for referrals, and the best referrals are friends. A salesperson who calls you quoting the name of a friend "who suggested I call you" is difficult to refuse. It's almost like refusing a friend.

Top salespeople almost always start by searching for similarities in backgrounds and interests with their clients. Similarities deepen trust and rapport, increase liking, and speed up the sales process.

Physical Attractiveness Increases Liking

Would you allow your opinions to be swayed by someone simply because he or she was physically attractive? Although most of us want to say no, the research suggests physical appearance plays a much bigger part than we like to admit.

Experiments show that a beautiful woman could sway an audience on a topic that had nothing to do with her looks. When males saw an automobile advertisement featuring a beautiful female model, they rated the car as better designed, more expensive, and more appealing than male subjects who did not see a model promote the car.[3]

If you are good-looking, you are more likely to be labeled as talented, kind, honest and intelligent. Furthermore, these labels are given without the labeler ever being aware of his or her bias.[4]

In a study of Canadian federal elections, researchers found physically attractive candidates received over twice the number of votes as unattractive politicians.[5]

What Is Attractiveness?

Just what do we mean by attractive? Two researchers, Murray Webster and Jama Driskell, found the most important component of beauty is conventionality.

After examining hundreds of photographs rated by panels as attractive and unattractive, they found: "The overall impression from these pictures is that very minor and superficial changes in hairstyle, weight and perhaps clothing would be significant to make the unattractive people attractive, or the reverse."[6]

They then conclude: "Attractiveness is a characteristic that gives us an instant impression of a person's status. Similarly when a person sits in a meeting 'dressed for success,' looking solemn, saying nothing, many people automatically attribute depth and wisdom."[7]

Attractiveness and Attitudes

When you meet strangers of the opposite sex whom you find attractive, you will probably automatically assume that you share their attitudes.

On the other hand, if you express an attitude shared by a stranger, that person will probably see you as more attractive than he or she would if your attitudes differed.

Attractiveness and Sex

Good-looking men have a head start over good-looking women. Good-looking men almost always are more liked and more respected than their less handsome rivals.

Good-looking women however, can, sometimes find their attractiveness works against them.

Recent research reveals that attractive women are more likely to win promotions over their less attractive rivals – except when they are competing for a nontraditional role.

Here is a sample finding: "If you are an executive in a traditional 'man's world,' you can expect to have a harder time than an unattractive woman in winning recognition for your capability and integrity, and in getting promoted, although your attractiveness will probably give you an advantage in a more typically 'feminine' executive job, say as a head dietitian or women's wear buyer."[8]

Attractiveness and Justice

Attractiveness also influences your chances of success in court. If you are found guilty of burglary or a crime where your good looks appear to play no part, a jury is more likely to find you innocent than it would a less attractive defendant.

However, if you used your good looks to commit a fraud or run a con game, the jury is more prone to throw the book at you.

Similarity Increases Liking

Of course you don't have to be physically attractive to be liked. People also like those who are similar to themselves.

As a national politician, Jimmy Carter was a virtual unknown in 1975. In his get-to-know-America campaign, Carter delivered thousands of speeches. Nearly every speech began:

"I'm Jimmy Carter. I come from a small town in the South; I'm a farmer, a churchgoer, and a family man. I live with my wife, Rosalynn, and my young daughter Amy. I served in the Navy and I was a nuclear engineer. I was governor of Georgia."

In those few lines, Carter stressed some attributes he had in common with a large part of his audience – who were "small towners," farmers, churchgoers, families, and veterans. He also provided proof of his occupational and political status.

Researchers McCroskey, Richmond, and Daly say there are four critical keys to similarity: attitude, morality, background, and appearance. When receiving a persuasive message, we ask:

1. Does the speaker think like me?
2. Does the speaker share my morals?
3. Does the speaker share my background?
4. Does the speaker look like me?

Of the four keys, similar attitudes and morals are the most important.[9]

Praise Increases Liking

The Guinness Book of Records called Joe Girard the "world's greatest salesman." For twelve years, he was America's "number one car salesman." On average, he sold five vehicles a day, when most of his peers struggled to sell one.

"Flattery will get you anywhere."
— *Jane Russell*

Joe attributed his success to just two things: the right price and being someone customers liked to buy from. To keep in contact with his huge customer base, each month he sent his 13,000 former customers a greeting card. While the card changed every month according to the season, the message was always the same.

It read, "I like you." It seems corny, but Joe thought it worked. Joe understood how humans fall for flattery. Compliments increase liking and compliance.[10]

In one remarkable experiment, praise given did not even have to be true to work. We are so gullible when it comes to praise that we can easily be seduced by false flattery.

Political insiders report that even Margaret Thatcher, with her Iron Lady image, "was apparently heavily influenced by ministers such as Cecil Parkinson who lavished compliments upon her."[11]

Association Increases Liking

Most of us like to be associated with success, so when celebrities and athletes we like and admire endorse products, we tend to follow their recommendations.

In 1996, *Forbes* reported U.S. companies put more than $1 billion into the pockets of 2,000 athletes for endorsement deals and licensing rights – a tenfold increase from just a decade ago.

Forbes reports that when it comes to endorsements, "Nice guys finish first." Bad guys, like Chicago Bulls cross-dressing Dennis Rodman, attract the publicity and the fad marketers but not long-term endorsements.

In 1997, Rodman earned just $6 million in endorsements compared to Michael Jordan's $47 million. Jordan's sponsors include Nike, Sarah Lee, McDonald's, Wilson Gatorade, Rayovac, World Cam, and Bijan.

Arnold Palmer, golf's legendary nice guy, at the age of sixty-seven could only win $100,000 on the fairway, yet he managed to pull $16 million in endorsements from blue chips Cadillac, Rolex, and Pennzoil.[12]

Golfing sensation and nice guy Tiger Woods earns $24 million a year in endorsements.

Appealing to Our Self-Image

We know celebrities and athletes are being handsomely paid for their endorsements, but we still buy. Why?

Psychologists Anthony Pratkanis and Elliot Aronson say that "we hold our beliefs and attitudes to define and make sense of our *selves*. By shaving with the right razor or eating the right cereal, we are saying, 'I am just like that ball player; I am part of the attractive in-group.' By purchasing the 'right stuff,' we enhance our own egos and rationalize away our inadequacies as we become just like our favorite celebrity."[13]

Are we trapped into following the wants of the good-looking? Not always. If we are motivated to think hard about the quality of the messages and arguments, we downplay the attractiveness of the source when it comes to being swayed. That is, the attractiveness of a source has less of an impact when we operate in the central as opposed to the peripheral route to persuasion.

Attractiveness is also of little advantage in situations when it seems inappropriate. We expect endorsers of shampoo to be attractive; the endorsers' attractiveness is part of the pitch. We don't expect our family doctor to be sensationally attractive, so great looks are not likely to be a persuasive asset.

Finally, the impact of attractiveness is often short-lived. We go along with attractive persuaders because we like and identify with them. Once we stop identifying with an attractive persuader, the reason for the opinion evaporates along with the attractiveness. Advertisers quickly drop any endorser who has lost his or her luster.

PERSUASION
POINTERS

 The best referrals in business and politics are usually friends of the person you want to influence.

2 Emphasize the similarities you share with the person you want to influence.

3 Look for areas where you can work and socialize together.

4 Be cautious before taking a strong stand on a controversial topic. People we like usually share our attitudes and morals.

5 Use praise whenever possible. Identify areas for which you can legitimately compliment the other person.

Part 4

PERSUASION AT ITS BEST

"*My life has been nothing but continuous persuasion.*"

ADOLF HITLER

Icons of Influence

The Most Influential Persuaders of the Twentieth Century

HEROIC GIANTS

Six men dominate the political history of the twentieth century: Lenin, Stalin, Hitler, Mao, Roosevelt, and Churchill.

Four – Lenin, Stalin, Hitler, and Mao – created barbaric dictatorships. Two – Roosevelt and Churchill – were democractic leaders who saved the world from tyranny.

Great democratic leaders have to be great persuaders. Without the consent of the people, they are rendered impotent. Dictators such as Hitler and Stalin, who used murder, torture, and arbitrary arrest to shore up support and destroy dissent, cannot be seriously considered great persuaders. In a century of tumultuous change, Roosevelt and Churchill stand out as two heroic giants.

In today's image-driven world, Roosevelt and Churchill seem unlikely candidates for greatness as persuaders. Roosevelt was certainly the more handsome of the two, but, crippled by polio, he had to lead and cajole from the confines of a wheelchair. Churchill was "short and fat," "pink and cuddly," said one journalist's wife.

He "waddled rather than walked and lectured rather than listened."[1] "A pugnacious looking bastard," one lowly ranked soldier called him.

Franklin Roosevelt

Franklin Delano Roosevelt is the only U.S. President to be elected four times. During his twelve years in office from 1933 to 1945, FDR guided America through the Great Depression and World War II – the two greatest crises to face the United States in the twentieth century. In the process, he remade the presidency, restored America's faith in democracy, and left a legacy of political freedom and domestic security.

"Under Roosevelt," historian William Leuchtenberg observed, "the White House became the focus of all government – the fountainhead of ideas, the initiator of action, the representative of the national interest."[2]

Roosevelt became President at the height of the Great Depression when one in four Americans was out of work. In his first inaugural address, Roosevelt offered hope and vision: "The only thing we have to fear, is fear itself," he asserted. Against fierce opposition, he sold the need for radical change. He called for a New Deal program for the "third of the nation, ill-housed, ill-clad, ill-nourished." Roosevelt declared, "The Nation asks for action and action now." During his first hundred days, Congress passed more than a dozen major pieces of legislation. In later years, the New Deal lost momentum, but the hundred days still remain the benchmark against which to measure a new President.

In dramatic contrast to Lenin, Stalin, Hitler, and Mao, Roosevelt was never an ideologue. Consider this interview with a young reporter:

Reporter: Mr. President, "are you a communist?
Roosevelt: No.
Reporter: Are you a capitalist?
Roosevelt: No.
Reporter: Are you a socialist?

Roosevelt: No.

Reporter: Well, what is your philosophy, then?

Roosevelt: Philosophy? Philosophy? I am a Christian and a Democrat
– that's all.

During the Depression, Roosevelt experimented with one economic
fix after another. Critics claimed "he switched economic plans as
often as he changed treatments for polio." The New Deal did
not cure the Depression; it took World War II and massive
spending on tanks, planes, and destroyers to slash the numbers
of jobless.

In foreign affairs, he successfully fought those who wanted to
keep America cotton-wooled in isolation. His partnership with
Winston Churchill during World War II became the most
important wartime alliance of the twentieth century. As
commander-in-chief, he picked a remarkable team of generals and
admirals to run the war effort.

Before he was cut down by polio and made a cripple in 1921,
Roosevelt was seen by his fellows as "vain," "superficial," and
"spoiled." But his fight with polio gave him grit, patience, and a
new ability to empathize with the poor and down-and-out.

Churchill said meeting Roosevelt was like opening your first
bottle of champagne. At a personal level, Roosevelt charmed and
beguiled. French leader Charles de Gaulle called him "that artist"
and a "seducer." Roosevelt loved to be liked. "If he thought you
didn't like him," remarked an aide, "he'd practically jump over a
chair to get you."[3]

Handling the press under Roosevelt became an art form. He was
the first President to give the press direct access to the White
House. Before then, face-to-face meetings between reporters and
the President were largely ceremonial. In his four terms, he held
998 press conferences, an all-time record. Reporters called a
Roosevelt press conference the "best show in town." The President

simplified complex policies into words reporters could understand and he could always deliver a colorful metaphor to spice up a story.

According to historian Nathan Miller, "the President's triumph over the press corps was so complete that some correspondents found it necessary to make a spirited defense against the charge they had become propagandists for the New Deal."[4]

With the support of reporters, Roosevelt was able to hide his physical disability from the American people and concentrate on running the world's largest democracy during the Depression and the war. His personal magnetism also allowed him to win over working journalists at a time when their bosses, the newspaper publishers, were openly hostile.

Roosevelt transformed the face of political communication with his use of radio. In 1924, there were 3 million radios in America; by 1935, there were over 30 million. Up to 60 million listeners tuned into Roosevelt's fireside chats. During the first ten months of his presidency, he used radio to communicate directly to the nation on twenty occasions. Roosevelt loved radio; radio, he believed, could "restore direct contact between the masses and their chosen leaders."

Roosevelt's radio style was intimate and conversational. His famous "fireside chats" were organized as civics lessons. Roosevelt would first explain the nature of the problem his government faced in simple, calmly spoken words. Then he would tell his listeners what he proposed to do about it. The explanations were simple but never simplistic. Unlike Hitler and Stalin, FDR respected the public's intelligence.

Roosevelt could be a "shameless schemer."[5] During the 1944 presidential campaign, after booking fifteen minutes of airtime, Roosevelt heard that his opponent Thomas E. Dewey had booked the next time slot to make a reply. Roosevelt spoke for fourteen minutes and then stopped. Baffled by the long silence, millions of listeners started fiddling with their dials, switching stations to find something to listen to. By the time Dewey began speaking most of his audience had disappeared.

No other politician has ever matched Roosevelt at softening up public opinion before introducing a major change. Take Social Security. First, FDR convinced the public that Social Security did not threaten the American ideals of self-help and independence. Then he used press conferences, a message to Congress, two fireside chats, and a State of the Union Address before introducing legislation.[6]

More than any other President, he studied public opinion, analyzed polls, trawled the daily newspapers for subtle changes in the public mood, and dispatched his wife, Eleanor, to different parts of the country to gather intelligence. "A government," said Roosevelt, "can be no better than the public opinion that sustains it."

Clare Boothe Luce, playwright wife of publisher Henry Luce, said, "Churchill had his fingered V for victory; Hitler, a stiff arm raised above his head; Mussolini, a strut." When she described Roosevelt, she moistened her index finger and held it aloft to test the wind.[7]

Above all, Roosevelt possessed an uncanny sense of timing. "I am like a cat," he once said. "I make a quick stroke and then I relax."

Unlike Churchill, Roosevelt didn't compose the details of all his speeches. Nevertheless, he was actively involved in the planning, writing, and editing of all his major addresses. A major speech typically went through a dozen drafts. By the time he came to deliver the speech, Roosevelt was word-perfect.

Roosevelt's speeches are littered with memorable, vivid phrases. A sampling:

- "This generation of Americans has a rendezvous with destiny." (speech accepting renomination as President, June 27, 1936)
- "We have earned the hatred of entrenched greed." (message to Congress, January 1936)

- "Repetition does not transform a lie into a truth." (radio address, October 1939)
- "We have the men – the skill – the wealth – and above all the will. ... We must be the great arsenal of democracy." (fireside chat radio broadcast, December 29, 1940)
- "Yesterday, December 7, 1941 – a date which will live in infamy – the United States of America was suddenly and deliberately attacked by naval and air forces of the Empire of Japan." (address to Congress, December 8, 1941)
- "When you get to the end of your rope, tie a knot and hang on." (quoted in the *Kansas City Star*)

Although Roosevelt is the most loved, he is also the most hated President of the twentieth century. He was denounced as a "traitor to his class." To this day, Roosevelt symbolizes big government and the controlled economy.

In his memoirs, Churchill painted a picture of himself as the wise, forward-thinking defender of the free world and portrayed Roosevelt as naïve but well-meaning, but Roosevelt was never naïve. If anything, Roosevelt was more Machiavellian by nature than Churchill. Roosevelt once described himself as a juggler. He told his Secretary of the Treasury, Henry Morgenthau, "You know I am a juggler and I never let my right hand know what my left hand does."[8]

Stalin, when comparing Roosevelt with Churchill, remarked, "Churchill is the kind who, if you don't watch him, will slip a kopek out of your pocket. ... And Roosevelt! Roosevelt is not like that. He dips his hand only for bigger coins."

Ronald Reagan, often called the great communicator, modeled himself after FDR. Reagan became to television what Roosevelt was to radio. The picture replaced the word; in the process, substance was sacrificed for image and style. Policy was replaced with sound bites expertly crafted to echo the latest opinion polls. Unlike Roosevelt, Reagan rarely ever talked to, let alone worked with, the large team of wordsmiths who wrote his speeches.

Surveys of presidential historians rank Roosevelt as far and away the most effective President of the twentieth century.

Winston Churchill

Time magazine made Churchill "man of the half-century" in 1950. On his death in 1965, Labour Prime Minister and long-time opponent Clement Atlee called him "the greatest citizen of the world of our time."

The Churchill legend obscures what was, until 1940, a mixed record. Churchill lost more elections than any other British politician of his time. For twenty-five years, he wandered with little support in the political wilderness. "He was regarded," writes biographer William Manchester, "as erratic, unreliable, shallow, impetuous, a hatcher of 'wild cat schemes'. ... A genius without judgment."[9]

As an orator Churchill had no peer, but too often Churchill used words to bludgeon opponents. Often gloomy and full of invective, his speeches inspired more suspicion than trust. Harold Begbie wrote, "His power is the power of gifts, not character. Men watch him but do not follow him. He beguiles their reason but never warms their emotions."[10]

As a radio broadcaster, Churchill seemed to lack the intimate conversation that Roosevelt had perfected. Churchill's speaking talents seemed more suited to a previous age.

Then World War II provided a theatre tailor-made for Churchillian-style performances. Churchill's warnings not to appease but to stand resolute against Hitler suddenly seemed prophetic. Faced with the threat of German invasion, Churchill stood out as the one man who could offer salvation from tyranny. In 1940, when Chamberlain lost the confidence of Parliament, Churchill was asked to become prime minister.

For Churchill, Britain's options were simple: "victory or defeat, survival or annihilation, freedom or tyranny, civilisation or barbarism."[11] The crisis was perfectly attuned to Churchill's rhetoric. "His words at last made the historic impact he had always wanted to make."[12]

Only six weeks after taking office, Germany's panzer divisions stood poised, ready to strike across the English Channel. The French had collapsed; Belgium had surrendered. The remnants of the British and French armies had been evacuated from Dunkirk.

> "The nation had the lion's heart. I had the luck to give the roar."
> — *Winston Churchill*

The Führer was now master of Europe. Hitler informed Göring: "The war is finished. I'll come to an understanding with England."

Britain stood alone. The nation's survival, the Chiefs of Staff advised Churchill, depended on stiffening morale. Churchill responded, in the words of American broadcaster Ed Murrow, "by mobilizing the English language and sending it into battle." When victory was unthinkable, Churchill's soaring prose became the difference between survival and defeat.

Churchill's speeches of 1940-1941 include many of history's most memorable phrases:

- *"I have nothing to offer but blood, toil, tears and sweat."* (on becoming prime minister, House of Commons, May 13, 1940)
- *"We shall fight on the beaches, we shall fight on the landing grounds, we shall fight in the fields and in the streets, we shall fight in the hills; we shall never surrender."* (House of Commons, 4 June, 1940)
- *"If the British Commonwealth and its Empire lasts for a thousand years, men will say this was their finest hour."* (referring to Dunkirk evacuation, House of Commons, June 18, 1940)
- *"Never in the field of human conflict was so much owed by so many to so few."* (referring to Battle of Britain pilots, House of Commons, August 20, 1940)
- *"Give us the tools, and we will finish the job."* (request to Roosevelt for aid, radio broadcast, February 9, 1941)
- *"You do your worst, we will do our best."* (addressed to Hitler, speech, July 14, 1941)

- *"Do not let us speak of darker days; let us speak of sterner days. These are not dark days. These are great days – the greatest days our country has ever lived."* (address, Harrow School, October 29, 1941)

Churchill's speeches sent shivers down his listeners' spines. Even today, his words retain their ability to stir. From May 1940 to December 1941, 70 percent of Britons tuned in to Churchill's twenty-five broadcasts. Churchill's popularity soared as he toured the country, marching from one bomb site to the next. In June 1940, 88 percent of the population supported him as prime minister – a figure that remained high for most of the war. Everywhere Churchill traveled, press and newsreel photographers projected him as the irrepressible John Bull.

Britain never really had a chance without American help, and Churchill's persuasive powers played a critical role in winning aid from America. Between 1939 and Roosevelt's death in 1945, Churchill and Roosevelt exchanged nearly 2,000 letters, memorandums, and messages.

Although clearly the junior partner in the Grand Alliance, Churchill was able to influence Roosevelt on many occasions. It is a tribute to both of them that, for the most part, both leaders put the common good of the alliance ahead of their national interests.

If Churchill was such a convincing persuader, why were he and the Conservative Party defeated by the Labour Party in 1945? The short answer is: Churchill failed to come up with a peacetime program that offered Britons economic and social security. Not one of Churchill's wartime broadcasts after March 1943 highlighted social policy. Churchill's focus never shifted from winning the war. In frustration, war-weary Britons, still haunted by memories of the Great Depression, turned to a Labour Party promising jobs and social security.

An exhausted and bewildered Churchill confessed during the 1945 election campaign, "I've tried them with pep and I've tried them with pap, and I still don't know what they want."

In the postwar years, Churchill's influence waned. His 1946 iron curtain speech, delivered in Fulton, Missouri, alerted the West to the danger of an expansionist Soviet Union. However, historian Norman Rose writes: Churchill was not a success as a peacetime prime minister.

Was Churchill the greatest Englishman of his time, of all times? All that can be said with certainty is that between 1940 and 1941, at a moment of his country's greatest peril, and by virtue of his unique abilities, Churchill saved his country from a dreadful tyranny. And by doing so, through his courage and leadership, he inspired the rest of the free world and gave hope to those already crushed under despotic rule. No man was ever more prepared, more fitted, more willing to fulfill this historic task, one that he completed with consummate artistry. If the test of true greatness is that a statesman leaves a positive imprint on the course of history, then Churchill passes the test with flying colors.[13]

Who, then, deserves the title as the most influential persuader of the twentieth century – Churchill or Roosevelt? If the main criteria include sustained success, the victor is undoubtedly Roosevelt. If the criteria center on sheer brilliance under pressure, then Churchill's majestic performance as Britain's wartime leader ranks him the best.

Both men were giants. Both played monumental roles in saving democracy. In the process, they redefined the art of persuasion.

As professional persuaders, we can only try to emulate them.

Footnotes

Preface

1 Jeffrey Robinson, *The Manipulators*. Simon and Schuster, 1998, p. 83.

Chapter 2

1 Charles J. Margerison, *If Only I Had Said ....* Mercury, 1987, pp. 73-79.

Chapter 3

1 Douglas L. Wilson, *Honor's Voice*. Knopf, 1998, p. 302.

Chapter 4

1 Gerry Spence, *How to Argue and Win Every Time*. St. Martin's Press, 1995, p. 4.
2 Paul Ekman, *Telling Lies*. W. W. Norton and Company, 1992, pp. 15–16.
3 James C. Humes, *The Ben Franklin Factor*. William Morrow and Company, 1992, p. 84.
4 Anthony R. Pratkanis and Elliot Aronson, *Age of Propaganda*. W. H. Freeman and Company, 1992, p. 95.
5 Anthony R. Pratkanis and Elliot Aronson, *Age of Propaganda*. W. H. Freeman and Company, 1992, p. 95.
6 Sharon Beder, *Global Spin*. Scribe Publications, 1997, p. 27.
7 John Stauber and Sheldon Rampton, *Toxic Sludge Is Good For You*. Common Courage Press, 1995, p. 96.
8 John Stauber and Sheldon Rampton, *Toxic Sludge Is Good For You*. Common Courage Press, 1995, p. 96.
9 Anthony R. Pratkanis and Elliot Aronson, *Age of Propaganda*, W. H. Freeman and Company, 1992, p. 98.
10 Anthony R. Pratkanis and Elliot Aronson, *Age of Propaganda*. W. H. Freeman and Company, 1992, p. 99.
11 Al Ries and Jack Trout, *The 22 Immutable Laws of Marketing*. HarperBusiness, 1993, p. 89.
12 Al Ries and Jack Trout, *The 22 Immutable Laws of Marketing*. HarperBusiness, 1993, p. 89.
13 Quoted in Luke Sullivan, *"Hey Whipple, Squeeze This."* John Wiley and Sons, 1998, p. 4.
14 Al Ries and Jack Trout, *The 22 Immutable Laws of Marketing*. HarperBusiness, 1993, p. 91.
15 Roger Ailes, *You Are the Message*. Dow Jones-Irwin, 1988, p. 140.
16 Roger Ailes, *You Are the Message*. Dow Jones-Irwin, 1988, pp. 19–20.
17 Gerry Spence, *How to Argue and Win Every Time*. St. Martin's Press, 1995, p. 131.
18 Lawrence Susskind and Patrick Field, *Dealing With an Angry Public*. The Free Press, 1996, p. 9.
19 Bill Brooks and Tom Travisano, *You're Working Too Hard to Make the Sale!* Irwin, 1995, p. 16.
20 M. Hirsh Goldberg, *The Book of Lies*. Quill/William Morrow, 1990, p. 120.
21 Jonathan Bond and Richard Kirshenbaum, *Under the Radar*. John Wiley and Sons, 1998, p. IX.
22 Jonathan Bond and Richard Kirshenbaum, *Under the Radar*. John Wiley and Sons, 1998, p. 91.
23 *Fortune*, August 3, 1998, p. 33.
24 Jonathan Bond and Richard Kirshenbaum, *Under the Radar*. John Wiley and Sons, 1998, pp. 20–21.
25 P. R. Wilson, "The Perceptual Distortion of Height as a Function of Ascribed Academic Status." *Journal of Social Psychology* 74 (1968): p. 97–102.
26 Thomas C. Reeves, *A Question of Character*. Arrow Books, 1991, p. 49.
27 Thomas C. Reeves, *A Question of Character*. Arrow Books, 1991, p. 49.
28 Thomas C. Reeves, *A Question of Character*. Arrow Books, 1991, p. 128.

Chapter 5

1 Susan Kismeric, *American Politicians: Photographs from 1945 to 1993*. New York. 1994, pp. 14–15.
2 Hugh Gregory Gallagher, *Franklin D. Roosevelt's Splendid Deception*. 1985, pp. 93–94.
3 Hugh Gregory Gallagher, *Franklin D. Roosevelt's Splendid Deception*. 1985, pp. 93–94.
4 Stuart Ewen, *PR! A Social History of Spin*. Basic Books, 1996, p. 395.
5 Stuart Ewen, *PR! A Social History of Spin*. Basic Books, 1996, p. 254.
6 Christopher Matthews, *Kennedy and Nixon*. Touchstone, 1996, p. 155.
7 Christopher Matthews, *Kennedy and Nixon*. Touchstone, 1996, p. 152.
8 Christopher Matthews, *Kennedy and Nixon*. Touchstone, 1996, p. 155.
9 Judee K. Burgoon, David B. Buller, and W. Gill Woodall, *Nonverbal Communication*. McGraw-Hill, 1996, pp. 136-137.
10 Judee K. Burgoon, David B. Buller, and W. Gill Woodall, *Nonverbal Communication*. McGraw-Hill, 1996, p. 140.
11 Judee K. Burgoon, David B. Buller, and W. Gill Woodall, *Nonverbal Communication*. McGraw-Hill, 1996, p. 140.

12 Andrew Thompson, *Margaret Thatcher, The Woman Within*. 1989, p. 219.

13 *The Australian*, April 8, 1997, p. 12.

14 *The Dominion*, November 26, 1998, p. 11.

15 *The Australian*, April 8, 1997, p. 12.

16 *USA Today*, August 18, 1985.

17 Roger E. Axtell, *Gestures*. John Wiley and Sons, 1998, p. IX.

18 Julius Fast, *Body Language in the Workplace*. Penguin Books, 1991, p. 15.

19 Harry A. Mills, *Negotiate: The Art of Winning*. Gower, 1991, pp. 79-80.

20 Julius Fast, *Body Language in the Workplace*. Penguin Books, 1991, p. 13.

21 Julius Fast, *Body Language in the Workplace*. Penguin Books, 1991, p. 60.

22 Andrew Thompson, *Margaret Thatcher: The Woman Within*. 1989, p. 48.

23 Mary Bragg, *Reinventing Influence*. Pitman Publishing, 1996, p. 123.

24 *The Dominion*, February 11, 1998, p. 5.

25 Also see Jo-Allan Dimitrius and Mark Mazzarella, *Reading People*. Random House, 1998, pp. 245–249.

26 *Bernard Asbell with Karen Wynn, What They Know About You*. Random House, 1991, p. 49.

27 Mary Bragg, *Reinventing Influence*. Pitman Publishing, 1996, pp. 73-74.

28 Elaina Zuker, *Influence*. Crisp, 1994, p. 72.

29 Steven Drozdeck, Joseph Yeager, and Linda Sommer, *What They Don't Teach You in Sales 101*. McGraw-Hill, 1991, p. 119.

30 D. Goleman, *New York Times*, April 8, 1986, pp. C1, C6.

31 Steven A. Beebe and Susan J. Beebe, *Public Speaking*. Allyn and Bacon, 1997, p. 293.

32 Suzette Haden Elgin, *Success with the Gentle Art of Verbal Self-Defense*. Prentice Hall, 1989, p. 153.

33 William Safire, *Lend Me Your Ears*. W. W. Norton and Company, 1992, p. 25.

34 Morey Stettner, *The Art of Winning Conversation*. Prentice Hall, 1995, pp. 286-287.

35 Noelle C. Nelson, *Winning!* Prentice Hall, 1997, p. 130.

36 *Newsweek*, February 2, 1998, p. 13.

37 AFP *Dominion*, February 8, 1998, p. 6.

38 Paul Ekman, *Telling Lies*. W. W. Norton and Company, 1992, p. 271.

39 Paul Ekman, *Telling Lies*. W. W. Norton and Company, 1992, p. 57.

40 Daniel McNeill, *The Face*. Little Brown, 1998, p. 245.

41 Daniel McNeill, *The Face*. Little Brown, 1998, p. 245.

42 Michelle Marchetti, "Whatever It Takes." *Sales and Marketing Management*. December 1997, p. 30.

43 Michelle Marchetti, "Whatever It Takes." *Sales and Marketing Management*. December 1997, p. 30.

44 Paul Ekman, *Telling Lies*. W. W. Norton and Company, 1992, p. 28.

45 Daniel McNeill, *The Face*. Little Brown, 1998, p. 247.

46 Gerhard Gschwandtner, "Lies and Deception in Selling." *Personal Selling Power* (15th anniversary issue), p. 63.

47 Gerhard Gschwandtner, "Lies and Deception in Selling." *Personal Selling Power* (15th anniversary issue), pp. 64–65.

Chapter 6

1 Paul D. Tieger and Barbara Barron-Tieger, *The Art of Speedreading People*. Little Brown, 1998, p. 19.

2 Paul D. Tieger and Barbara Barron-Tieger, *Do What You Are*. Little Brown, 1995, p. 336.

3 Paul D. Tieger and Barbara Barron-Tieger, *Do What You Are*. Little Brown, 1995, p. 336.

Chapter 7

1 Quentin de la Bedoyere, *How to Get Your Own Way in Business*. Gower, 1990, p. XI.

2 Godfrey Howard, *Getting Through!* David and Charles, 1989, p. 15.

3 Jean Aitchison, *The Language Web*. Cambridge University Press, 1997, p. 62.

4 George R. Walther, *Say What You Mean and Get What You Want*. Piatkus, 1993.

5 Godfrey Howard, *Getting Through!* David and Charles, 1989, p. 89.

6 Mark Hempshell, *How to Write Sales Copy That Really Sells*. Thorsons, 1992, pp. 44–45.

7 Bob Stone, *Successful Direct Marketing Methods*. NTC Business Books, 1994, p. 378.

8 Bob Stone, *Successful Direct Marketing Methods*. NTC Business Books, 1994, p. 379.

9 Herschell Gordon Lewis, *Sales Letters That Sizzle*. NTC Business Books, 1995, p. 6.

10 Herschell Gordon Lewis, *Sales Letters That Sizzle*. NTC Business Books, 1995, p. 8.

11 Garrett Soden, *Hook, Spin, Buzz*. Peterson's/Pacesetter Books, 1996, p. 24.

12 Godfrey Howard, *Getting Through!* David and Charles, 1989, p. 113.

13 Nido R. Qubein, *How to Be a Great Communicator.* John Wiley and Sons, 1997, p. 44.

14 Charles U. Larson, *Persuasion.* Wadsworth Publishing Company, 1995, pp. 122–123.

15 Godfrey Howard, *Getting Through!* David and Charles, 1989, p. 115.

16 Aaron Delwiche, *Examples: How Newt Gingrich Uses These Techniques.* Institute for Propaganda Analysis, World Wide Web.

17 Anthony R. Pratkanis and Elliot Aronson, *Age of Propaganda.* W. H. Freeman and Company, 1992, p. 43.

18 John Caples (revised by Fred E. Hahn), *Tested Advertising Methods*, 5th edition. Prentice Hall, 1997, p. 31.

19 Garrett Soden, *Hook, Spin, Buzz.* Peterson's/ Pacesetter Books 1996, p. 46.

20 Bob Stone, *Successful Direct Marketing Methods.* NTC Business Books, 1994, p. 77.

21 Bob Stone, *Successful Direct Marketing Methods.* NTC Business Books, 1994, p. 4.

22 Anthony R. Pratkanis and Elliot Aronson, *Age of Propaganda.* W. H. Freeman and Company, 1992, pp. 56–59.

23 Aaron Delwiche, *Wordgames – Glittering Generalities.* Institute for Propaganda Analysis, 1995, World Wide Web.

24 Charles U. Larson, *Persuasion.* Wadsworth Publishing Company, 1995, p. 134.

25 Quoted by Aaron Delwiche, *Wordgames – Euphemisms.* Institute for Propaganda Analysis, 1995, World Wide Web.

26 Ronald H. Carpenter, *Choosing Powerful Words.* Allyn and Bacon, 1999, p. 32.

27 Ronald H. Carpenter, *Choosing Powerful Words.* Allyn and Bacon, 1999, pp. 26–53.

28 Ronald H. Carpenter, *Choosing Powerful Words.* Allyn and Bacon, 1999, p. 44.

29 Ronald H. Carpenter, *Choosing Powerful Words.* Allyn and Bacon, 1999, p. 47.

30 *The Weekend Australian* December, 13–14, 1997, p. 29.

Chapter 8

1 Stuart Sutherland, *Irrationality.* Penguin Books, 1992, p. 15.

2 Gerard J. Tellis, *Advertising and Sales Promotion Strategy.* Addison-Wesley, 1998, pp. 160–161.

3 Jeffrey Pfeffer, *Managing With Power.* Harvard Business School Press, 1992, p. 279.

4 James C. Humes, *The Language of Leadership.* Information Australia, 1991, p. 54.

5 Anthony R. Pratkanis and Elliot Aronson, *Age of Propaganda.* W. H. Freeman and Company, 1992, p. 128.

6 Anthony R. Pratkanis and Elliot Aronson, *Age of Propaganda.* W. H. Freeman and Company, 1992, p. 130.

7 James C. Humes, *The Language of Leadership.* Information Australia, 1991, p. 61.

8 George Lakoff and Mark Johnson, *Metaphors We Live By.* University of Chicago Press, 1980, pp. 7–8.

9 George Lakoff and Mark Johnson, *Metaphors We Live By.* University of Chicago Press, 1980, p. 33.

10 Suzette Haden Elgin, *Genderspeak.* John Wiley and Sons, 1993, p. 162.

11 James A. Belasco and Ralph C. Stayer, *Flight of the Buffalo.* Warner Books, 1993, pp. 17–18.

12 Lee Iacocca with William Novak, *Iacocca.* Bantam Books, 1984, p. 212.

13 John Machado, *Creating Desire.* Sympress, 1996, pp. 129–131.

14 Gerald J. Tellis, *Advertising and Sales Promotion Strategy.* Addison-Wesley, 1998, p. 4.

15 Dorothy Leeds, *Powerspeak.* Piatkus, 1988, p. 101.

16 *The Economist*, March 1, 1997, p. 80.

17 *The Economist*, March 1, 1997, p. 80.

18 Donald J. Moine and John H. Herd, *Modern Persuasion Strategies.* Prentice Hall, 1984, p. 157.

19 *Forbes*, February 9, 1998, p. 27.

20 Robert J. Kriegel and Louis Patler, *If It Ain't Broke … Break It!* The Business Library, 1991, p. 89.

21 Donald J. Moine and John H. Herd, *Modern Persuasion Strategies.* Prentice Hall, 1984, p. 161.

22 Anthony R. Pratkanis and Elliot Aronson, *Age of Propaganda.* W. H. Freeman and Company, 1992, p. 165.

23 Peter L. Bernstein, *Against the Gods.* John Wiley and Sons, 1996, p. 274.

24 Anthony R. Pratkanis and Elliot Aronson, *Age of Propaganda.* W. H. Freeman and Company, 1992, pp. 62–63.

25 Gary Blake and Robert W. Bly, *The Elements of Copywriting.* Macmillan, 1997, p. 86.

26 Malcolm L. Kushner, *The Light Touch.* Simon and Schuster, p. 30.

27 Malcolm L. Kushner, *The Light Touch.* Simon and Schuster, p. 31.

28 Malcolm L. Kushner, *The Light Touch.* Simon and Schuster, p. 18.

29 Joanna Slan, *Using Stories and Humor.* Allyn and Bacon, 1998, p. 203.

30 Malcolm L. Kushner, *The Light Touch*. Simon and Schuster, p. 32.

31 Malcolm L. Kushner, *The Light Touch*, Simon and Schuster, p. 31.

Chapter 9

1 Noelle C. Nelson, *Winning!* Prentice Hall, 1997, p. 231.

2 Gerard J. Tellis, *Advertising and Sales Promotion Strategy*. Addison-Wesley, 1998, p. 138.

3 Gerry Spence, *How to Argue and Win Every Time*. St. Martin's Press, 1995, p. 126.

4 Jeffrey Toobin, *The Run of His Life*. Touchstone, 1997, pp. 10–12.

5 Lawrence S. Wrightsman, Michael T. Nietzel, and William H. Fortune, *Psychology and the Legal System*. Brooks/Cole Publishing Company, 1994, pp. 319–320.

6 Andrzej Huczynski, *Influencing Within Organizations*. Prentice Hall, 1996, p. 226.

7 Adapted from Ron Hoff, *Say It In Six*. Andrews and McMeel, 1996, p. 67.

8 Godfrey Howard, *Getting Through!* David and Charles, 1989, p. 62.

9 Bob Stone, *Successful Direct Marketing Methods*. NTC Business Books, 1994, p. 4.

10 Gerry Spence, *With Justice for None*. Penguin Books, 1989, pp. 81–83.

11 Charles U. Larson, *Persuasion*. Wadsworth Publishing Company, 1995, pp. 222–225.

12 *Business Week*, February 23, 1998, McGraw Hill, p. 46.

13 Jean Farinelli, "Succeeding in Business." *Vital Speeches of the Day*, 1994, 60(17): 531.

14 Jean Farinelli, "Succeeding in Business." *Vital Speeches of the Day*, 1994, 60(17): 531.

15 Gerard J. Tellis, *Advertising and Sales Promotion Strategy*. Addison-Wesley, 1998, p. 106.

16 David Michie, *The Invisible Persuaders*. Bantam Books, 1998, p. 300.

17 Garrett Soden, *Hook, Spin, Buzz*. Peterson's/Pacesetter Books, 1996, p. 149.

18 Garrett Soden, *Hook, Spin, Buzz*. Peterson's/Pacesetter Books, 1996, p. 152.

19 Marilyn Vos Savant, *The Power of Logical Thinking*. St. Martin's Press, 1996, pp. 65–66.

20 Larry Laudan, *The Book of Risks*. John Wiley and Sons, 1994, pp. 18–19.

21 Eric K. Meyer, *Designing Inforgraphics*. Hayden, 1997, pp. 89–90.

22 John Allen Paulos, *Innumeracy*. Penguin Books, 1988, p. 10.

23 John Allen Paulos, *Innumeracy*. Penguin Books, 1988, p. 12.

24 Bernice Kanner, *Are You Normal*. St Martin's Press, 1995, p. 108.

25 Steven A. Beebe and Susan J. Beebe, *Public Speaking*. Allyn and Bacon. 1997, p. 178.

Chapter 10

1 David A. Peoples, *Presentations Plus*. John Wiley and Sons, 1988, p. 66.

2 The 3M Meeting Management Team, *How to Run Better Business Meetings*. McGraw-Hill, 1987, pp. 114–115.

3 The ideas for these graphs came from Gregory Joseph, *Modern Visual Evidence*, New York: 1992, pp. A42–A43, and Edward R. Tufte, *Visual Explanations*, Graphics Press, 1994, p. 36.

4 Lou Cannon, *Official Negligence*. Times Books, 1997, p. xix.

5 Lou Cannon, *Official Negligence*. Times Books, 1997, p. xix.

6 Scott Heimes, *Nothing Matches Video for Pure Communication Power*. www.presentations.com.

7 Kathleen Hall Jamieson, *Packaging the Presidency*. New York: Oxford, 1996, p. 484.

8 Kathleen Hall Jamieson, *Dirty Politics*. New York: Oxford, 1992 pp. 15–42.

Chapter 11

1 Steven Pinker, *How the Mind Works*. Penguin Books, 1997, pp. 378–379.

2 Anthony R. Pratkanis and Elliot Aronson, *Age of Propaganda*. W. H. Freeman and Company, 1992, pp. 123–124.

3 Gregory, Cialdini, and Carpenter, "Mediators of Likelihood Estimates and Compliance: Does Imagining Make It So?" *Journal of Personality and Social Psychology* 43, pp. 89–99.

4 Jonathan Bond and Richard Kirshenbaum, *Under the Radar*. John Wiley and Sons, 1998, p. IX.

5 Jean-Marie Dru, *Disruption*. John Wiley and Sons, 1996, p. 170.

6 Neil Rackham, *Account Strategy for Major Sales*. Gower, 1988, p. 143.

7 Harry A. Mills, *Negotiate: The Art of Winning*. Gower, 1991, pp. 64–65.

8 Neil Rackham, *Making Major Sales*. Gower, 1987, p. 27.

9 Neil Rackham, *Spin Selling*. McGraw-Hill, 1988, pp. 15–16.

[10] Ben Feldman, *Creative Selling for the 1990's*. Dearborn, 1989, p. 59.

[11] Neil Rackham, *Spin Selling*. McGraw-Hill, 1988, pp. 73–81.

[12] Lawrence S. Wrightsman, Michael T. Nietzel, and William H. Fortune, *Psychology and the Legal System*. Brooks/Cole Publishing Company, 1994, p. 147.

[13] Lawrence S. Wrightsman, Michael T. Nietzel, and William H. Fortune, *Psychology and the Legal System*. Brooks/Cole Publishing Company, 1994, p. 147.

[14] Vincent Bugliosi, *Outrage*. W. W. Norton and Company, 1996, pp. 221–222.

[15] Harry A. Mills, *Negotiate: The Art of Winning*. Gower, 1991, pp. 73–75.

[16] Harry A. Mills, *Negotiate: The Art of Winning*. Gower, 1991, pp. 75–76.

Chapter 12

[1] William L. Nothstine, *Influencing Others*. Crisp, 1989, pp. 32–33.

[2] Carol Gelderman, *All the President's Words*. Walker, 1997, p. 18.

[3] Carol Gelderman, *All the President's Words*. Walker, 1997, p. 32.

[4] Carol Gelderman, *All the President's Words*. Walker, 1997, p. 33.

[5] Carol Gelderman, *All the President's Words*. Walker, 1997, p. 33.

Chapter 13

[1] Charles U. Larson, *Persuasion*. Wadsworth, 1995, p. 15.

[2] "Is Good Marketing Good Medicine." *Business Week*, April 20, 1998, p. 60.

[3] Carol Gelderman, *All the Presidents' Words*. Walker, 1998, p. 99.

[4] "Papers You Weren't Ever Supposed to See." *U.S. News & World Report*, April 5, 1998.

Chapter 14

[1] Ellen J. Langer, *Mindfulness*. Harvill, 1989, p. 26.

[2] Henry Mintzberg, "The Manager's Job: Folklore and Fact" in J Gabarro (ed.), *Managing People and Organizations*. Harvard Business School Publications, 1992, pp. 13–32.

[3] Anthony R. Pratkanis and Elliot Aronson, *The Age of Propaganda*. W. H. Freeman and Company, 1992, p. 121.

Chapter 15

[1] Kenrick and Sara Gutierres, "Contrast Effects in Judgments of Attractiveness: When Beauty Becomes a Social Problem," *Journal of Personality and Social Psychology, 38* (1980): 131–140.

[2] Mary Bragg, *Reinventing Influence*. Pitman Publishing, 1996, p. 42.

[3] *U.S. News & World Report*, "Don't Die Before You Read This." March 23, 1998, p. 52.

Chapter 16

[1] Robert B. Cialdini, *Influence*. Quill, 1984, pp. 34–35.

[2] Dennis Regan, "Effects of a Favor on Liking and Compliance. *Journal of Experimental Social Psychology,* 1971, pp. 627–639.

[3] Donald E. Brown, *Human Universals*. 1991.

[4] Stephen Pinker, *How the Mind Works*. Penguin Books, 1997, p. 404.

[5] Anthony R. Pratkanis and Elliot Aronson, *Age of Propaganda*. W. H Freeman and Company, 1992, p. 181.

[6] Robert B. Cialdini, *Influence*. Quill. 1984, pp. 39–40.

[7] Bob Stone, *Successful Direct Marketing Methods*. NTC Business Books, 1994, p. 92.

[8] Robert Cialdini and Karen Ascani, "Test of a Concession Procedure for Industry Verbal, Behavioral and Further Compliance with a Request to Give Blood." *Journal of Applied Psychology, 61* (1976): pp. 295–300.

Chapter 17

[1] Jonathan Freedman and Scott Fraser, "Compliance Without Pressure: The Foot-in-the-Door Technique." *Journal of Personality and Social Psychology, 4* (1966): pp. 195–202.

[2] P. Pliner, et al. "Compliance Without Pressure: Some Further Data on the Foot-in-the-Door Technique." *Journal of Social Psychology, 10* (1974): pp. 17–22.

[3] Robert B. Cialdini, *Influence*. Information Australia, 1984, p. 79.

[4] Stuart Sutherland, *Irrationality*. Penguin Books, 1992, pp. 98–99.

[5] John C. Mowen, *Judgement Calls*. Simon and Schuster, 1993, p. 66.

[6] Barbara W. Tuchman, *The March of Folly*. Abacus, 1984, p. 357.

7 H. R. McMaster, *Dereliction of Duty*. HarperCollins, 1997, p. 325.

8 Barbara W. Tuchman, *The March of Folly*. Abacus, 1984, p. 481.

9 Stanley I. Kutler, *Abuse of Power*. The Free Press, 1997, p. xxi.

10 Stanley I. Kutler, *Abuse of Power*. The Free Press, 1997, p. xxi.

11 David Michie, *Invisible Persuaders*. Bantam Books, 1988, p. 104.

12 David Michie, *Invisible Persuaders*. Bantam Books, 1988, p. 104.

13 David Michie, *Invisible Persuaders*. Bantam Books, 1988, p. 95.

14 John Vidal, *McLibel*. Pan Books, 1997, pp. 96–97.

15 John Vidal, *McLibel*. Pan Books, 1997, p. 97.

Chapter 18

1 Harry A. Mills, *Negotiate: The Art of Winning*. Gower, 1991, pp. 148–150.

2 Stuart Sutherland, *Irrationality*. Penguin Books, 1992, p. 40.

3 Robert Cialdini, *Influence*. Quill, 1984, p. 218.

4 Stuart Sutherland, *Irrationality*. Penguin Books, 1992, p. 40.

5 *New Zealand Herald,* March 27, 1998.

6 Robert Cialdini, *Influence*. Quill, 1984, p. 220.

7 Robert Cialdini, *Influence*. Quill, 1984, pp. 220–221.

8 Robert Cialdini, *Influence*. Quill, 1984, pp. 222–223.

Chapter 19

1 Anthony R. Pratkanis and Elliot Aronson, *Age of Propaganda*. W. H. Freeman and Company, 1991, p. 188.

2 *U.S. News & World Report,* "Beanie Baby Prices Are Insane." July 28, 1998.

3 Charles J. Frombrun, *Reputation*. Harvard Business School Press, 1996, pp. 1–2.

4 *The Economist,* December 20, 1997, p. 118.

5 Barry J. Nalebuff and Adam M. Brandenburger, *Co-opetition*. HarperCollins, 1996, p. 114.

6 *The Economist,* December 20, 1997, p. 118.

7 *The Economist,* December 20, 1997, p. 118.

8 Barry J. Nalebuff and Adam M. Brandernburger, *Co-opetition*. HarperCollins, 1996. p. 114.

9 Charles J. Frombrun, *Reputation*. Harvard Business School Press, 1996, p. 232.

10 Charles J. Frombrun, *Reputation*. Harvard Business School Press, 1996, p. 233.

11 Jeffrey Pfeffer, *Managing with Power*. Harvard Business School Press, 1992, p. 202.

12 Anthony R. Pratkanis and Elliot Aronson, *Age of Propaganda*. W. H. Freeman and Company, 1992, p. 191.

13 Robert C. B. Cialdini, *Influence*. William Morrow, 1984, pp. 225–226.

14 Robert C. B. Cialdini, *Influence*. William Morrow, 1984, pp. 255–256.

15 D.A. Zellinger, et al., "A Commodity Theory Analysis of the Effects of Age Restrictions upon Pornographic Materials." *Applied Psychology, 60* (1975): pp. 94–99.

16 Anthony R. Pratkanis and Elliot Aronson, *Age of Propaganda*. W. H. Freeman and Company, 1992, p. 189.

17 Harry A. Mills, *Negotiate: The Art of Winning*. Gower, 1991, pp. 137–138.

18 *Time,* May 6, 1996, pp. 55–61.

Chapter 20

1 Max Sutherland, *Advertising and the Mind of the Consumer*. Allen and Unwin, 1993, pp. 38–39.

2 Altheide and Johnson, "Counting Souls, A Study of Counseling at Evangelical Crusades." *Pacific Sociological Review 20* (1977): 323–348.

3 Max Sutherland, *Advertising and the Mind of the Consumer*. Allen and Unwin, 1993, p. 47.

4 Irving Janis, *Victims of Groupthink*. Houghton Mifflin, 1983, p. 3.

5 Daniel Goleman, *Vital Lies, Simple Truths*. Bloomsbury, 1985, pp. 184–187.

Chapter 21

1 Roger Ailes with Jon Kraushar, *You Are the Message*. Dow Jones-Irwin, 1988, p. 69.

2 Robert B. Cialdini, *Influence*. Quill, 1984, p. 164.

3 G.H. Smith and R. Engel, "Influence of a Female Model on Perceived Characteristics of an Automobile." *Proceedings of the 76th Annual Convention of the American Psychological Association,* 1968, pp. 681-682.

4 Robert B. Cialdini, *Influence*. Quill, 1984, p. 167.

5 Robert B. Cialdini, *Influence*. Quill, 1984, p. 167.

6 Bernard Asbell with Karen Wynn, *What They Know About You*. Random House, 1991, p. 28.

7 Bernard Asbell with Karen Wynn, *What They Know About You*. Random House, 1991, p. 28.

8 Bernard Asbell with Karen Wynn, *What They Know About You*. Random House, 1991, pp. 28-33.

9 Richard M. Perloff, *The Dynamics of Persuasion.* Lawrence Erlbaum, 1993, p. 146.

10 Robert Cialdini, *Influence.* Quill, 1984, pp. 165–166.

11 11 Mary Bragg, *Reinventing Influence.* Pitman Publishing, 1996, p. 56.

12 Forbes, "1997 Top 40 Athletes." World Wide Web.

13 Anthony R. Pratkanis and Elliot Aronson, *Age of Propaganda.* W. H. Freeman and Company, 1992, p. 93.

Chapter 22

1 Warren Kemball, *Forged in War.* HarperCollins, 1997, p. 8.

2 William Leuchtenberg, *Franklin D. Roosevelt and the New Deal.* Harper and Row, 1963, p. 327.

3 Nathan Miller, *F.D.R.* Madison Books, 1983, p. 350.

4 Nathan Miller, *F.D.R.* Madison Books, 1983, p. 354.

5 Gerald Parshall, *U.S. News & World.* April 28, 1997, p. 64.

6 Carol Gelderman, *All the Presidents' Words.* Walker, 1997, p. 17.

7 Carol Gelderman, *All the Presidents' Words.* Walker, 1997, p. 34.

8 Willian Kimball, *Forged in War.* HarperCollins, 1997, p. 11.

9 William Manchester, *The Last Lion.* Sphere, 1983, p. 17.

10 William Manchester, *The Last Lion.* Sphere, 1983, p. 17.

11 David Cannadine, *The Speeches of Winston Churchill.* Penguin Books, 1989, p. 11.

12 David Cannadine, *The Speeches of Winston Churchill.* Penguin Books, 1989, p. 11.

13 Norman Rose, *Churchill, An Unruly Life.* Simon and Schuster, 1994, p. 345.

INDEX